DIFFERENTIATION FOR GIFTED AND TALENTED STUDENTS

ESSENTIAL READINGS IN GIFTED EDUCATION

SERIES EDITOR

SALLY M. REIS

1 **ROBERT J. STERNBERG**
DEFINITIONS AND CONCEPTIONS OF GIFTEDNESS

2 **JOSEPH S. RENZULLI**
IDENTIFICATION OF STUDENTS FOR GIFTED AND TALENTED PROGRAMS

3 **LINDA E. BRODY**
GROUPING AND ACCELERATION PRACTICES IN GIFTED EDUCATION

4 **JOYCE VANTASSEL-BASKA**
CURRICULUM FOR GIFTED AND TALENTED STUDENTS

5 **CAROL ANN TOMLINSON**
DIFFERENTIATION FOR GIFTED AND TALENTED STUDENTS

6 **ALEXINIA Y. BALDWIN**
CULTURALLY DIVERSE AND UNDERSERVED POPULATIONS OF GIFTED STUDENTS

7 **SUSAN BAUM**
TWICE-EXCEPTIONAL AND SPECIAL POPULATIONS OF GIFTED STUDENTS

8 **SIDNEY M. MOON**
SOCIAL/EMOTIONAL ISSUES, UNDERACHIEVEMENT, AND COUNSELING OF GIFTED AND TALENTED STUDENTS

9 **ENID ZIMMERMAN**
ARTISTICALLY AND MUSICALLY TALENTED STUDENTS

10 **DONALD J. TREFFINGER**
CREATIVITY AND GIFTEDNESS

11 **CAROLYN M. CALLAHAN**
PROGRAM EVALUATION IN GIFTED EDUCATION

12 **JAMES J. GALLAGHER**
PUBLIC POLICY IN GIFTED EDUCATION

Carol Ann Tomlinson
EDITOR

DIFFERENTIATION FOR GIFTED AND TALENTED STUDENTS

A Joint Publication of Corwin Press and the National Association for Gifted Children

ESSENTIAL READINGS IN GIFTED EDUCATION
Sally M. Reis, SERIES EDITOR

CORWIN PRESS
A Sage Publications Company
Thousand Oaks, California

For information:

Corwin Press
A Sage Publications Company
2455 Teller Road
Thousand Oaks, California 91320
www.corwinpress.com

Sage Publications Ltd
1 Oliver's Yard
55 City Road
London EC1Y 1SP
United Kingdom

Sage Publications India Pvt. Ltd.
B-42, Panchsheel Enclave
Post Box 4109
New Delhi 110 017 India

Printed in the United States of America

Library of Congress Cataloging-in-Publication Data

Differentiation for gifted and talented students / Carol Ann Tomlinson, editor.
    p. cm. — (Essential readings in gifted education ; 5)
"A joint publication of Corwin Press and the National Association for Gifted Children."
Includes bibliographical references and index.
ISBN 1-4129-0430-7 (pbk.)
    1. Gifted children—Education (Middle school)—United States. I. Tomlinson, Carol A.
II. National Association for Gifted Children (U.S.) III. Series.
LC3993.23.D54 2004
371.95—dc22

                                        2004001090

This book is printed on acid-free paper.

04   05   06   07   08   10   9   8   7   6   5   4   3   2

Acquisitions Editor:	Kylee Liegl
Editorial Assistant:	Jaime Cuvier
Production Editor:	Sanford Robinson
Typesetter:	C&M Digitals (P) Ltd.
Cover Designer:	Tracy E. Miller
Graphic Designer:	Lisa Miller

NAGC Publications Coordinator: Jane Clarenbach

Contents

About the Editors

Sally M. Reis is a professor and the department head of the Educational Psychology Department at the University of Connecticut where she also serves as principal investigator of the National Research Center on the Gifted and Talented. She was a teacher for 15 years, 11 of which were spent working with gifted students on the elementary, junior high, and high school levels. She has authored more than 130 articles, 9 books, 40 book chapters, and numerous monographs and technical reports.

Her research interests are related to special populations of gifted and talented students, including: students with learning disabilities, gifted females, and diverse groups of talented students. She is also interested in extensions of the Schoolwide Enrichment Model for both gifted and talented students and as a way to expand offerings and provide general enrichment to identify talents and potentials in students who have not been previously identified as gifted.

She has traveled extensively conducting workshops and providing professional development for school districts on gifted education, enrichment programs, and talent development programs. She is co-author of *The Schoolwide Enrichment Model*, *The Secondary Triad Model*, *Dilemmas in Talent Development in the Middle Years*, and a book published in 1998 about women's talent development titled *Work Left Undone: Choices and Compromises of Talented Females*. Sally serves on several editorial boards, including the *Gifted Child Quarterly*, and is a past president of the National Association for Gifted Children.

Carol Ann Tomlinson's career as an educator includes 21 years as a public school teacher, including 12 years as a program administrator of special services for struggling and advanced learners. She was Virginia's Teacher of the Year in 1974. More recently, she has been for 13 years a faculty member at the University of Virginia's Curry School of Education, where she is currently Professor of Educational Leadership, Foundations and Policy. Special interests throughout her career have included curriculum and instruction for struggling learners and advanced learners, effective instruction in heterogeneous settings, and encouraging creative and critical thinking in the classroom.

Carol is a reviewer for eight journals and a section editor for one. She is author of more than 100 articles, book chapters, books, and other professional development materials. For ASCD, she has authored seven books including *How to Differentiate Instruction in Mixed Ability Classrooms,* and *The Differentiated Classroom: Responding to the Needs of all Learners,* a professional inquiry kit on differentiation, and facilitator's guides for four video staff development sets. For NAGC, she is a coauthor of *The Parallel Curriculum Model: A Design to Develop High Potential and Challenge High Ability Learners.* Carol is a past president of the National Association for Gifted Children.

Series Introduction

Sally M. Reis

The accomplishments of the last 50 years in the education of gifted students should not be underestimated: the field of education of the gifted and talented has emerged as strong and visible. In many states, a policy or position statement from the state board of education supports the education of the gifted and talented, and specific legislation generally recognizes the special needs of this group. Growth in our field has not been constant, however, and researchers and scholars have discussed the various high and low points of national interest and commitment to educating the gifted and talented (Gallagher, 1979; Renzulli, 1980; Tannenbaum, 1983). Gallagher described the struggle between support and apathy for special programs for gifted and talented students as having roots in historical tradition—the battle between an aristocratic elite and our concomitant belief in egalitarianism. Tannenbaum suggested the existence of two peak periods of interest in the gifted as the five years following *Sputnik* in 1957 and the last half of the decade of the 1970s, describing a valley of neglect between the peaks in which the public focused its attention on the disadvantaged and the handicapped. "The cyclical nature of interest in the gifted is probably unique in American education. No other special group of children has been alternately embraced and repelled with so much vigor by educators and laypersons alike" (Tannenbaum, 1983, p. 16). Many wonder if the cyclical nature to which Tannenbaum referred is not somewhat prophetic, as it appears that our field may be experiencing another downward spiral in interest as a result of current governmental initiatives and an increasing emphasis on testing and standardization of curriculum. Tannenbaum's description of a valley of neglect may describe current conditions. During the late 1980s, programming flourished during a peak of interest and a textbook on systems and models for gifted programs included 15 models for elementary and secondary programs (Renzulli, 1986). The Jacob Javits Gifted and Talented Students Education Act passed by Congress in 1988 resulted in the creation of the National Research Center on the Gifted and Talented, and dozens of model programs were added to the collective knowledge in the field in areas related to underrepresented populations and successful practices. In the 1990s, reduction or elimination of gifted programs occurred, as budget pressures exacerbated by the lingering recession in the late 1990s resulted in the reduction of services mandated by fewer than half of the states in our country.

Even during times in which more activity focused on the needs of gifted and talented students, concerns were still raised about the limited services provided to these students. In the second federal report on the status of education for our nation's most talented students entitled *National Excellence: A Case for Developing America's Talent* (Ross, 1993), "a quiet crisis" was described in the absence of attention paid to this population: "Despite sporadic attention over the years to the needs of bright students, most of them continue to spend time in school working well below their capabilities. The belief espoused in school reform that children from all economic and cultural backgrounds must reach their full potential has not been extended to America's most talented students. They are under-challenged and therefore underachieve" (p. 5). The report further indicates that our nation's gifted and talented students have a less rigorous curriculum, read fewer demanding books, and are less prepared for work or postsecondary education than the most talented students in many other industrialized countries. Talented children who come from economically disadvantaged homes or are members of minority groups are especially neglected, the report also indicates, and many of them will not realize their potential without some type of intervention.

In this anniversary series of volumes celebrating the evolution of our field, noted scholars introduce a collection of the most frequently cited articles from the premiere journal in our field, *Gifted Child Quarterly*. Each volume includes a collection of thoughtful, and in some cases, provocative articles that honor our past, acknowledge the challenges we face in the present, and provide hopeful guidance for the future as we seek the optimal educational experiences for all talented students. These influential articles, published after a rigorous peer review, were selected because they are frequently cited and considered seminal in our field. Considered in their entirety, the articles show that we have learned a great deal from the volume of work represented by this series. Our knowledge has expanded over several decades of work, and progress has been made toward reaching consensus about what is known. As several of the noted scholars who introduce separate areas explain in their introductions, this series helps us to understand that some questions have been answered, while others remain. While we still search for these answers, we are now better prepared to ask questions that continue and evolve. The seminal articles in this series help us to resolve some issues, while they highlight other questions that simply refuse to go away. Finally, the articles help us to identify new challenges that continue to emerge in our field. Carol Tomlinson suggests, for example, that the area of curriculum differentiation in the field of gifted education is, in her words, an issue born in the field of gifted education, and one that continues to experience rebirth.

Some of the earliest questions in our field have been answered and time has enabled those answers to be considered part of our common core of knowledge. For example, it is widely acknowledged that both school and home experiences can help to develop giftedness in persons with high potential and that a continuum of services in and out of school can provide the greatest likelihood that this development will occur. Debates over other "hot" issues such as grouping and acceleration that took place in the gifted education community 30 years ago are now largely unnecessary, as Linda Brody points out in her introduction to a series of articles in this area. General agreement seems to have been reached, for example, that grouping, enrichment and acceleration are all necessary to provide appropriate educational opportunities for gifted and talented learners. These healthy debates of the past helped to strengthen our field but visionary and reflective work remains to be done. In this series, section editors summarize what has been learned and raise provocative questions about the future. The questions alone are some of the most thoughtful in our field, providing enough research opportunities for scholars for the next decade. The brief introductions below provide some highlights about the series.

DEFINITIONS OF GIFTEDNESS (VOLUME 1)

In Volume 1, Robert Sternberg introduces us to seminal articles about definitions of giftedness and the types of talents and gifts exhibited by children and youth. The most widely used definitions of gifts and talents utilized by educators generally follow those proposed in federal reports. For example, the Marland Report (Marland, 1972) commissioned by the Congress included the first federal definition of giftedness, which was widely adopted or adapted by the states.

The selection of a definition of giftedness has been and continues to be the major policy decision made at state and local levels. It is interesting to note that policy decisions are often either unrelated or marginally related to actual procedures or to research findings about a definition of giftedness or identification of the gifted, a fact well documented by the many ineffective, incorrect, and downright ridiculous methods of identification used to find students who meet the criteria in the federal definition. This gap between policy and practice may be caused by many variables. Unfortunately, although the federal definition was written to be inclusive, it is, instead, rather vague, and problems caused by this definition have been recognized by experts in the field (Renzulli, 1978). In the most recent federal report on the status of gifted and talented programs entitled *National Excellence* (Ross, 1993), a newer federal definition is proposed based on new insights provided by neuroscience and cognitive psychology. Arguing that the term *gifted* connotes a mature power rather than a developing ability and, therefore, is antithetic to recent research findings about children, the new definition "reflects today's knowledge and thinking" (p. 26) by emphasizing talent development, stating that gifted and talented children are children and youth with outstanding talent performance or show the potential for performing at remarkably high levels of accomplishment when compared with others of their age, experience, or environment. These children and youth exhibit high performance capability in intellectual, creative, and/or artistic areas, possess an unusual leadership capacity, or excel in specific academic fields. They require services or activities not ordinarily provided by the schools. Outstanding talents are present in children and youth from all cultural groups, across all economic strata, and in all areas of human endeavor. (p. 26)

Fair identification systems use a variety of multiple assessment measures that respect diversity, accommodate students who develop at different rates, and identify potential as well as demonstrated talent. In the introduction to the volume, Sternberg admits, that just as people have bad habits, so do academic fields, explaining, "a bad habit of much of the gifted field is to do research on giftedness, or worse, identify children as gifted or not gifted, without having a clear conception of what it means to be gifted." Sternberg summarizes major themes from the seminal articles about definitions by asking key questions about the nature of giftedness and talent, the ways in which we should study giftedness, whether we should expand conventional notions of giftedness, and if so, how that can be accomplished; whether differences exist between giftedness and talent; the validity of available assessments; and perhaps most importantly, how do we and can we develop giftedness and talent. Sternberg succinctly summarizes points of broad agreement from the many scholars who have contributed to this section, concluding that giftedness involves more than just high IQ, that it has noncognitive and cognitive components, that the environment is crucial in terms of whether potentials for gifted performance will be realized, and that giftedness is not a single thing. He further cautions that the ways we conceptualize giftedness greatly influences who will have opportunities to develop their gifts and reminds readers of our responsibilities as educators. He also asks one of the most critical questions in our field: whether gifted and talented individuals will use their knowledge to benefit or harm our world.

IDENTIFICATION OF HIGH-ABILITY STUDENTS (VOLUME 2)

In Volume 2, Joseph Renzulli introduces what is perhaps the most critical question still facing practitioners and researchers in our field, that is how, when, and why should we identify gifted and talented students. Renzulli believes that conceptions of giftedness exist along a continuum ranging from a very conservative or restricted view of giftedness to a more flexible or multidimensional approach. What many seem not to understand is that the first step in identification should always be to ask: identification for what? For what type of program or experience is the youngster being identified? If, for example, an arts program is being developed for talented artists, the resulting identification system must be structured to identify youngsters with either demonstrated or potential talent in art.

Renzulli's introductory chapter summarizes seminal articles about identification, and summarizes emerging consensus. For example, most suggest, that while intelligence tests and other cognitive ability tests provide one very important form of information about one dimension of a young person's potential, mainly in the areas of verbal and analytic skills, they do not tell us all that we need to know about who should be identified. These authors do not argue that cognitive ability tests should be dropped from the identification process. Rather, most believe that (a) other indicators of potential should be used for identification, (b) these indicators should be given equal consideration when it comes to making final decisions about which students will be candidates for special services, and (c) in the final analysis, it is the thoughtful judgment of knowledgeable professionals rather than instruments and cutoff scores that should guide selection decisions.

Another issue addressed by the authors of the seminal articles about identification is what has been referred to as the distinction between (a) convergent and divergent thinking (Guilford, 1967; Torrance, 1984), (b) entrenchment and non-entrenchment (Sternberg, 1982), and (c) schoolhouse giftedness versus creative/productive giftedness (Renzulli, 1982; Renzulli & Delcourt, 1986). It is easier to identify schoolhouse giftedness than it is to identify students with the potential for creative productive giftedness. Renzulli believes that progress has been made in the identification of gifted students, especially during the past quarter century, and that new approaches address the equity issue, policies, and practices that respect new theories about human potential and conceptions of giftedness. He also believes, however, that continuous commitment to research-based identification practices is still needed, for "it is important to keep in mind that some of the characteristics that have led to the recognition of history's most gifted contributors are not always as measurable as others. We need to continue our search for those elusive things that are left over after everything explainable has been explained, to realize that giftedness is culturally and contextually imbedded in all human activity, and most of all, to value the value of even those things that we cannot yet explain."

ACCELERATION AND GROUPING, CURRICULUM, AND CURRICULUM DIFFERENTIATION (VOLUMES 3, 4, 5)

Three volumes in this series address curricular and grouping issues in gifted programs, and it is in this area, perhaps, that some of the most promising practices have been implemented for gifted and talented students. Grouping and curriculum interact with each other, as various forms of grouping patterns have enabled students to work on advanced curricular opportunities with other talented students. And, as is commonly known now about instructional and ability grouping, it is not the way students are grouped that matters most, but rather, it is what happens within the groups that makes the most difference.

In too many school settings, little differentiation of curriculum and instruction for gifted students is provided during the school day, and minimal opportunities are offered. Occasionally, after-school enrichment programs or Saturday programs offered by museums, science centers, or local universities take the place of comprehensive school programs, and too many academically talented students attend school in classrooms across the country in which they are bored, unmotivated, and unchallenged. Acceleration, once a frequently used educational practice in our country, is often dismissed by teachers and administrators as an inappropriate practice for a variety of reasons, including scheduling problems, concerns about the social effects of grade skipping, and others. Various forms of acceleration, including enabling precocious students to enter kindergarten or first grade early, grade skipping, and early entrance to college are not commonly used by most school districts.

Unfortunately, major alternative grouping strategies involve the reorganization of school structures, and these have been too slow in coming, perhaps due to the difficulty of making major educational changes, because of scheduling, finances, and other issues that have caused schools to substantially delay major change patterns. Because of this delay, gifted students too often fail to receive classroom instruction based on their unique needs that place them far ahead of their chronological peers in basic skills and verbal abilities and enable them to learn much more rapidly and tackle much more complex materials than their peers. Our most able students need appropriately paced, rich and challenging instruction, and curriculum that varies significantly from what is being taught in regular classrooms across America. Too often, academically talented students are "left behind" in school.

Linda Brody introduces the question of how to group students optimally for instructional purposes and pays particular concern to the degree to which the typical age-in-grade instructional program can meet the needs of gifted students—those students with advanced cognitive abilities and achievement that may already have mastered the curriculum designed for their age peers. The articles about grouping emphasize the importance of responding to the learning needs of individual students with curricular flexibility, the need for educators to be flexible when assigning students to instructional groups, and the need to modify those groups when necessary. Brody's introduction points out that the debate about grouping gifted and talented learners together was one area that brought the field together, as every researcher in the field supports some type of grouping option, and few would disagree with the need to use grouping and accelerated learning as tools that allow us to differentiate content for students with different learning needs. When utilized as a way to offer a more advanced educational program to students with advanced cognitive abilities and achievement levels, these practices can help achieve the goal of an appropriate education for all students.

Joyce VanTassel-Baska introduces the seminal articles in curriculum, by explaining that they represent several big ideas that emphasize the values and relevant factors of a curriculum for the gifted, the technology of curriculum development, aspects of differentiation of a curriculum for the gifted within core subject areas and without, and the research-based efficacy of such curriculum and related instructional pedagogy in use. She also reminds readers of Harry Passow's concerns about curriculum balance, suggesting that an imbalance exists, as little evidence suggests that the affective development of gifted students is occurring through special curricula for the gifted. Moreover, interdisciplinary efforts at curriculum frequently exclude the arts and foreign language. Only through acknowledging and applying curriculum balance in these areas are we likely to be producing the type of humane individual Passow envisioned. To achieve balance, VanTassel-Baska recommends a full set of curriculum options across domains, as well as the need to nurture the social-emotional needs of diverse gifted and talented learners.

Carol Tomlinson introduces the critical area of differentiation in the field of gifted education that has only emerged in the last 13 years. She believes the diverse nature of the articles and their relatively recent publication suggests that this area is indeed, in her words, "an issue born in the field of gifted education, and one that continues to experience rebirth." She suggests that one helpful way of thinking about the articles in this volume is that their approach varies, as some approach the topic of differentiation of curriculum with a greater emphasis on the distinctive mission of gifted education. Others look at differentiation with a greater emphasis on the goals, issues, and missions shared between general education and gifted education. Drawing from an analogy with anthropology, Tomlinson suggests that "splitters" in that field focus on differences among cultures while "lumpers" have a greater interest in what cultures share in common. Splitters ask the question of what happens for high-ability students in mixed-ability settings, while lumpers question what common issues and solutions exist for multiple populations in mixed-ability settings.

Tomlinson suggests that the most compelling feature of the collection of articles in this section—and certainly its key unifying feature—is the linkage between the two areas of educational practice in attempting to address an issue likely to be seminal to the success of both over the coming quarter century and beyond, and this collection may serve as a catalyst for next steps in those directions for the field of gifted education as it continues collaboration with general education and other educational specialties while simultaneously addressing those missions uniquely its own.

UNDERREPRESENTED AND TWICE-EXCEPTIONAL POPULATIONS AND SOCIAL AND EMOTIONAL ISSUES (VOLUMES 6, 7, 8)

The majority of young people participating in gifted and talented programs across the country continue to represent the majority culture in our society. Few doubts exist regarding the reasons that economically disadvantaged, twice-exceptional, and culturally diverse students are underrepresented in gifted programs. One reason may be the ineffective and inappropriate identification and selection procedures used for the identification of these young people that limits referrals and nominations and eventual placement. Research summarized in this series indicates that groups that have been traditionally underrepresented in gifted programs could be better served if some of the following elements are considered: new constructs of giftedness, attention to cultural and contextual variability, the use of more varied and authentic assessments, performance-based identification, and identification opportunities through rich and varied learning opportunities.

Alexinia Baldwin discusses the lower participation of culturally diverse and underserved populations in programs for the gifted as a major concern that has forged dialogues and discussion in *Gifted Child Quarterly* over the past five decades. She classifies these concerns in three major themes: *identification/selection, programming,* and *staff assignment and development.* Calling the first theme **Identification/Selection**, she indicates that it has always been the Achilles' heel of educators' efforts to ensure that giftedness can be expressed in many ways through broad identification techniques. Citing favorable early work by Renzulli and Hartman (1971) and Baldwin (1977) that expanded options for identification, Baldwin cautions that much remains to be done. The second theme, **Programming**, recognizes the abilities of students who are culturally diverse but often forces them to exist in programs designed "for one size fits all." Her third theme relates to **Staffing and Research,** as she voices concerns about the diversity of teachers in these programs as well as the attitudes or mindsets of researchers who develop theories and conduct the research that addresses these concerns.

Susan Baum traces the historical roots of gifted and talented individuals with special needs, summarizing Terman's early work that suggested the gifted were healthier, more popular, and better adjusted than their less able peers. More importantly, gifted individuals were regarded as those who could perform at high levels in all areas with little or no support. Baum suggests that acceptance of these stereotypical characteristics diminished the possibility that there could be special populations of gifted students with special needs. Baum believes that the seminal articles in this collection address one or more of the critical issues that face gifted students at risk and suggest strategies for overcoming the barriers that prevent them from realizing their promise. The articles focus on three populations of students: twice-exceptional students—gifted students who are at risk for poor development due to difficulties in learning and attention;

gifted students who face gender issues that inhibit their ability to achieve or develop socially and emotionally, and students who are economically disadvantaged and at risk for dropping out of school. Baum summarizes research indicating that each of these groups of youngsters is affected by one or more barriers to development, and the most poignant of these barriers are identification strategies, lack of awareness of consequences of co-morbidity, deficit thinking in program design, and lack of appropriate social and emotional support. She ends her introduction with a series of thoughtful questions focusing on future directions in this critical area.

Sidney Moon introduces the seminal articles on the social and emotional development of and counseling for gifted children by acknowledging the contributions of the National Association for Gifted Children's task forces that have examined social/emotional issues. The first task force, formed in 2000 and called the Social and Emotional Issues Task Force, completed its work in 2002 by publishing an edited book, *The Social and Emotional Development of Gifted Children: What Do We Know?* This volume provides an extensive review of the literature on the social and emotional development of gifted children (Neihart, Reis, Robinson, & Moon, 2002). Moon believes that the seminal studies in the area of the social and emotional development and counseling illustrate both the strengths and the weaknesses of the current literature on social and emotional issues in the field of gifted education. These articles bring increased attention to the affective needs of special populations of gifted students, such as underachievers, who are at risk for failure to achieve their potential, but also point to the need for more empirical studies on "what works" with these students, both in terms of preventative strategies and more intensive interventions. She acknowledges that although good counseling models have been developed, they need to be rigorously evaluated to determine their effectiveness under disparate conditions, and calls for additional research on the affective and counseling interventions with specific subtypes of gifted students such as Asian Americans, African Americans, and twice-exceptional students. Moon also strongly encourages researchers in the field of gifted education to collaborate with researchers from affective fields such as personal and social psychology, counseling psychology, family therapy, and psychiatry to learn to intervene most effectively with gifted individuals with problems and to learn better how to help all gifted persons achieve optimal social, emotional, and personal development.

ARTISTICALLY AND CREATIVELY TALENTED STUDENTS (VOLUMES 9, 10)

Enid Zimmerman introduces the volume on talent development in the visual and performing arts with a summary of articles about students who are talented in music, dance, visual arts, and spatial, kinesthetic, and expressive areas. Major themes that appear in the articles include perceptions by parents, students, and teachers that often focus on concerns related to nature versus nurture in arts talent development; research about the crystallizing experiences of artistically talented students; collaboration between school and community members about identification of talented art students from diverse backgrounds; and leadership issues related to empowering teachers of talented arts students. They all are concerned to some extent with teacher, parent, and student views about educating artistically talented students. Included also are discussions about identification of talented students from urban, suburban, and rural environments. Zimmerman believes that in this particular area, a critical need exists for research about the impact of educational opportunities, educational settings, and the role of art teachers on the development of artistically talented students. The impact of the standards and testing movement and its relationship to the education of talented students in the visual and performing arts is an area greatly in need of investigation. Research also is needed about students' backgrounds, personalities, gender orientations, skill development, and cognitive and affective abilities as well as cross-cultural contexts and the impact of global and popular culture on the education of artistically talented students. The compelling case study with which she introduces this volume sets the stage for the need for this research.

Donald Treffinger introduces reflections on articles about creativity by discussing the following five core themes that express the collective efforts of researchers to grasp common conceptual and theoretical challenges associated with creativity. The themes include **Definitions** (how we define giftedness, talent, or creativity), **Characteristics** (the indicators of giftedness and creativity in people), **Justification** (Why is creativity important in education?), **Assessment** of creativity, and the ways we **Nurture** creativity. Treffinger also discusses the expansion of knowledge, the changes that have occurred, the search for answers, and the questions that still remain. In the early years of interest of creativity research, Treffinger believed that considerable discussion existed about whether it was possible to foster creativity through training or instruction. He reports that over the last 50 years, educators have learned that deliberate efforts to nurture creativity are possible (e.g., Torrance, 1987), and further extends this line of inquiry by asking the key question, "What works best, for whom, and under what conditions?" Treffinger summarizes the challenges faced by educators who try to nurture the development of creativity through effective teaching and to ask which experiences will have the greatest impact, as these will help to determine our ongoing lines of research, development, and training initiatives.

EVALUATION AND PUBLIC POLICY (VOLUMES 11, 12)

Carolyn Callahan introduces the seminal articles on evaluation and suggests that this important component neglected by experts in the field of gifted education for at least the last three decades can be a plea for important work by both evaluators and practitioners. She divides the seminal literature on evaluation, and in particular the literature on the evaluation of gifted programs into four categories, those which (a) provide theory and/or practical guidelines, (b) describe or report on specific program evaluations, (c) provide stimuli for the discussion of issues surrounding the evaluation process, and (d) suggest new research on the evaluation process. Callahan concludes with a challenge indicating work to be done and the opportunity for experts to make valuable contributions to increased effectiveness and efficiency of programs for the gifted.

James Gallagher provides a call-to-arms in the seminal articles he introduces on public policy by raising some of the most challenging questions in the field. Gallagher suggests that as a field, we need to come to some consensus about stronger interventions and consider how we react to accusations of elitism. He believes that our field could be doing a great deal more with additional targeted resources supporting the general education teacher and the development of specialists in gifted education, and summarizes that our failure to fight in the public arena for scarce resources may raise again the question posed two decades ago by Renzulli (1980), looking toward 1990: "Will the gifted child movement be alive and well in 2010?"

CONCLUSION

What can we learn from an examination of our field and the seminal articles that have emerged over the last few decades? First, we must **respect the past** by acknowledging the times in which articles were written and the shoulders of those persons upon whom we stand as we continue to create and develop our field. An old proverb tells us that when we drink from the well, we must remember to acknowledge those who dug the well, and in our field the early articles represent the seeds that grew our field. Next, we must **celebrate the present** and the exciting work and new directions in our field and the knowledge that is now accepted as a common core. Last, we must **embrace the future** by understanding that there is no finished product when it comes to research on gifted and talented children and how we are best able to meet their unique needs. Opportunities abound in the work reported in this series, but many questions remain. A few things seem clear. Action in the future should be based on both qualitative and quantitative research as well as longitudinal studies, and what we have completed only scratches the surface regarding the many variables and issues that still need to be explored. Research is needed that suggests positive changes that will lead to more inclusive programs that recognize the talents and gifts of diverse students in our country. When this occurs, future teachers and researchers in gifted education will find answers that can be embraced by educators, communities, and families, and the needs of all talented and gifted students will be more effectively met in their classrooms by teachers who have been trained to develop their students' gifts and talents.

We also need to consider carefully how we work with the field of education in general. As technology emerges and improves, new opportunities will become available to us. Soon, all students should be able to have their curricular needs preassessed before they begin any new curriculum unit. Soon, the issue of keeping students on grade-level material when they are many grades ahead should disappear as technology enables us to pinpoint students' strengths. Will chronological grades be eliminated? The choices we have when technology enables us to learn better what students already know presents exciting scenarios for the future, and it is imperative that we advocate carefully for multiple opportunities for these students, based on their strengths and interests, as well as a challenging core curriculum. Parents, educators, and professionals who care about these special populations need to become politically active to draw attention to the unique needs of these students, and researchers need to conduct the experimental studies that can prove the efficacy of providing talent development options as well as opportunities for healthy social and emotional growth.

For any field to continue to be vibrant and to grow, new voices must be heard, and new players sought. A great opportunity is available in our field; for as we continue to advocate for gifted and talented students, we can also play important roles in the changing educational reform movement. We can continue to work to achieve more challenging opportunities for all students while we fight to maintain gifted, talented, and enrichment programs. We can continue our advocacy for differentiation through acceleration, individual curriculum opportunities, and a continuum of advanced curriculum and personal support opportunities. The questions answered and those raised in this volume of seminal articles can help us to move forward as a field. We hope those who read the series will join us in this exciting journey.

REFERENCES

Baldwin, A.Y. (1977). Tests do underpredict: A case study. *Phi Delta Kappan, 58*, 620-621.

Gallagher, J. J. (1979). Issues in education for the gifted. In A. H. Passow (Ed.), *The gifted and the talented: Their education and development* (pp. 28-44). Chicago: University of Chicago Press.

Guilford, J. E. (1967). *The nature of human intelligence*. New York: McGraw-Hill.

Marland, S. P., Jr. (1972). *Education of the gifted and talented: Vol. 1. Report to the Congress of the United States by the U.S. Commissioner of Education*. Washington, DC: U.S. Government Printing Office.

Neihart, M., Reis, S., Robinson, N., & Moon, S. M. (Eds.). (2002). *The social and emotional development of gifted children: What do we know?* Waco, TX: Prufrock.

Renzulli, J. S. (1978). What makes giftedness? Reexamining a definition. *Phi Delta Kappan, 60*(5), 180-184.

Renzulli, J. S. (1980). Will the gifted child movement be alive and well in 1990? *Gifted Child Quarterly, 24*(1), 3-9. **[See Vol. 12.]**

Renzulli, J. (1982). Dear Mr. and Mrs. Copernicus: We regret to inform you . . . *Gifted Child Quarterly, 26*(1), 11-14. **[See Vol. 2.]**

Renzulli, J. S. (Ed.). (1986). *Systems and models for developing programs for the gifted and talented*. Mansfield Center, CT: Creative Learning Press.

Renzulli, J. S., & Delcourt, M. A. B. (1986). The legacy and logic of research on the identification of gifted persons. *Gifted Child Quarterly, 30*(1), 20-23. **[See Vol. 2.]**

Renzulli J., & Hartman, R. (1971). Scale for rating behavioral characteristics of superior students. *Exceptional Children, 38*, 243-248.

Ross, P. (1993). *National excellence: A case for developing America's talent.* Washington, DC: U.S. Department of Education, Government Printing Office.

Sternberg, R. J. (1982). Nonentrenchment in the assessment of intellectual giftedness. *Gifted Child Quarterly, 26*(2), 63-67. **[See Vol. 2.]**

Tannenbaum, A. J. (1983). *Gifted children: Psychological and educational perspectives.* New York: Macmillan.

Torrance, E. P. (1984). The role of creativity in identification of the gifted and talented. *Gifted Child Quarterly, 28*(4), 153-156. **[See Vols. 2 and 10.]**

Torrance, E. P. (1987). Recent trends in teaching children and adults to think creatively. In S. G. Isaksen (Ed.), *Frontiers of creativity research: Beyond the basics* (pp. 204-215). Buffalo, NY: Bearly Limited.

Introduction to Differentiation for Gifted and Talented Students

Carol Ann Tomlinson

With a quick read, the eleven articles in this volume appear loosely connected. They are qualitative, quantitative, and narrative reports. They deal with specific models, general curriculum guidelines, particular instructional strategies, varied populations of interest, preservice and inservice teachers, teacher characteristics, learner responses, student achievement, teacher change—and that just begins the list. In addition, the articles span not twenty-five years, as is the case with many of the collections in this series, but only the last thirteen. Both the seeming scatter of focus and the relatively recent publication dates might suggest a topic newly and not definitively formed. To the contrary, the set of articles represents an issue born in the field of gifted education, and one that continues to experience rebirth.

CREATING A FRAME FOR READING

One article at the chronological midpoint in the group offers a useful way to frame the collection. Entitled "Interface between Gifted Education and General Education: Toward Communication, Cooperation, and Collaboration," (Tomlinson, et al., 1996) the report stemmed from a Task Force formed during the NAGC presidency of James Gallagher. Task Force researchers and authors used a three-tiered interview and qualitative synthesis process to sample attitudes among general educators and educators of the gifted regarding linkages between the two practices. The dominant theme of the fifty interviews conducted with general educators and gifted educators at state and local levels was an urgent need for communication, cooperation, and collaboration between the two facets of education.

While emphasizing potential benefits of movement from improved communication to extended cooperation to persistent collaboration, respondents representing both perspectives also issued a cautionary note. They pointed out that while general education and gifted education share many of the same goals, they do not have identical missions and messages. The field of gifted education cannot thrive unless it aligns itself with the broader field of education, respondents explained. Neither can it thrive, they pointed out, if it abandons its distinctive birthright.

A helpful way of thinking about the articles in this volume, then, is that some approach the topic of differentiation of curriculum with a greater emphasis on the distinctive mission of gifted education. Others look at differentiation with a greater emphasis on the goals, issues, and missions shared between general education and gifted education. Drawing from an analogy with anthropology, Tomlinson et al. (1996) remind us that "splitters" in that field focus on differences among cultures while "lumpers" have a greater interest in what cultures share in common. That analogy provides a second way of looking at the focus of the articles in this volume, with one set working more as "splitters" and posing questions about what happens for high-ability students in mixed-ability settings, while the second set functions more as "lumpers," questioning what common issues and solutions exist for multiple populations in mixed-ability settings.

The message of the group of articles as a whole could be construed in two complementary ways. First, there is knowledge and insight to be gained from the "distinctive mission" or "splitter" approach. Second, there is knowledge and insight to be gained from the "shared mission" or "lumper" approach. Different as they are in many ways, however, all of the pieces point to inevitable and desirable interfaces between gifted education and general education—interfaces that work to the benefit of both groups and the students they inevitably join in serving.

A SHARED INQUIRY

The eleven articles in this volume have a common focus on what we might call "differentiation" of curriculum and instruction. In one way or another, each of the articles probes what that concept means and what happens when it is implemented in some way.

As part of the literature reviews for several of the studies, authors capsule the long history of the concept of differentiation in the field of gifted education, reminding readers of contributions to that concept by educators of the gifted such as Virgil Ward (1961), Kaplan (1974), Renzulli (1977), Harry Passow (1982),

Maker (1982), VanTassel Baska (1985), and Tannenbaum (1986). These authors have given counsel on what it means to teach gifted learners in ways that respond appropriately to their particular learning needs. Work in this line of inquiry might be framed as focusing on differentiation from the distinctive focus of gifted education—or a "splitter" perspective.

Somewhat more recently, the term "differentiation" has been applied to a broader range of students and, in that context, has to do with ways in which teachers can respond effectively to the varied needs of students in academically diverse settings—including, but not limited to students with high-ability and/or advanced learning status (e.g., Tomlinson, 1999, 2001). Work in this line of inquiry might be framed as focusing on differentiation from the shared focus of general and gifted education (as well as other specialty areas such as second language learning, cultural diversity, literacy, and special education)—or from a "lumper" perspective.

As is evident from a closer reading of the eleven articles included here, themes and findings from both groups of articles reinforce both the assertion that gifted education and general education grapple with common issues and the assertion that the field of gifted education rightly addresses some special areas of concern that are its particular concern.

LOOKING THROUGH THE LENS OF GIFTED EDUCATION

While the eleven articles in this volume link gifted education and general education in a variety of ways, eight of the articles report on studies or provide guidance with particular emphasis on the learning needs of students identified as gifted, or students, while not identified as gifted, who have high degrees of ability or talent. A brief synopsis of the eight follows in the order of the articles' publication. The goal of the synopses is simply to highlight methods and key findings for each piece.

"Effectiveness of the Schoolwide Enrichment Model on Selected Aspects of Elementary School Change" (Olenchak & Renzulli, 1989) used both qualitative and quantitative methods to study impacts on 1698 K-6 students, 236 parents, and 10 principals in schools where the Schoolwide Enrichment Model (SEM) (Renzulli & Reis, 1985, 1997) was used over the span of a year. While the researchers were not able to obtain an effective control population, findings from the SEM schools studied indicated that student creative products increased; attitudes of classroom teachers, the general student population, and parents about education of gifted learners improved; numbers of enrichment and interest-based activities increased in classrooms; and cooperation between classroom teachers and gifted education specialists improved. A conclusion of particular interest is that teachers in the study were able to change their classroom practice without great angst because they could see the benefit of the changes for their students.

"The Impact of Staff Development on Teachers' Ability to Modify Curriculum for Gifted and Talented Students" (Reis & Westberg, 1994) studied the impact of three treatment conditions for training teachers of 300 grade 2–6 teachers in 20 schools to use curriculum compacting (Renzulli, Smith, & Reis, 1982) in their classrooms. Treatment Group 1 worked with video training modules as well as books and articles on compacting. Treatment Group 2 used the same materials as well as a two-hour group simulation on compacting. Treatment Group 3 worked with the training materials, the simulation, local consultant services, and 6–10 hours of peer coaching.

Researchers used quantitative methods to look for possible impacts of the treatments on the degree to which teachers modify curricular and instructional practices to address needs of gifted and talented students in their classrooms, teacher decisions about future use of compacting, and quality of teacher use of compactor forms used to plan for students. Teachers in Treatment 3 were significantly different from those in the other two groups in the amount of curriculum eliminated for their advanced learners. Over half of teachers in all three groups indicated intent to continue using compacting, and there were no statistical differences among the groups regarding intent. While quality of compactor forms was higher for each successive treatment, there were no statistically significant differences among ratings for teachers in the three groups on quality of compactor form. As was the case in the previous study, teachers showed little resistance to change in their practice because they saw benefits for students.

"A Multi-Site Case Study of Successful Classroom Practices for High Ability Students" (Westberg & Archambault, 1997) used qualitative method to study 10 elementary classrooms (2 urban, 6 rural, 2 suburban) in various parts of the country with a reputation for addressing the learning needs of high-ability students. Among hallmarks of the teachers across sites were: (1) advanced training and knowledge, (2) willingness to embrace change, (3) collaboration with peers, (4) teacher awareness of student differences and willingness to reflect on and plan for students as individuals, (5) supportive leaders, and (6) a teacher sense of both autonomy and support.

"Open-Ended Activities: Differentiation through Learner Response" (Hertzog, 1998) approached differentiation for high-ability learners in an unusual way. The researcher poses the question of whether differentiation may occur, not so much because of curricular modification, but as a result of varied student responses to the same curriculum. In other words, she asked whether open-endedness in tasks can become an effective tool for differentiation for high-ability learners because it allows these students to work on topics of greater interest, in modes that are more comfortable, with materials that are more suitable, and so on.

The study included 3 heterogeneous third and fourth-grade classrooms. Drawing from observation and interviews with students and teachers, the researcher ultimately used qualitative data analysis to examine student responses to over 33 open-ended activities. She concluded that differentiation occurred for high-ability students because they responded to the tasks in greater depth, with higher levels of skills, and were guided by their own learning preferences—not because the teacher offered tasks that were more complex or abstract. Hertzog also observed that open-endedness often led to student groupings segregated by ability, raising potential questions about equity in such groupings. Further, she noted that open-endedness often resulted in high-ability learners selecting comfortable rather than challenging options.

"Curriculum Compacting and Achievement Test Scores: What Does the Research Say?" (Reis et al., 1998) studied achievement of 436 students in grades 2–5 in 27 districts who experienced curriculum compacting in math, language arts, science, social studies, and spelling. Achievement of students whose curricula were compacted was compared with students in control groups who did not participate in compacting. Out-of-level testing was used (Iowa Test of Basic Skills) to avoid possible ceiling effects.

Using statistical treatments, researchers found that students who participated in compacting had ITBS scores that were not statistically different from control students who completed all prescribed classroom work. This was the case even when students had as much as 40–50% of course content eliminated or streamlined via compacting. Researchers concluded that the findings should assuage the concerns of teachers who fear that student achievement will be depressed if they omit prescribed coursework.

"Building Bridges Between General Practitioners and Educators of the Gifted: A Study of Collaboration" (Purcell & Leppien, 1998) reports on a survey of 289 enrichment specialists, classroom teachers, and administrators focusing on the nature of collaborative efforts on behalf of high-ability learners in general education classrooms. Using qualitative coding methods, researchers examined expectations of general classroom teachers of enrichment specialists who might collaborate with them, and vice versa. Both classroom teachers and enrichment specialists emphasized the key role of the specialists in serving as the initial catalyst for collaboration. Classroom teachers expected specialists to be resourceful in addressing a variety of classroom elements and to communicate consistently, effectively, and empathetically. Enrichment specialists expected classroom teachers to be flexible, to know how to monitor learner needs and adapt curriculum accordingly, to appreciate differences among students, and to be highly curious learners with an interest in creativity. Researchers concluded that enrichment specialists likely expect more than classroom teachers can deliver and need to support teachers in professional growth in the attributes rather than assuming, or even hoping for, their presence at the outset of collaborative relationships. Findings have implications for both initiating and sustaining successful collaboration.

"Changing General Education Classroom Practices to Adapt for Gifted Students" (Johnsen et al., 2002) reports on a multi-year study in which researchers supported teacher change in differentiating curriculum for gifted learners in general education classrooms. There were 74 teacher participants from 6 sites. Extensive teacher training included 22 units on a variety of topics with emphasis on teachers selecting their own goals for change and staff development options supporting those goals. Mentor teachers provided ongoing support to teachers. Administrators and community liaison representatives also participated in training. A classroom observation scale, designed to enable observers to watch systematically for change in teacher practices related to organization of content, use of time and pacing, use of assessment, environment adaptations, and attention to student preferences was important in tracking teacher change over time. Quantitative analysis was used to analyze data obtained with the observation scale. Computer assisted qualitative data analysis was employed in finding trends and patterns across sites from field notes, classroom observation notes, and interviews in the six sites.

Almost all of the project teachers made observable changes in their practice over the two-year project span. Many of the changes were more conservational (allowing teachers to retain core frameworks of practice) than transformational (calling for significant changes in the core frameworks of practice). In general, teachers preferred making changes relative to environment and student preference rather than the more demanding areas of content and assessment, for example. Nonetheless, over the span of the study, 66 of the 74 teacher participants made transformational changes in one or more areas.

Factors cited as important in promoting the high rate of teacher change in practice were positive attitudes among participants and leaders; a clear vision of goals provided by the project; freedom to select goals for change; the nature of staff development; support from mentors, peers, and leaders; and positive effects of the project on students.

"A Curriculum Study of Gifted-Student Learning in the Language Arts" (VanTassel-Baska et al., 2002) reported on use of a quasi-experimental study of impacts of the William and Mary language arts curriculum on gifted students (K-8) in 46 schools in 17 school districts. The concept-based curriculum units are designed to develop analytic and interpretive skills in literature, persuasive writing, linguistic competency, listening and oral communication skills, and reasoning in language arts. Using a range of statistical treatments, researchers examined comparisons between treatment and comparison groups, gender comparisons, impacts of treatment on various student proficiencies, impact of grouping model on effects of treatment, comparisons of single-year and multi-year exposure to the model, and comparisons between low and high SES groups. Treatment impact was generally positive under all conditions. Use of the model proved effective for students at all grades, with both genders, across economic lines, and in all grouping arrangements.

LOOKING THROUGH
THE LENS OF GENERAL EDUCATION

Two articles in the section examine issues surrounding the concept of differentiation from the general education perspective. Rather than taking a particular focus on any one group of learners and concomitant needs, these two studies look at issues related to teachers addressing academic diversity in general. This perspective encourages examination of barriers to and mechanisms for addressing learning needs that may be systemic in nature. Again, a brief synopsis of the two studies follows.

"Practices of Preservice Teachers Related to Gifted and Other Academically Diverse Learners" (Tomlinson et al., 1994) is both a quantitative and qualitative study of 70 novice teachers and their cooperating teachers at five universities in three states in the South, Southeast, and Mid-Atlantic regions of the U.S. In the portion of the study reported in the article, novice teachers took part in one of two treatment groups related to addressing academic diversity or in a control group. Novices in Treatment 1 participated in a full-day workshop on differentiation for academic diversity. The workshop was planned with a reflective and problem-solving focus for participants and was equivalent to a day-long staff development session common in schools. Novices in Treatment 2 participated in the same workshop, but were also assigned a coach who would work with them to problem solve regarding needs of academically diverse learners encountered during their student teaching. Control novices did not participate in the workshops or work with coaches.

The study sought to answer questions about impacts of the treatments on practices of novice teachers, attitudes and practices of cooperating teachers, how preservice teachers seek out students for whom differentiation may be necessary, how preservice teachers assess the effectiveness of approaches to differentiation they employ, and how preservice teachers evolve as problem solvers in meeting the needs of academically diverse populations.

Observations and interviews were primary modes of data collection for the qualitative portion of the study. Data were analyzed for redundancy of codes and development of themes. Several themes are reported: (1) the novice teachers acknowledged the presence of student differences but early on began to believe it impossible to respond to those differences, (2) the novice teachers were ill-prepared to diagnose and reflect on student differences, (3) the novices were generally unclear about what differentiation meant or how it might be enacted in the classroom, and the novices typically had a small repertoire of instructional approaches they might use to address learner variance. There were also several common factors which discouraged the young teachers from addressing academic diversity. Those included: (1) discomfort with classroom management, (2) views of teaching and learning that emphasize the teacher as dispenser of knowledge and students as consumers of what teachers dispense, (3) a weak sense of how to assess student proficiency and how to link assessment results to instructional planning, and (4) lack of emphasis from cooperating teachers, university supervisors, university instructors, and building principals on addressing academic diversity.

"Deciding to Differentiate Instruction in Middle School: One School's Journey" (Tomlinson, 1995) is a qualitative case study of a middle school with a district mandate to differentiate instruction. The case study extended over an

18-month period, including 28 hours of interviews, 30 hours of classroom observation, as well as attendance at and participation in team meetings (11 hours), faculty meetings (4 hours), and staff development sessions (34 hours). Data were analyzed for codes and themes.

Among early barriers to differentiation were: (1) a rationale for differentiating instruction, (2) a need for clarity of definition. In regard to the former, teachers often felt their students were doing well enough without individual modifications. In regard to the latter, teachers tended to define differentiation in ways that were more reactive than proactive and thus to believe they already differentiated instruction adequately. Other early barriers included the presence of a top-down mandate, perceived emphasis on coverage of prescribed curricula, rejection of an initiative that might turn out to be a fad, and a need for more flexible time use in a school with short class periods.

As teachers moved beyond early barriers and began to grapple with changes necessary to differentiate instruction, they needed to develop: (1) multiple ways to approach instruction, (2) a definition of management as facilitation of learning vs. control of behavior, and (3) ways of fostering student-centered vs. teacher-centered classrooms. Teachers who were early subscribers to the concept of differentiation tended to: (1) be inquirers about students, (2) accept teaching as an organic enterprise in which disequilibrium was necessary for growth, and (3) practice their way into new beliefs.

UTILITY OF MULTIPLE LENSES

The articles that follow are just a sampling, of course, of what has been researched and written on curriculum differentiation—from either the "splitter" or "lumper" perspective. Nonetheless, the collection reveals some interesting similarities across this diverse set of contributions. The juxtaposition of perspectives achieved by using multiple lenses to examine the same topic also suggests some provocative questions for research and action.

There are at least four findings that occur in more than one study. First, some approaches to differentiation may provide an effective starting point for moving toward broader change. Such approaches may be easier for teachers to accept if they do not call for teachers to abandon core curricular and instructional practices so much as to augment them in some way, if they provide choice about the nature of the change, or if student curriculum in essence closely guides teachers in making required changes. In such instances, teachers may be less resistant to change because basic teaching routines are left largely intact, because teachers can see positive benefits for learners from the change, and/or because ambiguity about required changes is removed. In several of the studies, there is evidence that teacher attitude may shift in more positive directions as a result of early, more incremental action—thus giving credence to the possibility that broader change in attitude can evolve from initial successes.

Second, there may be some common characteristics among teachers who are more open to changing their practice. Among these characteristics are being an inquirer about students, having a desire to collaborate with colleagues, being a persistent and hungry learner, and accepting the ambiguities of change as positive catalysts for growth. This set of characteristics offers dual possibilities for further exploration—first developing methods for identifying such teachers and enlisting their participation in the early stages of change toward more academically responsive classrooms, and second, formulating professional development continuums that foster the development of such characteristics in a larger number of teachers.

A third finding with some redundancy across articles in this section is the importance of support for teachers who are attempting to become more responsive to academically diverse student populations—including, but not limited to high-ability learners. In these articles, evidence of support from superordinates and/or from colleagues was an encourager for teacher change. Its absence was a discourager. This was the case for both preservice and veteran teachers and suggests a need to work as assiduously with educational leaders as with teachers toward more effectively differentiated classrooms. These studies suggest that such support for change may variously signal necessity, agency, or professional efficacy for different teachers at different times in their development. It would be interesting to study the roles and forms of support for a wide array of teachers at differing points in the process of confronting academic diversity in their classrooms.

A fourth finding shared across multiple studies in this section relates to the potential of "gifted education technology" (Olenchak & Renzulli, 1989, p. 36) to benefit a broad array of learners. Several studies included here suggest potential benefits to a range of teachers and/or students from application of both general and specific approaches often associated with the field of gifted education. It would certainly be worthwhile to examine the ripple effect of such applications over time and populations. Among avenues worthy of examination would be the impact of effectively designed and implemented professional development for a wide range of educators (including curriculum developers, content experts, and teachers) using guidelines and "gifted education technologies" outlined in these articles to strengthen learning for many students—again including, but not limited to, those identified as gifted.

The studies included in this section were largely conducted in elementary settings, with fewer focused on middle and high school contexts. There is a need to more fully examine secondary settings to identify specific needs for differentiation, approaches that are successful for teachers and students in supporting effective differentiation, and impacts of teachers and students of such change.

A final question raised, but not answered, by the articles that follow is a critical one and returns us again to "splitter" vs. "lumper" approaches to fostering more effectively differentiated classrooms. That question has to do with the relative roles of systemic change vs. incremental change in addressing the needs of high ability and other academically diverse learners. It would be useful to examine the impacts of changes indicated in the research studies here to determine the degree to which they were sustained over time, led to extended change in teacher attitude and practice, and/or evolved to patterns that had positive impacts on multiple populations in general classroom settings, or conversely, whether these early changes were transitory or limited in scope. The larger question not answered for either general education or gifted education is the degree to which classrooms can become robustly effective for any learners over time until issues related to quality of curriculum, role of management, community building, flexibility of instruction, and so on are impacted in ways likely both to cause major change in the professional lives of teachers and in the nature of classrooms.

It is almost certainly the case that fundamental changes in general classrooms and collaborative relationships within those classrooms will have to occur if the needs of high-ability learners are to be substantively and durably addressed in those classrooms. The same changes will be required before the needs of second language learners, students with learning problems, students from various cultures, students with high creative potential, and a host of other exceptionalities can be effectively addressed over time in those same classrooms. The field of gifted education needs to continue its quest to understand and contribute to meaningful change for all learners in general classrooms.

It is also the case that gifted education has a mission to address those needs unique to high-ability learners. If the field of gifted education does not attend to those very particular needs, it is likely they will go untended.

Thus we can return to "Interface Between Gifted Education and General Education" (Tomlinson et al., 1996). Perhaps the most compelling feature of the collection of articles in this volume—and certainly its key unifying feature—is the linkage between the two areas of educational practice in attempting to address an issue likely to be seminal to the success of both over the coming quarter century and beyond. A series of suggestions regarding school reform issues is offered in the Tomlinson et al. (1996) article. The suggestions include: (1) advocating and working for educational environments in which all students have an opportunity to explore meaningful content, think critically and creatively, and become engaged in worthwhile production, and (2) forming alliances with other groups that have an interest in flexible classrooms designed to appropriately address student diversity. This collection of articles certainly begins addressing those recommendations. Perhaps gathering them into one place can serve as a catalyst for next steps in those directions for the field of gifted education as it continues collaboration with general education and other educational specialties while simultaneously addressing those missions uniquely its own.

REFERENCES

Hertzog, N. B. (1998). Open-ended activities: Differentiation through learner response. *Gifted Child Quarterly, 42*(4), 212–227. **[See Vol. 5, p. 77].**

Johnsen, S. K., Haensly, P. A., Ryser, G. R., & Ford, R. F. (2002). Changing general education classroom practices to adapt for gifted students. *Gifted Child Quarterly, 46*(1), 45–63. **[See Vol. 5, p. 133].**

Kaplan, S. (1974). *Providing programs for the gifted and talented: A handbook.* Ventura, CA: Office of the Ventura County Superintendent of Schools.

Maker, J. (1982). *Curriculum development for the gifted.* Rockville, MD: Aspen Systems Corporation.

Olenchak, F. R., & Renzulli, J. S. (1989). The effectiveness of the Schoolwide Enrichment Model on selected aspects of elementary school change. *Gifted Child Quarterly, 33*(1), 36–46. **[See Vol. 5, p. 17].**

Passow, H. (1982). *Differentiated curricula for the gifted/talented.* Ventura, CA: Office of the Ventura County Superintendent of Schools.

Purcell, J. H., & Leppien, J. H. (1998). Building bridges between general practitioners and educators of the gifted: A study of collaboration. *Gifted Child Quarterly, 42*(3), 172–181. **[See Vol. 5, p. 117].**

Reis, S. M., & Westberg, K. L., (1994). The impact of staff development on teachers' ability to modify curriculum for gifted and talented students. *Gifted Child Quarterly, 38*(3), 127–135. **[See Vol. 5, p. 39].**

Reis, S. M., Westberg, K. L., Kulikowich, J. M., & Purcell, J. H. (1998). Curriculum compacting and achievement test scores: What does the research say? *Gifted Child Quarterly, 42*(2), 123–129. **[See Vol. 5, p. 105].**

Renzulli, J. S. (1977). *The enrichment triad model: A guide for developing defensible programs for the gifted and talented.* Mansfield Center, CT: Creative Learning Press.

Renzulli, J. S., & Reis, S. M. (1985). *The schoolwide enrichment model: A comprehensive plan for educational excellence.* Mansfield Center, CT: Creative Learning Press.

Renzulli, J. S., & Reis, S. M. (1997). *The schoolwide enrichment model: A comprehensive plan for educational excellence* (2nd ed.). Mansfield Center, CT: Creative Learning Press.

Renzulli, J. S., Smith, L., & Reis, S. M. (1982). Curriculum compacting: An essential strategy for working with gifted students. *The Elementary School Journal, 82*(3), 185–194.

Tannenbaum, A. (1986). The enrichment matrix model. In J.S. Renzulli (Ed.), *Systems and models for developing programs for the gifted and talented* (pp. 126–152). Mansfield Center, CT: Creative Learning Press.

Tomlinson, C. A. (1995). Deciding to differentiate instruction in middle school: One school's journey. *Gifted Child Quarterly, 39*(2), 77–87. **[See Vol. 5, p. 209].**

Tomlinson, C. A. (1999). *The differentiated classroom: Responding to the needs of all learners.* Alexandria, VA: Association for Supervision and Curriculum Development.

Tomlinson, C. A. (2001). *How to differentiate instruction in mixed-ability classrooms (2nd Edition).* Alexandria, VA: Association for Supervision and Curriculum Development.

Tomlinson, C. A., Coleman, M. R., Allan, S., Udall, A., & Landrum, M. (1996). Interface between gifted education and general education: Toward communication, cooperation, and collaboration. *Gifted Child Quarterly, 40*(3), 165–171. **[See Vol. 5, p. 1].**

Tomlinson, C. A., Tomchin, E. M., Callahan, C. M., Adams, C. M., Pizzat-Tinnin, P., Cunningham, C., Moore, B., Lutz, L., Roberson, C., Eiss, N., Landrum, M., Hunsaker, S., & Imbeau, M. (1994). Practices of preservice teachers related to gifted and other academically diverse learners. *Gifted Child Quarterly, 38*(3), 106–114. **[See Vol. 5, p. 191].**

VanTassel-Baska, J. (1985). Appropriate curriculum for the gifted. In J. Feldhusen (Ed.), *Toward excellence in gifted education* (pp. 175–189). Denver: Love.

VanTassel-Baska, J., Zuo, L., Avery, L., & Little, C. A. (2002). A curriculum study of gifted-student learning in the language arts. *Gifted Child Quarterly, 46*(1), 30–44. **[See Vol. 5, p. 165].**

Ward, V. (1961). *Education for the gifted: An axiomatic approach.* Columbus, OH: Charles E. Merrill Books.

Westberg, K. L., & Archambault, F. X. (1997). A multi-site case study of successful classroom practices for high ability students. *Gifted Child Quarterly, 41*(1), 42–51. **[See Vol. 5, p. 59].**

Interface Between Gifted Education and General Education: Toward Communication, Cooperation and Collaboration

Carol Ann Tomlinson

University of Virginia

Mary Ruth Coleman

University of North Carolina at Chapel Hill

Susan Allan

Grosse Pointe Michigan Public Schools

Anne Udall

Charlotte Mecklenburg Public Schools

Mary Landrum

University of Nebraska, Kearney

Gifted education has often seemed isolated from general education, in part because of differing perspectives on equity and excellence goals and tensions

---

Editor's Note: From Tomlinson, C. A., Coleman, M. R., Allan, S., Udall, A., & Landrum, M. (1996). In the public interest: Interface between gifted education and general education: Toward communication, cooperation and collaboration. *Gifted Child Quarterly, 40*(3), 165–171. © 1996 National Association for Gifted Children. Reprinted with permission.

resulting from those divergent viewpoint. Recently however, there have been calls from both educators of the gifted and general educators for an increased interface between the two fields. This article reports findings and suggestions from a study conducted by a task force commissioned by the National Association of Gifted Children to determine attitudes of educators of the gifted and general educators regarding linkage between the practices, and to provide guidance from practitioners in both fields on increasing communication, cooperation and collaboration between the fields.

BACKGROUND

During the current educational environment characterized by serious and sustained efforts at school reform (as often in past times as well), there have been evident tensions between general education and gifted education born largely from (1) the view of gifted education by general educators as elitist (Margolin, 1994; Oakes, 1985; Sapon-Shevin, 1995; Wheelock, 1992), and (2) the view of general education by educators of the gifted as insensitive to the needs of high ability learners (Council for Exceptional Children, 1994; Renzulli & Reis, 1991). Flashpoints representative of differences between the two groups of educators have included reform initiatives such as heterogeneous grouping, cooperative learning, site-based management, and the middle school concept (Council for Exceptional Children, 1994; Gallagher, 1991, 1992; Robinson, 1990; Rogers, 1991; Tomlinson, 1992, 1994).

Tensions notwithstanding, many educators of the gifted have noted that gifted learners also suffer from classrooms with a drill and skill, teacher-centered, text-based, test-driven profile (Tomlinson & Callahan, 1992), and that the school reform movement embodies many potential benefits for gifted learners as for all students (Council for Exceptional Children, 1994; Dettmer, 1993; Ford & Harris, 1993; Frank, 1992; Ross, 1993; Tomlinson & Callahan, 1992). The literature of gifted education has also recently included numerous calls for a closer linkage between gifted education and general education (Council for Exceptional Children, 1994; Hanninen, 1994; Treffinger, 1991; VanTassel-Baska, 1994). Nonetheless, there have been no systematic attempts to investigate ways in which practitioners in the two fields perceive the idea of linkage or to determine channels through which such a relationship might evolve.

During his tenure as President of the National Association for Gifted Children, James Gallagher established an NAGC Task Force commissioned to explore ways in which the field of gifted education might more effectively interface with the field of general education. The task force was charged with making recommendations to the NAGC Board for increased collaboration between the two fields. This article capsules the method and the content of the report of the NAGC Task Force on Interface Between Gifted Education and General Education with the expectation that both the general message of the report and many of its specific recommendations are useful not only at the national level, but at university, district, school and classroom levels as well.

METHOD: PROCESS EMPLOYED BY THE TASK FORCE

To encourage input from a larger number of participants than would likely be the case in a more typical committee structure, the task force chair devised a three-tiered data gathering process which would solicit ideas from a variety of professionals and parents across the country. The first tier of the process involved a collaboration between three members of a task force steering committee to develop an interview protocol and outline processes for data gathering and analysis. Each of the task force members had had lengthy professional experience with both general education and gifted education, each had served in both public school and university positions, and each had extensive training and practice in research. These participants also served as interviewers in the second tier of the process as well.

In the second tier of the process, steering committee members each contacted educators from various regions of the country, inviting them to participate in the work of the task force by interviewing two people in the field of gifted education whose role and contribution they respected, and two people from the field of general education whose role and contribution they respected. Those who accepted received an interview packet containing an explanation of the project and their role in it, a semi-structured interview protocol (Bogdan & Biklen, 1982), guidelines for interviewing (Bogdan & Biklen, 1982), and procedures for reporting data to the task force steering committee. (Supporting documents are available upon request.)

Interviewers tape recorded interviews, developed synthesis papers of each interview as well as reflection papers (Bogdan & Biklen, 1982) on their set of interviews, and submitted complete interview notes and syntheses to the steering committee who received and analyzed approximately 50 interviews. Interviews were conducted with professionals and parents in Arizona, California, Georgia, Illinois, Louisiana, Michigan, Missouri, New Mexico, North Carolina, South Dakota, Texas, Virginia, Washington, and Wisconsin. Categories of persons interviewed included: regular classroom teachers, school-level specialists in gifted education, district level administrators of programs for the gifted, state level administrators in gifted education, state level administrators in general education, university professors, school principals, assistant principals, superintendents of schools, assistant superintendents, a director of student learning and assessment, a program manager for federal funding, and parents. The goal of the task force was not to systematically sample from a universe, but rather to hear broadly ideas from a variety of individuals who have a stake in both gifted and general education. Members of the task force steering committee, joined by an additional member who had not been a part of the original design process, analyzed interview notes and syntheses, looking first for recurrent themes via content analysis (Lincoln & Guba, 1985), and then organizing those themes in a way which represented both the patterns and flow of ideas in the interviews as a group (Miles & Huberman, 1984). An audit trail for the project has been maintained (Lincoln & Guba, 1985).

The third tier of the task force process involved a review of the draft report by a committee convened by a public school educator with extensive professional experience in both gifted and general education. The intent of the review was to examine both the content and form of the report. The review committee was supportive of many of the recommendations in the draft version of the report. They were skeptical, however, of the draft focus on collaborative efforts between gifted education and general education, preferring instead to seek out and emphasize other avenues of interface which did not imply specific collaboration. Following review of the draft, the committee chair revised the draft to include the intent of the review committee report, presented it to steering committee members for approval, and subsequently to the President of NAGC who commissioned the work of the task force.

While those involved with the work of the task force do not doubt that other perspectives on the issue of a gifted education/general education collaboration exist, we do feel that the fifty interviews analyzed present noteworthy trends in thinking as well as an interesting and worthwhile range of suggestions.

AN OVERVIEW OF THE MESSAGE OF THE REPORT

The inescapable message which prevailed throughout the interviews, from educators of the gifted and general educators alike, was the urgency of need for communication, cooperation and/or collaboration between the fields. Virtually all interviewees talked about a rationale for joint efforts, included caveats in pursuing collaboration, noted obstacles to cooperation and collaboration, emphasized potential benefits to cooperation and collaboration, and made specific recommendations about how cooperation and collaboration might be nurtured. This report follows that format. In many instances, the words of interviewees are used to support or amplify generalizations developed through analysis of interview documents. It is important to note that interviewees as well as steering committee members and review committee members understand that cooperation and collaboration are not synonymous with assimilation. There was clarity among all participants that the field of gifted education has a unique mission in the larger field of education which must be preserved. Nonetheless, there was also a clear sense that communication, cooperation and collaboration between gifted education and general education are compelling goals which should be initiated and pursued by educators of the gifted. In this article, the term "collaboration" should be taken to mean those efforts which support mutual understanding and mutual action between the two fields, understanding that the missions of the two will not and should not be identical.

Rationale for Collaboration

Interviewees presented three distinct and recurrent rationales for fostering a collaboration between gifted education and general education.

1) *Collaboration between the two fields would facilitate balancing the roles of equity and excellence to the benefit of all students.* Often, general education emphasizes equity concerns in education while gifted education focuses on excellence concerns. When the two fields remain relatively distinct in dialogue, planning and execution of plans, the result is a sense of "haves" and "have nots" among identified gifted and non-identified students respectively. Collaboration would promote the idea of talent development for all students. It would "break the mold of treating all students the same" in general education, and yet be more inclusive in gifted education by intent "to provide a quality program for all students, not just a select few." Blending and balancing equity and excellence seems a compelling rationale for cooperation and/or collaboration to many interviewees. Equity becomes concerned with opportunity to maximize capacity for all learners, including the gifted. Excellence becomes concerned with talent development at all levels, including those not identified as gifted. American education (and democracy) benefits from recognition of the legitimate roles of both excellence and equity in schools (and society) and from balancing rather than devaluing either role.

2) *Collaboration between the two fields would reinforce the reality that we share many of the same goals.* Gifted students spend most of their time in the regular classroom setting. What benefits the health of the regular classroom contributes to the robustness of learning for all students, including the gifted. Therefore, rich content, regular expectations for critical and creative thinking, development of meaningful products, establishing expectations for high quality and hard work are goals shared by both sets of educators. (Reflecting opportunity rather than blame, one general educator said, "If you can't help make general education better, you're shortly not going to have the opportunity to make education of gifted students better, because there will be no public schools as we know them today.") Similarly, gifted students are part of the developmental continuum of learners, all of whom have specialized needs as well as shared needs. Therefore, "meeting the individualized needs of the child is a common philosophy of both groups (of educators)." Shared goals do not erase clear disagreements between general educators and educators of the gifted about how such goals should be enacted. They do, however, provide an important basis for discussion and cooperation between members of the two educational practices in developing implementation strategies beneficial to a broader group of students than might be the case without such dialogue and cooperation.

3) *Collaboration between the two fields would maximize the strengths of both generalists and specialists to the benefit of the total school community.* "General educators have an essential role to play in schools, but so do specialists, and they aren't

the same role, and they ought not to have to compete for status or recognition." Said a general educator, "As a teacher, I'd like to do a better job of providing for children. To do that, I need better training and support. I need a better repertoire of instructional strategies. I need to know about more resources and materials. And I need to have a better connection with what gifted education is all about." Said an educator of gifted learners, "The education a gifted student gets in my classroom could not be duplicated in the regular classroom, but I also know that gifted kids need to be a part of the larger environment." Gifted education has had and continues to have a role as a laboratory for testing, refining and disseminating ideas generated by and applicable to general education. Both generalists and specialists have particular contributions to make to the success of education, and a symbiotic relationship would enhance the possibilities of both groups of educators—and the children whom they serve.

The overall rationale for collaboration seemed to suggest the metaphor of an orchestra. Gifted education is one section of the larger group, with an important line of the score to contribute. The full expression of the music is only possible when all sections do their best to play their part—with regard for that part, and for the artistry of parts blended to become a more impressive end product. Gifted education is neither the whole orchestra—nor is the orchestra whole without it.

A Cautionary Note

A number of interviewees, while not veering from their commendation of collaboration, injected a caution. "We (gifted education) can be more collaborative with general education . . . Certainly we should share strategies and techniques that work broadly. It used to be that (these) strategies were used with just gifted students. Now we see the importance of using them with all students, and that's where we should collaborate. But we also have to have (a means) to meet the unique needs of gifted students." "Inclusion of students with unique needs into the regular classroom has a chance only if someone is out there insisting that we must address those needs in differing ways." "If we lose our identity, we lose our opportunity for advocacy."

One interviewee suggested that gifted education errs when it becomes exclusive, but not when it understands its separateness. Gifted education plays a role in advocating high-end excellence which no other group in education plays. "Don't reject your birthright," cautioned one general educator. "You must be what you are." An educator of the gifted said, "While our job must increasingly be to develop all talent, to take all kids as far as they can go, we must continue to be the models of high-end talent development in the context of general talent development." Another said, "Views of intelligence are broadening, but there are students still at the upper ends of each intelligence who are just putting in time in classrooms. We have to be there for them, even if it is not politically popular to do so."

Anthropologists are sometimes described as lumpers (those who look at commonalities of cultures) and splitters (those who look at cultural differences).

Currently, general education tends to take a "lumper" role. The similarities among students are real and important. Those similarities call upon gifted education to promote those instructional mechanisms which enrich all students. Nonetheless, educators of the gifted also have a role as "splitters." "Educators have to stop looking for a single way that will work for everybody. Kids need treatments according to their differing needs. Gifted education has to remind us that it is not acceptable to treat everybody the same—that one size never has fit all." "We cannot succumb to the bandwagon, to the mentality of the single quick fix." "Stop taking the temperature every 15 seconds. Stop saying the sky is falling. Let some things play out. Things are changing, and we need to see where they are going." "We tell our students that it is okay to be different. We'd better have the courage to be different when it's necessary too."

Clearly, gifted education exists to advocate for and serve a group of learners often overlooked in the planning and advocacy of other facets of educational practice. Articulating goals of and championing high-end excellence would likely be greatly diminished without the unique voice of gifted education. Collaborative efforts are not acceptable if they erode those roles. The caution seems to be that the field of gifted education adopt a sort of Janusian stance— looking both in the direction of our heritage and toward new opportunity.

Obstacles to Establishing Collaboration

Clearly there are obstacles which have impeded collaboration between general education and gifted education in the past. Some are implicit or explicit in previous sections of the article. Failure to understand the obstacles impairs our capacity to move forward toward collaboration. Three obstacles to collaboration pervaded the interviews of participants in the task force project: mutually negative attitudes between general educators and educators of the gifted, isolationism, and scarcity of resources.

Chief among the barriers to collaboration noted by interviewees falls under the heading of mutual suspicion and mistrust which permeates relationships between educators of the gifted and general educators. Educators of the gifted often seem to operate from an assumption that what happens in the regular classroom is not worthwhile, unimportant. "Gifted educators often exhibit an 'I know best' attitude. It's alienating." General educators seem to dismiss the value of gifted education. A regular classroom teacher said, "I'm a pessimist when it comes to this subject. I don't know if it's the times or the locality where I work, but among 45 faculty working in my school, I'd say there are about 44 who don't believe that gifted education exists or that gifted children do. It's very overt. People are filled with animosity . . ."

Related to mutually offensive attitudes about colleagues are defeating attitudes about students as well. "I get the feeling that educators of the gifted think the only important talent is in their classes. It's not true, of course. But sometimes, I don't think gifted educators want to see that." "There's misunderstanding, even fear of, gifted students on the part of many classroom teachers. This kind of negative reaction is born of a great . . . lack of information and knowledge about gifted students." A state-level general educator spoke from no-man's-land, "Many of us have a feeling of defensiveness, caused by so many little camps with their own focus and interests. None of them have what I believe ought to be the primary focus, and that is to educate the child. Children suffer because of it."

Related to the barrier of mistrust is one which stems from programs which appear remote and isolated from the general curriculum. Pullout programs per se were not cited as obstacles, but rather pullout programs which seem disintegrated from the regular education program were problematic. "I want to emphasize," said one regular classroom teacher, "that programs which separate do not support collaborative efforts." Another noted, "I have no ownership (in the pullout program) even though I am a gatekeeper for it." Another educator concluded, "This kind of program puts us into a 'my kids/your kids' mentality instead of an 'our kids' frame of mind."

A third impediment to collaboration recurrent in the interviews was the issue of resources. Paucity of time and money were evident concerns of both general educators and educators of the gifted. An educator of the gifted reflected, "I would like to collaborate with classroom teachers more. I think what it comes down to is time. I think they would like to work more with us too. It's hard to develop a working relationship when you are only in the building a few hours a week . . . (and when) the other person has no time to plan anyhow." A professor explained, "There are too few resources available to help teachers meet the needs of high ability learners. Teachers become overwhelmed and end up teaching to the middle."

Benefits from Establishing Collaboration

Obstacles to collaboration notwithstanding, virtually all interviewees elected to concentrate on benefits to education, educators and to learners which could result from collaborative relationships between general educators and educators of the gifted. In fact, it appeared evident that many respondents felt collaboration held the best promise to eroding the barriers, even as it held promise to enrich education.

Three categories of benefits of collaboration were common among interviews.

1. *Collaboration enhances understanding and trust between gifted education and general education.*

Collaboration:

- facilitates communication.
- promotes ownership of gifted learners by educators of the gifted.
- promotes ownership of non-identified students by educators of the gifted.

- encourages linking general and specialized learning opportunities for gifted students.
- helps each group of educators develop more accurate information about a broader group of learners.
- helps educators "act their way into new beliefs rather than believing their way into new actions."

2. *Collaboration supports professional development of all educators.*

Collaboration:

- encourages networking among educators.
- decreases the problem of the isolation of teaching.
- promotes sharing of competencies which could accelerate positive school change.
- promotes shared expertise, allowing educators of the gifted to share process skills and general educators to share content knowledge.
- promotes peer coaching and observation for professional growth.
- encourages mutually beneficial research on and evaluation of challenging instructional practices.

3. *Collaboration enhances student learning.*

Collaboration:

- promotes individualization and differentiation for all students.
- facilitates higher level thinking and higher expectations for content and production for more students.
- promotes talent development for all students.
- promotes continuity across school programs and services.
- promotes more fluid and flexible grouping of students.
- promotes speaking with a single voice for community support for education.

Several interviewees pointed to specific benefits to gifted education of collaboration. Said one, "It strengthens the voice of gifted education. Alone, gifted education has little impact on the field of education as a whole." Another explained that teachers of the gifted are often perceived as being "superhuman" and inaccessible simply because of their association with the term "gifted." "If educators of the gifted work in regular classrooms and take instructional and management risks right along with the classroom teacher, and make mistakes right along with the classroom teacher, we will ultimately become "real" teachers and our voices will be human voices again." By making themselves more accessible and inviting to general educators through collaboration, gifted educators who establish effective collaborations benefit general educators and gifted learners. One classroom teacher explained, "I need help . . . I'm frustrated . . . I have so many exceptionalities to deal with and I have only five front row seats." Another said, "Generalists don't feel they can do it all, even if reformers think so."

Recommendations in Behalf of Collaboration

Virtually all respondents emphasized the need for gifted education to take the lead in establishing collaborative efforts at national, state, district, school and classroom levels. Interviewees provided a diverse range of suggestions for moving toward gifted education/general education collaboration. Some of the recommendations would be best implemented by practitioners at the local level, some by organizations such as NAGC and at a national level. "We (gifted education) have to take the lead. We are not big, we are not valued (by the general education community), we are not important. We have to knock (on the wall that separates us) to see if someone is on the other side." Suggestions for enhancing collaboration are grouped here in six categories.

1. *Suggestions for Improved Perceptions about Gifted Education*

- Take clear, consistent, proactive public stands that make gifted education part of the movement to improve education for all students.
- Greet examples of acceptance and nurturing of gifted children by general educators with expressions of interest and excitement.
- Using broadened conceptions of intelligence, focus on gifted education as a resource for talent development in a broad range of students.
- Develop videotapes of effective examples of gifted education and share them broadly.
- Provide opportunities for general educators to see educators of the gifted at work in a variety of settings "to help more educators understand what gifted learners can do and what differentiation looks like."
- Provide in-depth training for educators of the gifted on topics which help them become active players in the larger perspectives of education (e.g. standards, rubrics, portfolios).
- "Plant the seed for the need." Create materials and conversations which help general educators understand the specific needs of gifted learners which could be effectively addressed by generalist/specialist collaborations.
- Provide assistance from public relations and communications professionals (through conferences such as those sponsored by state associations for the gifted and NAGC) to educators of the gifted in how to respond in positive ways to detractors and how to network with colleagues.
- In interactions with general education, be patient. Accept "a little progress each time. Don't push too hard."
- Support educators of the gifted in remaining active in professional organizations of general education.

2. *Suggestions Regarding Instructional Practice and Programming*

- Focus on how to assess student needs and interests, and how to design responsive instruction rather than focusing on identification and grouping.
- Provide leadership in using performance-based assessment.
- Focus on the regular classroom more than on special programs/classes.
- Share differentiated units broadly, demonstrating ways in which instructional strategies can be modified for most effective use with high ability learners.
- Focus on flexible use of time with gifted learners in the classroom.
- Emphasize a continuum of services necessary for and available to gifted learners in the school.
- Take the lead in establishing differential rubrics and performance outcomes for use with gifted learners in the regular classroom.
- Emphasize collaborative identification through the regular classroom.
- Emphasize both co-planning and co-teaching.
- Provide opportunities for general educators and educators of the gifted to swap roles.
- Proactively develop administrator understanding of the benefits of collaboration and support toward building collaboration.
- Promote collaboration between specialists in gifted education and special education as a means of addressing and supporting individualization and differentiation for more students in more settings.
- Create and share specific models of differentiated instruction and flexible grouping in the regular classroom.
- Find and share examples of general education teachers who are effective with gifted learners in the regular classroom.
- In special classes/learning opportunities for the gifted, be sure g/t specialists differentiate instruction rather than assuming all eligible students should fit a single mold.

3. *Suggestions Regarding Preservice, Inservice, and Graduate Preparation*

- Encourage university level educators of the gifted to volunteer to teach preservice courses, participate in preservice seminars, and serve as university supervisors for student teachers. "We need preservice teachers coming out of college ready to deal with student differences."
- Encourage university level educators of the gifted to collaborate with special educators to develop and teach models of differentiated instruction for academically diverse classrooms.
- Emphasize collaborative/consultative models and models of instructional differentiation in Master's level programs preparing educators of the gifted.

- Prepare educators of the gifted to model a variety of instructional strategies in the regular classroom.
- Take the lead in action research projects on topics related to high ability learners with general educators and educators of the gifted.
- Actively recruit and support minority teachers of the gifted at both preservice and graduate levels.
- Find out what kinds of collaboration and assistance general educators want and help educators of the gifted be ready to provide it. "Stay close to the classroom."

4. *Suggestions Regarding Policy and Political Action*

- Plan conferences such as state association conferences and NAGC conferences at times and in places where other professional groups are meeting, then encourage sharing of sessions, speakers, demonstrations.
- Give reduced cost or no cost admission to a general educator accompanying and state association or NAGC members to a state or NAGC conference, and plan sessions on collaboration designed to facilitate the working partnership between members of both groups.
- Become involved in the national standards movement.
- Seek involvement with the Holmes Group.
- Nurture support which now exists for gifted education in the National Education Association, American Federation of Teachers as well as state and local education associations.
- Link governors' schools and residential schools for the gifted to new mandates for alternative schools.
- Hold state association and NAGC conference sessions and strands on how to form liaisons with general education at the state department of education, school district, and school levels.
- Hold state association and NACG conference sessions and/or special workshops on political action and policy development. Provide financial support for a network of educators of the gifted with potential to make an impact in these areas to receive the training.
- Support educators of the gifted and other advocates for gifted child education in becoming administrators, school board members, site-based committee members, PTAs, and other policy-making groups and positions.
- Support educators of the gifted in attending and presenting at general education professional conferences at state and national levels (e.g., NCTM, ASCD, NMSA, NAASP, NCTE).
- Promote use of technology by educators of the gifted to form liaisons with general educators and general education groups.
- Encourage university level educators of the gifted to order general teacher education books, survey contents, and communicate with publishers regarding concepts which need to be included in future editions.

- Establish working relationships with businesses and industries which have an interest in high-end excellence.
- Assist in parent education with the goal of tapping into the political influence of parents of gifted learners in positive ways.

5. *Suggestions Regarding School Reform Issues*

- Advocate and work for educational environments in which all students have an opportunity to explore meaningful content, think critically and creatively, and become engaged in worthwhile production.
- Form alliances with other groups that have an interest in flexible classrooms designed to appropriately address student diversity.
- Stress teaching educators of the gifted how to understand and respond effectively to student diversity (including academic diversity, ethnic diversity, learning style diversity) and how to assist colleagues in doing likewise.
- Work closely with minority communities, learning from them ways in which the community would identify and develop talent.
- Encourage state association and NAGC conference proposals to integrate minority issues into topics presented rather than separating minority issues from other issues.
- Encourage development of curricula which are multicultural in emphasis and approach.
- Join other educators in working for reduced class size, longer blocks of instructional time, improved teacher salaries and other initiatives likely to improve the quality of instruction broadly in schools.
- Advocate adapting school schedules to accommodate collaborative teacher planning and shared instruction.
- Develop broad guidelines for working with gifted learners in site-based settings.

6. *Suggestions Regarding Research and Dissemination Efforts*

- Work to strengthen the research base for practices advocated for gifted learners.
- Provide leadership in reflective practitioner and action research to address issues of interest to teachers regarding gifted learners, diversity, and practices likely to impact instruction of gifted learners.
- Conduct longitudinal efforts to study and modify teacher attitudes about giftedness.
- Stress effective qualitative research as an evaluation tool for gifted education and as a way to help educators understand gifted learners.
- Invite more collaborative participation in gifted education journals.
- Develop publications for general educators discussing instructional issues and sharing instructional practices of interest to teachers. "Share your trade secrets broadly."

SUMMARY

A general educator said, "Generalists don't feel like they can do everything, even if reformers think they can," said one respondent. The broad consensus of the interviewees is that there is merit and urgency in collaboration, both from the vantage point of general educators as well as educators of the gifted. We both work at a moment in history when polar influences encourage us on the one hand to mask diversity and on the other to celebrate it. Gifted learners would benefit from the latter stance, as would many other learners in our schools. Gifted education has an opportunity and a history which could make a positive contribution toward moving in the direction of embracing diversity, There was a caution that gifted education must not jettison its reason for being in order to hop aboard educational bandwagons. Nonetheless, the voices of interviewees spoke as a chorus affirming that, with temperance and caution, the benefits of collaboration far outweigh the very real obstacles in the path of collaboration.

REFERENCES

Bogdan, R., & Biklen, S. (1982). *Qualitative research for education: An introduction to theory and methods*. Boston: Allyn & Bacon.

Council for Exceptional Children (1994). *Toward a common agenda: Linking gifted education and school reform*. Reston, VA: Council for Exceptional Children.

Dettmer, P. (1993). Gifted education: Window of opportunity. *Gifted Child Quarterly, 37*, 92–94.

Ford, D., & Harris, J. III. (1993). Educational reform and the focus on gifted African-American students. *Roeper Review, 15*, 200–204.

Frank, R. (1992, March). School restructuring: Impact on attitudes, advocacy, and educational opportunities for gifted and talented students. In *Challenges in gifted education. Developing potential and investing in knowledge for the 21st century*. Columbus, OH: Ohio State Department of Education.

Gallagher, J. (1991). Educational reform, values, and gifted students. *Gifted Child Quarterly, 35*, 12–19.

Gallagher, J. (1992, March). Gifted students and educational reform. In *Challenges in gifted education: Developing potential and investing in knowledge for the 21st century*. Columbus, OH: Ohio State Department of Education.

Hanninen, G. (1994). Blending gifted education and school reform. ERIC Digest #E525.

Lincoln, Y., & Guba, E. (1985). *Naturalistic inquiry*. Beverly Hills, CA: Sage.

Margolin, L. (1994). *Goodness personified: The emergence of gifted children*. New York: Aldine De Gruyter.

Miles, M., & Huberman, A. (1984). *Qualitative data analysis: A sourcebook of new methods*. Newbury Park, CA: Sage.

Oakes, J. (1985). *Keeping track: How schools structure inequality*. New Haven, CT: Yale University Press.

Renzulli, J., & Reis, S. (1991). The reform movement and the quiet crisis in gifted education. *Gifted Child Quarterly, 35*, 26–35.

Robinson, A. (1990). Cooperation or exploitation? The argument against cooperative learning for talented students. *Journal for the Education of the Gifted, 14*, 9–27.

Rogers, K. (1991). *The relationship of grouping practices to the education of the gifted and talented learner* Storrs, CT: National Research Center on the Gifted and Talented.

Ross, R. (1993). *National excellence: A case for developing America's talent*. Washington, DC: Office of Educational Research and Improvement.

Sapon-Shevin, M. (1995). Why gifted students belong in inclusive schools. *Educational Leadership, 52*(4), 64–70.

Tomlinson, C. (1991). Gifted education and the middle school movement: Two voices on teaching the academically talented. *Journal for the Education of the Gifted, 15*, 206–238.

Tomlinson, C. (1992). Gifted learners: The boomerang kids of middle school? *Roeper Review, 16*, 177–182.

Tomlinson, C. & Callahan, C. (1992). Contributions of gifted education to general education in a time of change. *Gifted Child Quarterly, 36*, 183–189.

Treffinger, D. (1991). School reform and gifted education: Opportunities and issues. *Gifted Child Quarterly, 35*, 6–11.

Van Tassel-Baska, J. (1991). Gifted education in the balance: Building relationships with general education. *Gifted Child Quarterly, 35*, 20–25.

Wheelock, A. (1992). *Crossing the tracks: How "untracking" can save America's schools.* New York: The New Press.

2

The Effectiveness of the Schoolwide Enrichment Model on Selected Aspects of Elementary School Change

F. Richard Olenchak

The University of Alabama

Joseph S. Renzulli

The University of Connecticut

This study examined the effectiveness of a yearlong application of the Schoolwide Enrichment Model in eleven schools. Subjects consisted of

Editor's Note: From Olenchak, F. R., & Renzulli, J. S. (1989). The effectiveness of the schoolwide enrichment model on selected aspects of elementary school change. *Gifted Child Quarterly*, 33(1), 36-46. © 1989 National Association for Gifted Children. Reprinted with permission.

1,698 elementary grade students, 236 teachers, 120 parents, and 10 principals. Data analysis revealed positive changes in student and teacher attitudes. Student creative products were numerous and exceeded the norm of typical student creative output. Most notable among qualitative data analysis were: remarkably favorable changes in attitudes toward education of the gifted on the part of classroom teachers and the general student population, large increases in student-centered enrichment activities and work on self-selected interests, greater cooperation between classroom teachers and gifted education specialists, and more favorable attitudes toward special programming on the part of parents.

INTRODUCTION

Although programs that serve gifted and talented students have traditionally been restricted to small and select groups, there has been a trend in recent years to experiment with more flexible approaches to both identification and programming. This trend is undoubtedly the result of recent research on the nature of human abilities (e.g., Sternberg, 1982; Gardner, 1983; Bloom, 1985) and a realization that some of the activities recommended for the gifted can successfully be applied to larger segments of the school population (Renzulli, 1977; Reis & Renzulli, 1982; Shore & Tsiamis, 1985; Feldman, 1983; and Birch, 1984). A greater interest in performance-based identification and a concern about the "condition of separateness" that often exists between special and regular programs have also contributed to a willingness to experiment with approaches that hold promise for overcoming some of the problems that historically have drawn criticism to the field of gifted education.

The purpose of this study was to examine the effects of a programming model that was specifically designed to apply some of the technology of gifted education to the overall process of schoolwide enrichment. The model employed as the experimental treatment was *The Schoolwide Enrichment Model* (*SEM*, Renzulli & Reis, 1985), and the experimental design used both qualitative and quantitative variables. The study compared differences between a control group and several groups participating in yearlong *SEM* programs. The specific factors examined were student attitudes toward learning, teacher attitudes toward teaching, the extent and quality of students' creative productivity, and the processes involved in the implementation of *SEM*. Two overall goals of the study were (1) to determine if a school's participation in this type of program would result in specific and quantifiable indicators of schoolwide change, and (2) to examine whether or not such participation would result in more favorable attitudes toward the entire concept of gifted education.

METHODS

Subjects, Site Selection, and Randomization

The subjects in this study were in 11 elementary schools and consisted of 1,698 students in grades K-6, 236 elementary grade teachers, and 120 parents, representative in general proportion to the grade levels involved. Qualitative data dealing with implementation procedures were also gathered from students, teachers, parents, and 10 elementary principals. The student sample represented 28% of the total population of approximately 6,000 pupils enrolled in the 11 participating schools. The student sample was stratified according to grade level and randomly selected from all K-6 classrooms. The teacher sample included all regular classroom teachers at each of the 11 school sites.

Putting the Research to Use

In exploring the program options available for the gifted and talented, both school personnel and parents should consider the impact such programs may have on various participant groups. Could a program offer numerous appropriate learning opportunities for some students yet restrict involvement in activities along perhaps indefensible lines? Might a program appeal to teachers but ultimately provide little for students? By examining the effects of the Schoolwide Enrichment Model (SEM) on students, teachers, principals, and parents, this study provides an opportunity for schools to examine a research-based approach as one among several alternative patterns of program organization. The results indicate that SEM is likely to enhance student attitudes toward learning and teacher attitudes toward teaching. Perhaps even more importantly, the schoolwide use of the high quality instructional technology prevalent in gifted education stands to improve education in general, gain much needed support and collaboration from general faculty, and insure consideration of the needs of gifted and talented students.

Because the *Schoolwide Enrichment Model* encompasses entire school units, control groups could not be located within the same school buildings. Therefore, entire schools had to be assigned to either treatment or control groups in order to protect control populations from contamination by aspects of the *SEM* treatment. A detailed demographic examination of each interested site was undertaken in an effort to locate similarities among schools prior to assignment. This investigation included a review of the most recent school and U.S. Census data pertaining to district socioeconomic levels, school attendance, staff educational levels, and the curriculum offered to students through both gifted and regular education programs. Schools selected enrolled between 350 and 750 students and served either urban or suburban populations.

After this review of demographic and curricular information, invitations were extended on a random basis for schools to participate as an experimental or control site. At this point, a major problem was encountered. Although over 25 schools were sought for control sites, a great hesitancy on the part of administrations was encountered, and despite our best efforts, only one school from the original pool agreed to serve as a control site. Moreover, school administrators evinced an offsetting desire to provide experimental subjects—so much so that the 10 treatment sites were randomly selected from over 30 that had indicated a willingness to experiment with the program model. At least superficially, the unequal number of control and treatment sites was a result of schools' general desire to participate in a novel treatment and general unwillingness to serve as a control for this experiment. For this reason, we will not report the results of hierarchical regression comparisons of student and teacher attitudes toward learning and teaching between the experimental groups and the single control group; however, the results of these analyses are available from the authors upon request.

Since true random assignment of either students or teachers to the treatment or control groups was impossible because of the all-encompassing school-wide nature of the treatment, extensive review of the demographic and curricular characteristics of the schools was undertaken in an effort to secure schools that were as alike as possible. Special consideration of demographic data was made in an attempt to equalize the student groups according to grade level, classroom teacher experience, classroom teaching style, and classroom climate. In order to enchance the demographic data collected and analyzed and to reflect more clearly the aforementioned variables, extensive interviews with central office administrators were conducted to obtain additional information.

Treatment

In order to be selected for participation in this study, school officials had to agree to a specified set of enrichment programming procedures set forth in the *Schoolwide Enrichment Model* (Renzulli & Reis, 1985). It was also necessary for each school to have an enrichment resource teacher on at least a half-time basis. In all cases, written agreement was obtained from administrations and boards of education as further assurance that actual *SEM* implementation would take place. Participating schools were expected to identify students who were of above average ability in one or more areas of performance or potential. Identification was based on achievement test scores, teacher nominations, student interests, and other procedures set forth in the model.

Space limitations prevent a detailed description of the *Schoolwide Enrichment Model*; however, we have attempted to summarize the major organizational and service delivery components in Figure 1. These service delivery components constitute the major focus of the experimental treatment so far as student services are concerned and are briefly described as follows:

Curriculum Compacting. Modifying or "streamlining" the regular curriculum in order to eliminate repetition of previously mastered material, upgrade the challenge level of the regular curriculum, and provide time for appropriate enrichment and/or acceleration activities while ensuring mastery of basic skills.

Assessment of Student Strengths. A systematic procedure for gathering and recording information about students' abilities, interests, and learning styles.

Type 1 Enrichment: General Exploratory Experiences. Experiences and activities that are designed to expose students to a wide variety of disciplines (fields of study), visual and performing arts, topics, issues, occupations, hobbies, persons, places, and events that are not ordinarily covered in the regular curriculum.

Type II Enrichment: Group Training Activities. Instructional methods and materials that are purposefully designed to promote the development of thinking and feeling processes.

Type III Enrichment: Individual and Small Group Investigations of Real Problems. Investigative activities and artistic productions in which the learner assumes the role of a firsthand inquirer; the student thinking, feeling, and acting like a practicing professional.

At each experimental school site, enrichment teams working in cooperation with resource teachers organized a wide variety of general enrichment activities. These activities (Types I and II in Figure 1) encompass exploration of topics, issues, and materials not ordinarily covered in the regular curriculum and a wide variety of systematically organized process training skills. General enrichment was provided to all students in the experimental schools for one academic year. Calendars of exploratory activities (Type I) were developed, and students participated through all-school events, grade level or single-classroom events, or through cross-grade special interest groups. Process training activities were organized in all classrooms in the treatment schools using a scope and sequence approach called the Type II Taxonomy (Renzulli & Reis, 1985). Whenever possible, these activities were integrated with regular experiences.

The ways in which individual students or small groups responded to particular activities served as the bases for determining which students would move into more advanced and self-selected follow-up studies related to a given topic or area of study (Type III). In other words, performance based "identification situations" served as a means for decision making about the nature and extent of subsequent program involvements. Type III enrichment opportunities were available for students who demonstrated above average ability in a self-selected area of interest and who also showed a willingness to develop task

Figure 1   Overview of the Schoolwide Enrichment Model

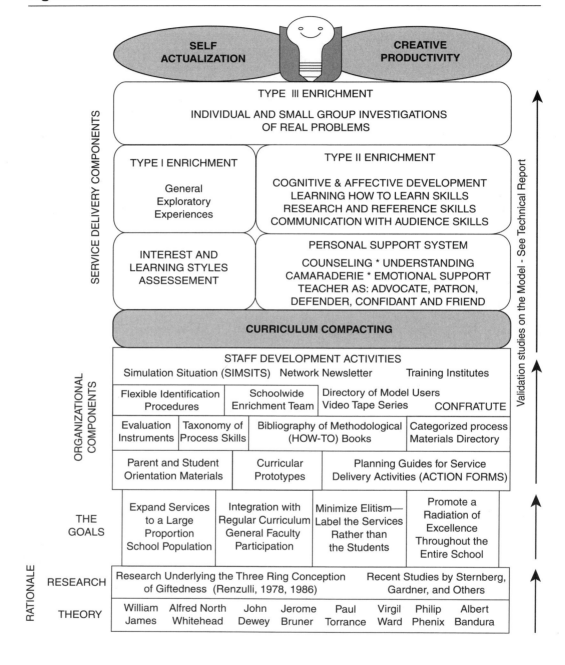

commitment and creativity in connection with the topic. Teachers were provided with information that would encourage students to pursue their topics using the *modus operandi* of the practicing professional.

In addition to participating in all aspects of the schoolwide enrichment process, high ability students also received supplementary services in the form of curriculum compacting in regular classrooms and advanced level enrichment experiences and acceleration provided by resource teachers in pull-out and cluster grouping arrangements. Cluster groups generally consisted of top level reading and math students or students who shared a similar interest in a particular topic or area of study. Experimental schools were expected to participate in inservice training related to the implementation of the treatment model and to maintain careful records through the use of various planning guides. These guides, referred to as Action Forms in the SEM, provide consistency of treatment and serve as management devices that provide form and structure to the model. Each participating school had to verify that all specified planning, inservice, and service delivery activities were in fact implemented throughout the course of the school year during which this experimental treatment took place.

Research Design and Instrumentation

The first portion of the research examined variations in students' and teachers' attitudes through the use of hierarchical multiple regression procedures. Analysis of the quality of student products was carried out through simple calculation of means from comparisons of tallies of the number of Type III investigations initiated to the number actually completed. In addition, mean rankings for each completed Type III product were determined from individual rankings of two independent raters. The group means were then compared to mean scores on the product assessment instrument (described below). A minimal inter-rater reliability criterion level of .75 was maintained. The quality of student products was determined through the use of *The Student Product Assessment Form* (Reis, 1981). This instrument operationally defines product quality by analyzing the degree of presence/absence of the following factors:

1. Early Statement of Purpose

2. Problem Focusing

3. Level of Resources

4. Diversity of Resources

5. Appropriateness of Resources

6. Logic, Sequence, and Transition

7. Action Orientation

8. Audience

9. Overall Assessment

    A. Originality of the Idea
    B. Achieved Objectives Stated in Plan
    C. Advanced Familiarity with Subject
    D. Quality Beyond Age/Grade Level
    E. Care, Attention to Detail, etc.

      F.   Time, Effort, Energy
      G.   Original Contribution

The instrument has an estimated reliability of .96, and levels of agreement among raters on individual items range from 86.4% to 100%. The test-retest (r = .96) reliability was established over a period of one year by having a group of independent raters assess the same set of student products on two separate occasions with an intervening period of time between the two assessments.

A two-pronged qualitative analysis was selected to examine the processes involved in the implementation of SEM. Data obtained from interviews, observations, and logs were reduced by selecting, focusing, simplifying, abstracting, and transforming into key themes (listed below) based on the methodology of natural history. Second, all themes were analyzed by a team of researchers who were selected because of their general experience in programming for the gifted and talented. The themes were examined for relevance to implementation of *SEM* and were sequenced according to the point at which each theme would be included in the implementation process. There was 95% agreement among the rating groups on the sequence of events. This process enabled the researchers to support placement of these themes into a particular events sequence based on both the data collected and on the judgment of the content experts.

Qualitative data were obtained from students, teachers, principals, and parents through the use of four separate interview agendas that were developed for the respective groups. Factors examined by these agendas will be discussed in the sections that follow. Additionally, enrichment activity logs were maintained by six randomly selected teachers at each experimental school site and field notes were recorded by the researchers as part of the observation process.[1]

RESULTS

Student Creative Productivity

A major aspect of this research concentrated on an examination of the quality of students' creative products that emerged as a result of Type III investigations (i.e., individual and small group studies of real problems) at the treatment schools. Although previous research has examined this issue from a comparative perspective involving Talent Pool and non–Talent Pool youngsters, the question of student products has not been explored in schools that have undertaken systematic schoolwide enrichment activities.

Tallies of the number of Type III investigations initiated and of the number actually completed were maintained at each treatment site. Calculation of a simple mean from the tallies yielded the mean number of Type III products that emerged from those initiated. Because control group students would not be expected to produce creative products of the Type III genre due to their lack of training in schoolwide enrichment processes that evoke such products, comparison to the control site was not carried out. Table 1 displays the relationship between the number of Type III investigations initiated and those completed.

Table I   Type III Investigations: Initiated Versus Completed

Treatment Site	N of Started Type III's	N of Completed Type III's	Percent
1	16	12	75.00
2	33	26	78.79
3	25	22	88.00
4	61	43	70.49
5	25	19	76.00
6	24	17	70.83
7	34	24	70.59
8	28	17	60.71
9	24	16	66.67
10	27	20	74.08
Number =	297	216	
Mean =	29.70	21.60	73.12
Standard Deviation =	11.47	8.11	6.93

In addition, a 20% random sample of the completed Type III products was submitted for assessment by two objective and independent raters using *The Student Product Assessment Form (SPAF)* (Renzulli & Reis, 1985a). The sample was stratified according to treatment sites so that each of the schools experimenting with schoolwide enrichment would have a portion of their students' creative products represented in the sample.

Mean ratings for the random sample of products selected for evaluation were calculated on the basis of each rater's scoring of his/her sample. Mean ratings were also calculated across raters. Inter-rater reliability was calculated for level of agreement between the two raters and a t-test was employed to locate any statistically significant differences between the raters.

The Type III investigations initiated in the 10 treatment schools were tallied by gifted education resource teachers. This information resulted in a total of 297 reported Type III investigations that had been initiated. Of this number, 216 were deemed by the students and the gifted education resource teachers to have been completed. This translates to 72.73% of Type III investigations initiated that actually came to fruition as completed products. The completion rate is quite high based on previous research about Type III investigations (Reis, 1981). Completed products ranged in frequency at each treatment school from 12 to 43, with the mean number of completed Type III investigations being 21.6.

Two independent raters evaluated each product.[2] The inter-rater reliability, using the results of the Type III ratings, was calculated at .886, exceeding the .75 criterion level that was established prior to the advent of the data collection for this study. The results of the t-test analysis indicated that there were no significant differences between the two raters based on the ratings of all of the sample Type III products ($p = .36$).

The results of this analysis revealed that students at the *SEM* sites produced a large number of individual and small group Type III investigations based on previous studies of Type III production (Reis, 1981). The quality of Type III products can be estimated by comparing the independent raters' scores with the range (0—80) and the mean scores (M = 45, SD = 5.30) from previous administrations of the *SPAF* used in assessing products of other students who had demonstrated above average ability, creativity, and task commitment. Treatment site scores ranged from a low of 48.25 to a high of 65.01. The lowest mean rating across raters at any treatment school was 49.50, and the average of all evaluated Type III products was 53.21. These results indicate that student creative productivity was clearly in the well above average to superior range based on previous SPAF administrations.

Enrichment Implementation Steps

Qualitative research techniques intended to trace patterns in descriptive data were pursued in response to an examination of enrichment implementation steps. Descriptive information ideally should be derived from several types of data sources so that conclusions are drawn across sources. This procedure offered a positive alternative to formulating conclusions based on only one type of data source. The Dynneson-Bastian Model for school ethnography (Hirsch, 1981) provided the researchers with a logical system for the collection and analysis of descriptive data from three sources using triangulated comparison analyses of the results of various types of interviews, observations, and logs. This procedure involved detailed examinations of interviews with students, teachers, principals, and parents. Augmenting the interviews were analyses of observations of students and teachers and reviews of teacher activity logs. Interviews, observations and activity log analyses focused on the extent and nature of implementation of the service delivery components described above, problems encountered in the implementation process (e.g., demands made upon students' and teachers' time, availability of resources, cooperation among regular and special program teachers), and general attitudes toward the program.

Using two-pronged analyses, the raw data were reduced by selecting, focusing, simplifying, abstracting, and transforming into key themes based on the inductive and deductive methodology of natural history (Dobbert, 1984; Spradley, 1979, 1980). The pretreatment and posttreatment interview data and the observational data were reduced to internal themes. Individual themes were then combined to form the following composite themes: Principals as School Leaders, Teachers as Encouragers of Student Creative Productivity, Curriculum Compacting in Basic Skills, Gifted Behaviors Can Be Developed, Teamwork Among School Personnel, Parents and the Community, and Importance of Student Interest in Creative Productivity. Once these procedures had been completed, the themes that had been identified were submitted to examination by a group of four experts who were well versed in the *Schoolwide Enrichment Model* and its service delivery components. These expert resource persons displayed 95% agreement on the sequence of events and characteristics of the key themes relating to the process of implementing schoolwide enrichment.

Teacher, student, and parent interview data were further examined by tallying the responses and comparing the percentages occurring in each category before and after treatment. Garrett's (1958) formula was used to determine the level of significance between correlated percentages. Percentage data from this procedure are presented in Tables 2, 3, and 5.

Results of Qualitative Analyses

Items on a Teacher Interview Agenda concentrated on the nature of activities within the framework of regular classrooms and whether there is time allocated for student exploration of self-determined topics. Based on the concept of enrichment as described in the *Schoolwide Enrichment Model*, items also focused on whether teachers accessed experts in fields of study. Such access encourages students to be exposed to practicing professionals. Hence, items also addressed whether or not this type of gifted education procedure actually encompassed some of the regular education activities as a means for fostering the emergence of gifted behavior in broader groups of youngsters.

Pre and Post teacher interviews were carried out with a 25% sample that was representative of all elementary grades in the treatment schools. This group can be described as having had a good deal of experience (Range = 1-35 years) and as adequately representing all elementary grades. Table 2 provides an overview of the alterations in teacher perceptions related to 12 concepts crucial to the implementation of enrichment and the statistical difference between correlated percentages. All 12 concepts were highly significant ($p < .001$). Teachers reported they could provide classroom exploration time without necessarily having students complete regular seatwork beforehand. Moreover, teachers grew to appreciate the need for and importance of teamwork in securing resource persons and sharing their expertise among many classrooms.

The student interview and observation sample of 120 randomly selected students was divided equally among the 10 treatment sites to provide 12 student interviews per site. This 14-item instrument concentrated on the nature of the school day from student perspectives: time for exploration of interests, how such time is allowed within the framework of the school day, knowledge of enrichment activities and their availability, and knowledge of the gifted program. As with teachers, the same students were interviewed twice, once prior to treatment and once after treatment. The results of these interviews are summarized in Table 3. The difference in percentages before and after treatment was significant on 13 of the 14 items ($p < .001$). After treatment, students indicated they had more school time, with teacher support, to spend in interest areas aside from regular school material. Increasingly, students among the general school population felt that they had some involvement with the gifted program, and a smaller posttreatment percentage viewed the gifted program as restricted to a special group.

Table 2   Teacher Interviews: A Pretreatment – Posttreatment Comparison
             N = 66

Topic	Pre Percent	Post Percent	Statistical Difference Between Correlated Percentages
can provide exploration within classroom	71	93.3	3.90*
students must complete seatwork before exploration	91.3	40.7	5.75*
gifted education teacher facilitates classroom exploring	0	66.4	6.65*
exploration built into classroom through learning centers or curriculum compacting	16	47	4.45*
view school library as the *only* place to send child for more exploration time	63.8	6	6.19*
view library as resource to be used in *combination* with gifted program, mentors, extra materials	0	94	9.55*
use community professionals as means for enrichment in classroom	31.9	88.7	6.19*
resource person arrangements made by myself	71.5	9.8	6.40
resource persons shared between classrooms and grade levels	33.4	94.9	6.40*
resource person arrangements facilitated by gifted teacher	2.3	69.8	6.65*
gifted education viewed negatively	84.6	18.8	6.65*
gifted education viewed positively	15.4	81.2	6.65*

*$p < .001$

Employing the same approach as with teachers and students, principals at the 10 treatment schools were interviewed in pre- and posttreatment fashion using a Principal Interview Agenda. Unlike the teacher and student interviews, however, the principal interviews did not evince very large changes in perceptions. For example, in the fall principals largely viewed the gifted education program as:

"important . . . regarded as part of our whole school plan . . . activities that are available to many students and not only those who have been assigned the label of 'gifted'";

"shifting to a schoolwide approach and as an enhancer of the basic curriculum . . . progress is tied directly to the type of gifted teacher and the amount of time allocated to each school";

"evolving from a rather elitist program for a few to one that serves many children"; and "starting to become more of an integral part of the school."

Table 3   Student Interviews: A Pretreatment – Posttreatment Comparison
             N = 120

Topic	Pre Percent	Post Percent	Statistical Difference Between Correlated Percentages
have time in school to study interests aside from regular school material	39.2	84.2	7.38*
must complete regular seatwork prior to exploring interests	100	62.5	6.75*
can pursue exploration of interests during regular class time in my classroom	44.2	57.3	3.95*
curriculum compacting understood as means of creating enrichment time	0	46	7.43*
currently want to work on an interest area project idea	78.3	50.8	5.80*
can have time to work on my interest area project with teacher support	8.4	94.2	10.16*
have *already* been provided with adequate time in school to work on interest projects this year	0	71.6	9.30*
have some involvement with the gifted program for interests	4.2	31.6	5.80*
have adequate time to leave my classroom to work on interests	33.3	84.2	7.83*
mostly work on interests in library	98.3	64.2	6.50*
work on interests through visits to gifted resource room	3.6	36.7	6.30*
have heard of the gifted program	90.8	96.6	.85
have something to do with the gifted program	9.2	72.6	8.70*
think gifted program is restricted to a particularly "smart" group	89.6	14.8	9.49*

*p < .001

In similar fashion, the postinterviews with principals revealed the following comments that described the schoolwide enrichment program as:

"serving many roles now . . . serving those children who are extremely bright and motivated to pursue an interest area to its depths . . . serving students who all need extension beyond the basics . . . enchancing the self-concepts of virtually every child in the building because of an increasingly positive school climate attributable to the gifted program";
"slowly progressing with a broadened conception of serving gifted children . . . teachers' thinking about what gifted programs are for has changed to consider that giftedness may not be just children with high

test scores . . . parents are frustrated with the slow pace of change but love the program";

"having much more impact on the school than ever before because kids, regardless of scores and grades, can possibly achieve high quality work in an area they love."

While principals became stronger in their convictions about implementing the *Schoolwide Enrichment Model* as the year progressed, the principals' roles in their schools as instructional leaders were clearly evident in both sets of interviews. It was the principals who offered positive impressions about the gifted program at the outset in order to motivate their schools to pursue implementation of schoolwide enrichment. Consequently, it follows logically that principals would have maintained those impressions as the treatment project began to be implemented. Perhaps it was most important that the perceptions of principals did not grow less positive during the course of the treatment. Table 4 summarizes the comparison of principals' perceptions.

Principals also did not alter their perceptions regarding enrichment or the roles of the gifted education teacher. Typically, this group described the term, "enrichment," as "something new and different beyond the basic curriculum" or as "creative extensions beyond the regular curriculum that are based on interests of students." From fall to spring interviews, these definitions changed very little. In the fall and again during the postinterviews, the principals viewed the role of the teacher of gifted as "acting as a key resource to classroom teachers by helping them plan and implement enrichment activities and process skill instruction across grade levels and by assisting students who want to work on a project of quality," or "as serving the needs of kids who seem to want to work at something in-depth and working with teachers to make classrooms more appropriate learning places for all children." During both interview series, every principal stressed that the gifted education teacher must maintain strong ties to the classroom in order to develop schoolwide enrichment teams as forums for sharing resources, planning events, and encouraging students.

A 10% randomly selected sample of 120 parents was interviewed twice, once prior to treatment and once after. There were 12 parents per treatment school who were selected by a computerized program for randomization from all of the parents of each of the 10 sites. Specific demographic information was intentionally not obtained in order to encourage parents to cooperate as openly as possible, though the computer selection process likely eliminated any possibility of interviewing only certain demographically typed parents. Items on the Parent Interview Agenda concentrated on an understanding of enrichment, knowledge of the gifted program, and the use of practicing professionals in classrooms as resource persons and as mentors. Table 5 provides a summary of parent responses and indicates that significant changes were made in most of their responses before and after the treatment ($p < .001$).

Teacher logs provided interesting documentation of the types of enrichment activities that were incorporated into regular classrooms during the course of

Table 4   Principal Interviews: A Pretreatment – Posttreatment Comparison

Topic	Pre Comments	Post Comments
perception of gifted program	important; activities for many children: starting to become integrated into the school	serves many children; helps self-concept of children; major role in school program; integrated more than ever thought
perceptions of enrichment	something new and different beyond basic curriculum; a nice break from the stress and rigor of basic instruction	creative extensions based on child interest beyond basic skills; provides opportunities for children to apply their basic skills to something they care about
role of gifted teacher	acting as key resource to classroom teachers in planning and implementing enrichment and process skill instruction	serving the needs of children who want to work at something and helping classroom teachers provide more appropriate instruction to all students

implementation of schoolwide enrichment. These logs were maintained by interviewed teachers using a semistructured format as a means for tracing the nature of activities that each teacher personally identified as enrichment. The log format allowed the researchers to assess the roles of teachers and students within the context of each activity listed.

Over the period from the fall of 1986 through May, 1987, the number of enrichment activities listed by teachers remained relatively consistent after some dramatic increases during the initial steps of the implementation of the *SEM* treatment (September-December), but the roles of teachers and students shifted greatly. With early log entries, activities tended to have a teacher-centered/passive student orientation; later log entries tended to emphasize a student-centered/active student orientation. The emphasis of *SEM* on students as active participants in learning clearly provided an indication that the enrichment activities were actually becoming integrated into the regular classroom program at the treatment schools. Table 6 presents numbers of enrichment activities offered per month and the nature of teacher and student roles in the activities.

Of the enrichment activities logged by teachers, all appeared to qualify as verifiable opportunities for students to become acquainted with information and areas of study that are not usually encompassed within each experimental school's basic curriculum. Although the logged activities span a wide range, several examples provide illustration of the manner in which teachers have worked to integrate enrichment into their programs:

First graders in one pilot school were familiarized with ornithology by their teacher through stories about birds. In order to increase the student opportunities for interest in the field, students constructed bird feeders,

Table 5   Parent Interviews: A Pretreatment – Posttreatment Comparison
N = 120

Topic	Pre Percent	Post Percent	Statistical Difference Between Correlated Percentages
enrichment is either outside of classrooms or for bright children	95	55	6.93*
enrichment includes activities for *all* children in our school	4.3	45	6.67*
my child has ample chance for enrichment in the regular classroom	19.2	81.6	8.70*
sufficient time for my child to pursue interest studies during school day	23.6	88.4	8.83*
does not *at all* understand the gifted program or what it is intended to do	52.5	29.2	5.25*
gifted program seems very restricted to certain children	34.2	26.6	3.10*
some understanding of the broader schoolwide approach and how it can help my child	13.3	44.2	6.10*
my child's class has some professionals come into the room as special resource persons	18.3	20.8	1.90
I have visited my child's classroom to share my profession or skills with the class	14.3	15	1.11

*p < .001
**p < .01

maintained observations of the birds visiting the feeders, and ultimately wrote about their experimentation in bird feeding.

Similarly, third grade students in another school were introduced to American Indian culture by a guest speaker from the Indian Cultural Center. While the study of the Plains Indians is part of the basic curriculum, the exposure to an expert in the field of Indian lore created high interest in preparation for student research work about Indians. Each student was encouraged to pursue in-depth study of a particular Indian-related interest.

Guest speakers also played an important part in the enrichment of sixth graders at one of the pilot schools. In studying careers, several guests visited and shared their knowledge about careers. Although some of the guests were practicing professionals, speakers also included a career counselor and an employment agent.

Although some of the treatment school teachers appear to have conducted a number of enrichment-type activities in their classrooms prior to the

Table 6   Summary of the Nature of Teacher-Logged Enrichment Activities

Month	Activities Logged Number	Teacher-Centered Percent	Student-Centered Percent
September	19	74	26
October	58	77	23
November	111	66	34
December	136	58	42
January	201	53	47
February	187	44	56
March	183	40	60
April	194	41	59
May	213	41	59
Mean =	144.67	54.89	45.11
Standard Deviation =	65.02	13.81	13.81

implementation of schoolwide enrichment, the logs clearly indicated that efforts to promote student interests increased. Not only had teachers tried to increase the active classroom involvement of students through enrichment, but the logs provided evidence that there was a new emphasis on encouraging students to become interested enough to continue study in enrichment topic areas.

DISCUSSION

The results of this study revealed that student attitudes toward learning were positively enhanced by participation in the schoolwide enrichment treatment. The descriptive data provided evidence that students had become increasingly positive about school and the variety of opportunities offered for learning. This was particularly evident in terms of students' beliefs that their interests were considered in determining the nature of classroom assignments in which they would become involved. The results also indicated that, after participation in the treatment, teachers had been involved in more frequent incidents of shared planning with fellow classroom teachers and with the gifted education resource teacher and that they developed a much more positive impression of gifted education. Perhaps more importantly, these results provide evidence that participation in the treatment did not negatively influence teacher attitudes toward teaching. Research on school change (Berman & McLaughlin, 1979; Fullan, 1982; Hord et al., 1987; Loucks, 1982; Louis & Kell, 1981; Sarason, 1982) has indicated that teachers tend to be slow in altering attitudes toward large-scale aspects of education. Such large-scale aspects include school as a total entity and teaching as a profession. The same group of researchers of school change have provided support for the notion that when teachers are confronted with new curricula or methods, they typically will become more negative in their attitudes about their positions in schools. Usually, these negative attitudes are ameliorated after the stress related to implementation of new programming has subsided and as the new methods begin providing positive outcomes for students.

The results of the present investigation make several important points about students and teachers. First, as schools implement schoolwide enrichment, it is likely that youngsters' attitudes toward school learning processes will be positively enhanced. In light of the plethora of research criticizing education on many counts, not the least of which is that schools produce poorly prepared graduates (National Commission on Excellence in Education, 1983), the results of this study appear to offer a possible solution. While there have been no comprehensive studies that have examined the relationship between student attitudes toward learning and students' eventual preparedness for future study or employment, it seems logical to hypothesize that heightened levels of student attitudes toward learning would ultimately enhance both the quantity and quality of pupils' learning.

Students consistently expressed positive attitudes about SEM. They collectively viewed school as a place that more accurately addressed their personal needs and that provided them with opportunities that they might not have ever had otherwise. Perhaps of even greater importance were some attitudinal changes expressed by students such as the following:

1. A general feeling that pursuit of individual interests is both acceptable and encouraged in school;

2. a perception that completion of workbook pages and other traditional classroom assignments is not an end but rather a means for obtaining opportunities for greater exploration, training, and creative production within topics based on one's interests;

3. beliefs that school is intended for students to become more attuned to their own personal needs and interests while acquiring the skills necessary for successful adulthood.

Second, implementation of a system of schoolwide enrichment activities is likely at least to maintain teachers' attitudes toward teaching. While there are many factors that contribute to teacher attitudes toward their work, the results of this examination suggest that teachers who teach in *SEM* schools will not become less enthusiastic about teaching. As changes evolve within schools, it is not unusual for teachers, particularly at the onset of an innovation, to become less enthused about their work because the innovations may not quite match the preimplementation promotion (Fullan, 1982). Further, teacher feelings of disappointment may be compounded by the pressures related to the acquisition of new innovation-induced skills or to the different expectations suddenly placed on them from administration. The results of this investigation provided no evidence that teachers' attitudes had grown less positive about teaching as a result of *SEM*.

Excellence Begets Excellence

Keeping in mind that traditional gifted education activities are made available to a restricted number of students, it appears fair to conclude that excellence in the gifted program evidently has been separate from excellence in the remainder of the school. Unfortunate by-products of this condition of separateness have been negative attitudes toward gifted education on the part of many people in general education and a reluctance to allocate funds and supplementary resources because they are perceived as favoritism toward a disproportionately small segment of the total school population.

As early as 1962, Ward suggested that an effective gifted education program should help to promote a "radiation of excellence" throughout the entire school (Ward, 1962). And in recent years a number of writers have recommended that various types of enrichment opportunities be made available to larger segments of the school population (Shore & Tsiamis, 1985; Birch, 1984; Feldman, 1983; and Renzulli, 1984). Research studies have been generally supportive of these efforts to extend certain aspects of gifted education technology to larger groups (Reis, 1981; Delisle & Renzulli, 1982; Gubbins, 1982; Cooper, 1983). The fact that the research reported here confirms previous findings adds further support to the broadened conception of giftedness that is recommended by numerous theorists and researchers (see especially Sternberg & Davidson, 1986). Perhaps even more importantly, this research clearly elevates the role that gifted education technology can play in overall school improvement and the promotion of educational excellence. Finally, this research offers a solution to the schism that traditionally has existed between programs for the gifted and general education. The gains that gifted education has made in instructional technology and the commitment that this field has made to serving our most potentially able youth will only have long-term endurance when they are woven into the fabric of general education rather than perceived as dangling threads that can be snipped off at any time.

NOTES

1. Sample copies of instruments available from the authors upon request.

2. Data available from authors upon request.

REFERENCES

Berman, P., & McLaughlin, M. (1979). *An exploratory study of school district adaptations*. Santa Monica, CA: Rand Corporation.

Birch, J. W. (1984). Is any identification procedure necessary? *Gifted Child Quarterly,* *28* (4), 157–161.

Bloom, B. S. (Ed.) (1985). *Developing talent in young people.* New York: Ballantine.

Cooper, C. R. (1983). *Administrators' attitudes towards gifted programs based on the Enrichment Triad/Revolving Door Identification Model: Case studies in decision-making.* Unpublished doctoral dissertation, The University of Connecticut.

Delisle, J. R., & Renzulli, J. S. (1982). The revolving door identification and programming model: Correlates of creative production. *Gifted Child Quarterly, 26,* 89–95.

Dobbert, M. L. (1984). *Ethnographic research: Theory and application for modern schools and societies.* Westport, CT: Praeger.

Feldman, D. H. (1983). Reconceptualizing excellence: Still a national priority. *Roeper Review, 6* (1), 2–4.

Fullan, M. (1982). *The meaning of educational change.* New York: Teachers College Press.

Gardner, H. (1983). *Frames of mind.* New York: Basic Books.

Garrett, H. E. (1958). *Statistics in psychology and education (5th Edition).* New York: David McKay, Inc.

Gubbins, E. J. (1982). *Revolving door identification model: Characteristics of talent pool students.* Unpublished doctoral dissertation, The University of Connecticut.

Hirsch, L. T. (1981). *The learning place: An ethnographic study of an elementary school principal.* Unpublished doctoral dissertation, The University of Connecticut.

Hord, S. M., Rutherford, W. L., Huling-Austin, L., & Hall, G. E. (1987). *Taking charge of change.* Alexandria, VA: Association for Supervision and Curriculum Development.

Loucks, S. F. (1982). *People, practices, and policies: Discoveries from school improvement research.* Paper presented at the joint annual meeting of the Pennsylvania and New Jersey Educational Research Associations, Philadelphia.

Louis, K. S., & Kell, D. (1981). *The human factor in knowledge use: Field agent roles in education.* Cambridge, MA: ABT Associates.

National Commission on Excellence in Education. (1983). *A nation at risk: The imperative for educational reform.* Washington, DC: National Science Foundation.

Reis, S. M. (1981). *An analysis of the productivity of gifted students participating in programs using the revolving door identification model.* Unpublished doctoral dissertation, The University of Connecticut.

Reis, S. M., & Renzulli, J. S. (1982). Case for a broadened conception of giftedness. *Phi Delta Kappan, 63* (9), 619–620.

Renzulli, J. S. (1977). *The enrichment triad model: A guide for developing defensible programs for the gifted.* Mansfield Center, CT: Creative Learning Press.

Renzulli, J. S. (1984). Technical report on research studies relating to the Revolving Door Identification Model. Bureau of Educational Research, The University of Connecticut.

Renzulli, J. S., & Reis, S. M. (1985). *The schoolwide enrichment model: A comprehensive plan for educational excellence.* Mansfield Center, CT: Creative Learning Press.

Renzulli, J. S., & Reis, S. M. (1985a). *Student product assessment form* (rev.). Mansfield Center, CT: Creative Learning Press.

Sarason, S. (1982). *The culture of the school and the problem of change* (2nd ed.). Boston: Allyn and Bacon.

Shore, B. M., & Tsiamis, A. (1985). Identification by provision: Limited field test of a radical alternative for identifying gifted students. In H. Collis (Chair), *Identification and guidance/counseling of highly gifted children.* Symposium conducted at the 6th World Conference on Gifted and Talented Children, Hamburg, West Germany.

Spradley, J. P. (1979). *The ethnographic interview*. New York: Holt, Rinehart and Winston.

Spradley, J. P. (1980) *Participant observation*. New York: Holt, Rinehart and Winston.

SPSS, Inc. (1986). *SPSS-X user's guide* (2nd ed.). New York: McGraw Hill.

Sternberg, R. J. (1982). Lies we live by: Misapplication of tests in identifying the gifted. *Gifted Child Quarterly, 26* (4), 157–161.

Sternberg, R. J., & Davidson, J. (1986). *Conceptions of giftedness*. New York: Cambridge University Press.

Ward, V. (1962). *The gifted student: A manual for program development*. A Report of the Southern Regional Project for Education of the Gifted.

3

The Impact of Staff Development on Teachers' Ability to Modify Curriculum for Gifted and Talented Students

Sally M. Reis

Karen L. Westberg

The National Research Center on the Gifted and Talented

The University of Connecticut

In this study, three levels of staff development were provided to elementary teachers to train them in a technique called curriculum compacting. Teachers in 20 school districts across the country were randomly assigned by district to one of three treatment groups that received different levels of staff development. After receiving training in curriculum compacting (a procedure that enables teachers to eliminate previously mastered curriculum and substitute more challenging alternatives), teachers were able to eliminate between 42% and 54% of the content for the high-ability students they selected. Teachers in Treatment Group 3, who received the most

Editor's Note: From Reis, S. M., & Westberg, K. L. (1994). The impact of staff development on teachers' ability to modify curriculum for gifted and talented students. *Gifted Child Quarterly*, *38*(3), 127-135. © 1994 National Association for Gifted Children. Reprinted with permission.

intensive staff development, completed the highest rated compactor forms. The majority of the teachers in the study were enthusiastic about the process of modifying curriculum for high-ability students, reinforcing Guskey's (1986) model of the process of teacher change.

The University of Connecticut site of The National Research Center on the Gifted and Talented conducted a study during the 1990–1991 academic year to examine the effects of three levels of staff development on elementary teachers' implementation of a technique designed to modify the regular curriculum to meet the needs of gifted and talented students in regular classrooms. Teachers in 20 school districts throughout the country were randomly assigned by district to three treatment groups that received different levels of staff development. After receiving staff development services, teachers implemented a technique called curriculum compacting with the students they selected for their advanced academic abilities.

STATEMENT OF THE PROBLEM

The research study drew upon two different bodies of knowledge. The first deals with the challenge level of regular curricular materials, and the second involves teachers' willingness and ability to modify curriculum and instruction for the gifted and talented.

Many educators would argue that the greatest problem facing gifted and talented students is the lack of challenge in the work they are assigned in the regular classroom. One need only enter a classroom to realize that the work assigned to gifted students is often too easy. The research literature also supports this claim. For example, a study conducted by the Educational Products Information Exchange Institute (1980–1981), a nonprofit educational consumer agency, revealed that 60% of the fourth graders in the school districts studied were able to achieve a score of 80% or higher on a test of the content of their math texts before they had opened their books in September. Similar findings were reported on content tests with 4th- and 10th-grade science texts and with 10th-grade social studies texts.

Putting the Research to Use

This study was undertaken to investigate whether different types of staff development resulted in different outcomes in the implementation of a teaching practice called curriculum compacting. The study also investigated teachers' attitudes toward the use of this teaching practice in the future. Teachers who received the most intensive staff development (videotaped inservice, books, simulations, peer coaching) completed the most highly rated compactor forms, indicating that the use of various types of sustained staff development produced different outcomes.

Guskey's model (1986) of teacher change indicates three outcomes to staff development: change in teachers' classroom practices, change in student learning outcomes, and change in teachers' beliefs and attitudes. Guskey further believes that the teaching practices that continue to be used are those found to improve student learning outcomes. The results of this study concur with Guskey's model, indicating that as teachers observed positive results with the curriculum compacting process with students, they became more positive about their future use of the practice.

This study suggests that to institute different teaching practices effectively, sustained staff development involving some type of peer coaching as suggested by Joyce and Showers (1987) is necessary. It further suggests that teachers will be more likely to change their practices if they perceive positive benefits for their students following an innovation. These positive changes in student learning outcomes then influence teachers' beliefs and attitudes about the use of the practice.

In a more recent study dealing with average and above-average readers. Taylor and Frye (1988) found that 78% to 88% of fifth- and sixth-grade average and above-average readers could pass pretests on basal comprehension skills before they were covered by the basal reader. The average students were performing at approximately 92% accuracy, and the better readers were performing at 93% on comprehension skill pretests. Unfortunately, a follow-up to the study revealed that many teachers were not using pretests to identify the students who previously had mastered reading skills. In fact, only 1 of 31 teachers in two of the schools studied were still using pretests even though their use had been encouraged by the district's elementary supervisor.

Michael Kirst discusses a related problem, the fact that textbooks have dropped two grade levels in difficulty over the past 10 to 15 years. Kirst (1982) reports that:

When Californians tried to reserve two slots on the statewide adoption list for textbooks that would challenge the top one-third of students, no publisher had a book to present. They could only suggest reissuing textbooks from the late sixties (now unacceptable because of their inaccurate portrayals of women and minorities) or writing new ones, a three to five year project. (p. 7)

In a speech before the American Association of School Administrators in February of 1984, former Secretary of Education, Terrel Bell, criticized the publishing industry for their textbook content as well as textbook adoption committees for their policies and procedures. Citing *A Nation at Risk*, Bell argued that too much concern with readability has resulted in a "dumbing down" of textbooks (Farr & Tulley, 1985). Lynn Arthur Steen, a professor of mathematics at St. Olaf College, aptly summarizes the problems associated with the lack of challenge in mathematics: "In practice, although not in law, we have a national curriculum in mathematics education. It is an 'underachieving' curriculum that follows a spiral of almost constant radius, reviewing each year so much of the past that little new learning takes place" (1989, p. 45). Similar statements have been made about social studies curricula and textbooks. For example, Tyson-Bernstein and Woodward (1989) said, "The banal content of elementary social studies books gets children off to a bad start. Young children are bored because they discuss things they already know" (p. 16).

Because of this change in the textbook industry, and because repetition is built into curricular approaches to reinforce learning, many gifted students spend much of their time in school practicing skills and reading content they already know. This is documented by the widespread dissatisfaction expressed by so many school personnel about the use of basal textbooks for high ability students. Despite research by Kulik and Kulik (1984); Slavin (1984, 1986); Slavin, Karweit, and Madden (1989) and others indicating that students learn skills and concepts at a faster rate when grouping and individualization take place, teachers still utilize whole-group instruction (Cuban, 1982; Goodlad, 1983, 1984).

Recent research conducted by The National Research Center on the Gifted and Talented indicated that the instructional and curricular practices provided to gifted students in the regular classroom are almost identical to those provided to average-ability students. The results of a survey administered to over 7,000 third- and fourth-grade classrooms throughout the country revealed that classroom teachers make only minor modifications in the regular classroom to meet the needs of gifted students (Archambault et al., 1993). The survey also indicated that 60.8% of public school teachers and 53.3% of private school teachers reported that they had never had any training in teaching gifted students. These results were corroborated by findings from observations in 46 third- or fourth-grade classrooms which indicated that gifted students received no differentiated experiences in 84% of the instructional activities in which they were involved (Westberg, Archambault, Dobyns, & Salvin, 1993).

A Staff Development Plan for Modifying
Regular Curriculum for Gifted and Talented Students

Because research indicates that the challenge level of textbooks has declined and that teachers often use whole-class instructional techniques, curriculum modification is necessary to meet the needs of gifted and talented students in regular classroom settings. One technique that has been designed to accomplish this goal is curriculum compacting (Renzulli, Smith, & Reis, 1982). Curriculum compacting is a part of a total educational program for gifted and talented students developed and field-tested over the past 15 years (Renzulli, 1977; Renzulli & Reis, 1985). It can be used, however, as a part of any educational program for gifted and talented students and has been mentioned by several other developers of programming models as a method for modifying curriculum for gifted students (Betts, 1986; Clifford, Runions, & Smythe, 1986; Feldhusen & Kolloff, 1986; Treffinger, 1986). Tannenbaum has advocated a related process called telescoping in which students "complete the basics in the least amount of time thereby sparing themselves the tedium of dwelling on content that they either know already or can absorb in short order" (1986, p. 409), and Van Tassel-Baska has labeled a similar practice "compression of content" (1985, p. 51).

Curriculum compacting is a system designed to adapt the regular curriculum to meet the needs of gifted students by either eliminating work that has been previously mastered or streamlining work that may be mastered at a pace commensurate with the students' abilities. Research indicates that the time gained through this system may then be used to provide students with appropriate enrichment and/or acceleration activities (Imbeau, 1991; Reed, 1987). Curriculum compacting has three major objectives: (a) to create a more challenging learning environment, (b) to guarantee proficiency in the basic curriculum, and (c) to "buy time" for more appropriate enrichment and/or acceleration activities. Teachers who implement the curriculum compacting procedure complete a form called "The Compactor" (Renzulli & Smith, 1978) on a student or group of students who demonstrate the need for this service. The compactor form is shown in Figure 1. Three types of information are documented on the form in three columns: curriculum areas to be considered for compacting, procedures for compacting basic material, and acceleration and/or enrichment activities.

Although the technology exists to enable teachers to compact curriculum for gifted students, most do not (Imbeau, 1991; Renzulli et al., 1982; Starko, 1986). Some teachers cite reasons such as lack of time, inability to group students adequately, lack of enrichment and acceleration materials to use in their classrooms, lack of training to deal with gifted and talented students, and lack of administrative support and school board policy. Other teachers do not believe that gifted students should be excused from doing work they already have mastered. It may be that in the 1970s and 1980s the return to basics and focus on mastery and achievement tests resulted in administrative pressure on teachers to spend more time on predetermined tasks. This has resulted in a cadre of teachers who are poorly prepared by their preservice training to deal with gifted students and do not allow their brightest students to skip any skills, even when mastery is clearly documented.

Current research on effective staff development in education suggests that traditional, single meeting inservice sessions on new approaches will not be sufficient to change practices used in classrooms (Guskey, 1986; Joyce & Showers, 1982, 1983; Knowles, 1978; Kolb, 1976; Showers, Joyce, & Bennett, 1987). Joyce

Figure 1   Individual Educational Programming Guide

The Compactor

NAME Liza_____   AGE 10_____   TEACHER(S) _____   Individual Conference Dates
and Persons Participating in
Planning of IEP

SCHOOL _____   GRADE 5_____   PARENTS _____   _____

CURRICULUM AREAS TO BE CONSIDERED FOR COMPACTING	PROCEDURES FOR COMPACTING BASIC MATERIAL	ACCELERATION AND/OR ENRICHMENT ACTIVITIES
Provide a brief description of basic material to be covered during this marking period and the assessment information or evidence that suggests the need for compacting.	Describe activities that will be used to guarantee proficiency in basic curricular areas.	Describe activities that will be used to provide advanced level learning experiences in each area of the regular curriculum.
English Unit on adjectives (identification, proper adjectives, comparing adjectives) Unit on nouns (proper, common, possessive plurals, identification) Unit on capital letters	Teacher-made tests in all areas described Continental Press dittos used as test Will work on individual tests on articles (a, an, the) and possessive adjectives.	Start a school newspaper to be published once a month Liza will edit the Geography and Travel section of the school newspaper. Liza will also write a monthly column.
Math Unit on fractions (adding, subtracting, multiplying, dividing)	Teacher-made tests Unit 7 test *Macmillan Mathematics 5* Math curriculum posttests	Will be able to move to multiplying and dividing since mastery was shown in other areas. Acceleration.
Spelling Words in Economy Press Kit on Individualizing Spelling—one week. Next week—works with teacher in directed activities from *Harper/Row Basic Speller 5.*	Is on highest level in spelling kit. Daily work Teacher-made tests where she shows knowledge of spelling rules.	School newspaper (see above) - independent study project
Social Studies U.S. Geography – Geography and the history of New England	Teacher-made tests to show basic understanding of geography, production, colonial history	Individual project work on history and geography of New England (specifically Rhode Island)

Check here if additional information is recorded on the reverse side.

and Showers (1983) found that only 5% of the teachers they studied were able to incorporate a new strategy without assistance. Sparks (1986) found that peer coaching was effective in changing teaching practices. Guskey and Sparks (1991) believe that the organizational climate has a major influence on the implementation of innovations and state, "Contexts that nurture support and trust, encourage shared decision making and responsibility, and provide ongoing assistance appear best in sustaining successful improvement efforts" (p. 74).

In addressing the issues related to the improvement of educators' teaching practices, Guskey (1986) suggests that staff development efforts are not influenced by teachers' beliefs and attitudes; rather, attitudes and beliefs are a result of teachers' implementation of new practices and the observation of changes in students' learning outcomes. Guskey's model of the process of teacher change suggests that there are three major outcomes to staff development efforts: teachers' practices, the learning outcomes of students, and teachers' beliefs and attitudes. The order of these outcomes is in contrast to the popular belief that staff development programs influence teachers' attitudes and beliefs first, which in turn influence teachers' implementation of new teaching practices in order to observe the effects of the new practice on student learning outcomes. Guskey believes instead that the teaching practices that are sustained are those found by teachers to be "useful in helping students attain desired learning outcomes . . . [and] evidence of improvement (positive change) in the learning outcomes of students generally precedes and may be a prerequisite to significant change in the beliefs and attitudes of most teachers" (1986, p. 7).

Current research on staff development suggests four key concepts are necessary for a successfully implemented innovation: coaching in the implementation phase (Joyce & Showers, 1983, 1987), attention to teachers' attitudes and beliefs (Guskey, 1986), the manner in which new practice is presented to the target audience (Guskey, 1986; Knowles, 1978), and the recognition of the special needs of special learners (Knowles, 1978). The different methods of training used in this study explored these concepts by providing different levels of staff development to teachers.

METHODS AND PROCEDURES

This study investigated the effects of participation in training sessions on regular classroom teachers' use of a curriculum modification technique for gifted and talented students called curriculum compacting. Three separate treatment groups were used to examine the most efficient but effective method for training teachers to modify curriculum. Classroom teachers in the experimental groups were each provided with different levels of support for curriculum compacting (see Figure 2). Teachers receiving Treatment 1 were provided with two instructional videotapes about the compacting process. They also received a book about the procedure and related articles. Teachers receiving Treatment 2 received everything that Treatment Group 1 received, as well as approximately 2 hours of group simulations on compacting conducted by the local gifted and talented resource teacher and/or consultant. The simulations developed by Starko (1986) have been a standard resource in this type of training Treatment Group 3 received the same training as the previous treatment group with the addition of local consultant services and further involvement in peer coaching experiences for approximately 6–10 hours during the academic year.

Figure 2   Description of Materials to Be Used by Different Treatment Groups

Treatment 1:
Two videotapes (1 hour total) explaining how to compact curriculum
One book including more explanatory information about how to implement curriculum compacting
   (130 pages)
Related articles/examples

Treatment 2:
Two videotapes (1 hour total)
One book including more explanatory information about how to implement curriculum compacting (130
   pages)
Related articles/examples
Group compacting simulations and practice conducted by local gifted and talented education consultant

Treatment 3:
Two videotapes (1 hour total)
One book including more explanatory information about how to implement curriculum compacting (130 pages)
Related articles/examples
Group compacting simulations and practice conducted by local gifted and talented education consultant
Local consultant services and peer coaching experiences

Classroom teachers were provided with the first level of treatment, the videotapes and written materials on compacting, during October and early November. Teachers were then asked to select one to three students in their second- through sixth-grade classrooms that would clearly qualify for curriculum compacting. In most cases, this group of students was participating in a school or district gifted and talented program. However, some of the participating districts did not provide gifted education services to students at all grade levels. In these situations, teachers selected their most able students, and a district research liaison person verified these students' advanced abilities.

The effects of the treatments were addressed by the several research questions in the study. The questions addressed and reported here include:

1. In what areas and to what degree do teachers modify instructional practices and regular curricular materials to meet the needs of gifted and talented students in regular classroom settings?

2. Is there a significant difference among treatment groups and teachers' decisions about whether they will compact curriculum in the future?

3. Is there a significant difference among treatment groups with regard to the quality of the compactor forms completed by teachers?

Sampling Procedures

A sample of 20 school districts and approximately 300 classroom teachers throughout the United States from collaborative school districts that are a part of The National Research Center on the Gifted and Talented (NRC/GT) were selected as treatment groups for this study. To participate, districts had to meet the following criteria: (1) previous training on curriculum compacting had not been provided to teachers, and (2) districts had to be willing to accept random assignment to treatment groups. Efforts were made to recruit districts with elementary student populations that included economically disadvantaged, limited English proficient, and handicapped students. The districts participating in the study represented a wide range of schools from across the United States, ranging from small rural schools in Wyoming to a magnet school of Hispanic students in California.

Instrumentation

In addition to using the curriculum compacting form, which was used by teachers to document the compacting services provided to students, two additional instruments were developed to assess the compacting procedures employed by teachers in the study. The first, the Classroom Practices Questionnaire (Reis et al., 1993), was developed for this study to ascertain the classroom practices and procedures used by teachers when providing compacting services to students. This self-report instrument included three open-ended questions about the content areas selected for compacting, the percentage of curriculum that was eliminated, and whether or not teachers would continue to use the process of compacting in the future. Teachers' responses to these three questions are reported below.

The second instrument developed for this study, the Curriculum Compactor Assessment Form (Reis, 1991), was designed to assess the effectiveness of the teachers' implementation of the curriculum compacting process. The following procedure was used to provide an estimate of the instrument's reliability. First, a nine-item checklist for assessing completed compactors was developed. The nine items on the checklist reflect the elements of quality compactor forms advocated by curriculum compacting experts (Renzulli et al., 1982; Starko, 1986). Four research team members with extensive experience in the compacting process used the checklist to evaluate independently five completed compactor forms. Items were rated 0 to 1, indicating the *absence* (0) or *presence* (1) of the characteristic on the form. After completing the checklists on the five forms, research team members discussed their evaluations to improve the reliability of their ratings. Eleven compactor forms were then assessed by the two team members who later evaluated all forms completed by teachers in the study. The mean interrater agreement on these ratings was 90.36%. After discussing the evaluations of the 11 compactors, a 10th (and final) item was added to the checklist that would provide a summative rating of each compactor. The final compactor assessment form is shown in Figure 3.

RESULTS

Descriptive, nonparametric, and parametric statistical procedures were used to address the three research questions listed earlier. The results of these analyses follow.

Figure 3   The Curriculum Compactor Assessment Form

Column on Compactor	Rating
Column 1	
1. Are curricular strength areas of the student(s) clearly identified (e.g., language arts, mathematics)?	_____
2 Are pretests or general assessments of student strength areas provided (such as language arts pretests or achievement test information)?	_____
Column 2	
3. Are specific areas of content to be eliminated or modified listed?	_____
4. Are various types of skills assessment to prove evidence of proficiency (i.e., passed various level tests) documented?	_____
Column 3	
5. Are alternative activities listed for students?	_____
6. Are the activities based on alternative enrichment activities, that is, *not* extensions of regular curricular exercises?	_____
7. Do the alternative activities listed appear to have taken into account the students' interests (e.g., independent study options, specific types of alternative reading assignments)?	_____
Columns 1-2-3	
8. Is it apparent that various pieces of information have been taken into account regarding students' curricular strengths, the documentation of proficiency, and the replacement of more appropriate enrichment and/or acceleration? In other words, is there connection between Columns 1-2-3 on the compactor?	_____
9. Does the teacher appear to have completed the form with care and attention to detail, and does the compactor form reflect appropriate time spent by the classroom teacher?	_____
10. Does the completed compactor form reflect the overall quality expected in the curriculum compacting process?	_____
Total Score (0 to 10 possible)	_____

Areas and Percent of Curriculum Completed

To address research question number one, teachers' responses to two questions on the Classroom Practices Questionnaire were tabulated, namely, the content areas selected for compacting and the percentage of curriculum eliminated by teachers in all treatment groups. Modifications to curriculum were most often made in mathematics and language arts, the two areas identified by the authors of the compacting procedure to be the most commonly used (Reis, Burns, & Renzulli, 1992). The majority of the teachers compacted curriculum in one content area for each student: however, teachers compacted more than one content area for some students. Two hundred and fifty-three students received compacting in mathematics; 164 students received compacting in language arts; 169 students received compacting in spelling; 31 students received compacting in social studies; and 20 students received compacting in science.

Teachers were also asked on the questionnaire to estimate the percentage of the regular curriculum material in each subject area that was eliminated for identified students. The mean percent of curriculum eliminated across all subject areas reported by teachers for students in Group 1 was 45%; for students in Group 2 it was 42%; and for students in Group 3 it was 54%. A one-way analysis of variance procedure was computed to determine if the amount of curriculum eliminated by teachers differed among the three groups. The results indicated significant differences among the groups ($F = 6.54$, $df = 2/333$, $p < .01$). A Scheffé post hoc procedure revealed that Group 3 was significantly different from Groups 1 and 2 ($p < .05$).

Intentions About Future Use of Compacting

To address research question number two, answers to the final, open-ended question on the Classroom Practices Questionnaire were coded. This item asked if teachers would continue to use curriculum compacting in the future and why they would make this decision. The responses to this question for all three treatment groups were placed into three categories: positive, negative, and uncertain. A high percentage of teachers indicated that they would use curriculum compacting again next year, and those who expressed some concern about doing this were anxious for more help or additional classroom materials. A 2×3 contingency table was produced to investigate the association between treatment group and response about future use of compacting. The frequencies and percentages of these responses within each group are summarized in Table 1. The calculated chi-square statistic for this analysis was not significant at the .05 alpha level, indicating the lack of a relationship between group membership and future use of curriculum compacting.

As indicated in Table 1, more than two thirds of all teachers who responded to this item on the Classroom Practices Questionnaire indicated that they would continue to use the curriculum compacting procedure in the future, and most of those who responded positively wrote comments about their experiences when using this procedure. A representative comment from each group is included below:

> Yes. I feel their time can be better spent than doing assignments on material they already know. When they share projects and reports with the class it also enriches their [other students'] learning experiences. (Treatment Group 1 teacher)
>
> Yes. I will continue this method because it has shown me a very meaningful strategy to use with students who know grade level material already. In turn this enables students to become interested in independent learning *they* would like to pursue. The capable students are less likely to be turned off by this approach. This was a strategy that kept all students challenged in my class. I will use this next year in math and hopefully other areas as well. (Treatment Group 2 teacher)

Table 1   Teachers' Responses About Future Use of Curriculum Compacting

	RESPONSES						
	Positive		Negative		Unsure		Total # of
GROUP	Frequency	Row %	Frequency	Row %	Frequency	Row %	Responses
Treatment 1	63	77.8	1	1.2	17	21	81
Treatment 2	62	72.1	5	5.8	19	22.1	86
Treatment 3	56	66.7	8	9.5	20	23.8	84
Total	181	72.1	14	5.6	56	22.3	251

The obtained $X^2 = 5.949$ (2) was not significant at .05 alpha level.

Definitely! This is such an exciting way to teach! I feel the students involved in the compacting program had the opportunity to become such active, *independent* learners. They had a taste of learning through their own actions not just the material spooned out through limited text books. It was amazing to watch this learning process in action! Sparks flew in my classroom this year!!! Now that I'm familiar with the program, I can't wait for next year to begin! (Treatment Group 3 teacher)

The teachers' responses placed in the uncertain category included comments about available planning time, a need to learn more about compacting, and students' independent study skills. The reasons cited by the small number of teachers who gave negative responses about the future use of compacting included comments about large class sizes and a preference for their own method of meeting students' needs.

Quality of Compactor Forms

To address research question number three, the differences among the treatment groups with regard to the characteristics reflected on teachers' curriculum compactor forms were examined. A total of 428 compactors were returned by teachers in the three treatment groups. The majority were completed for one student: however, some compactors were completed on more than one student. Each completed compactor was assessed by two raters using the Curriculum Compacting Assessment Form. The mean ratings for the compactors from each district are shown in Table 2. As indicated in the table, the mean ratings of the compactor forms are higher for each successive treatment group. The mean assessment of the forms in Treatment Group 1 was 6.3. Treatment Group 2 was 6.6, and Treatment Group 3 was 7.1. A one-way analysis of variance procedure indicated no significant differences on ratings of compactor forms among the treatment groups, $F(2, 427) = 2.06, p < .13$.

Table 2   Results From Assessment of Compactors

District Location	No. of Students	Rater 1's Mean Ratings	Rater 2's Mean Ratings	Both Raters' Mean Ratings
Treatment Group 1				
RI	16	5.5	5.4	5.5
MI	25	7.0	7.0	7.0
AR	34	6.0	7.0	6.5
VA	14	6.4	6.6	6.5
CA	7	4.7	4.7	4.7
CT	27	7.5	7.9	7.7
	123	6.2	6.3	6.3
Treatment Group 2				
IA	34	6.8	6.7	6.8
CT	12	6.4	6.6	6.5
NH	18	6.9	7.0	6.9
LA	35	7.1	7.7	7.4
MN	4	5.0	5.3	5.1
CT	9	5.9	6.2	6.1
CT	18	7.2	7.4	7.3
	130	6.5	6.7	6.6
Treatment Group 3				
UT	52	7.2	7.4	7.3
MT	25	7.2	7.7	7.5
MS	56	6.2	6.8	6.5
MN	12	7.8	8.0	7.9
NY	7	6.0	5.6	5.8
WY	7	7.7	8.0	7.9
OK	16	6.6	6.9	6.8
	175	7.0	7.2	7.1

DISCUSSION

Elimination of Content

As early as 1937 Leta Hollingworth, who started a school for gifted children in New York City, concluded that these students need only half of the time traditionally spent on regular school work. Over 50 years later, it is clear that a similar situation still exists for our most able students in school. The process of compacting curriculum in this study did not begin until November, after the students had been identified and the first level of staff development completed. Accordingly, many teachers indicated that if they had been able to begin the process in September, the percentage of curriculum eliminated would have been higher. The large amount of content that could be eliminated for these students suggests that many of our most able students spend a great deal of time in school doing work that they already know. Mathematics was the most frequently compacted content area by teachers in each of the three groups in this study. The next most frequently compacted subject area was language arts, which did not incorporate spelling, the third most frequently compacted area.

The finding about mathematics supports recent studies by Usiskin (1987) and Flanders (1987), who found that textbooks have decreased in difficulty *and* that they use a large percentage of repetition. Flanders (1987) investigated three separate mathematics textbook series to examine just how much new content is presented each year. His primary finding was that a relatively steady decrease occurs in the amount of new content over the years up through eighth grade, where less than one third of the material taught is new to students. Overall, students in Grades 2–5 encounter approximately 40% to 65% new content, an equivalent of new material 2 or 3 days a week. Flanders found that most of the new content in any text is found in the second half of the book. In Grades 7–8, where the total amount of new content is lowest, only 28% of the content in the first half of the books is new material. Flanders's study shows that the mathematical content of some textbooks is mostly review of previous topics. Flanders states:

> The result is that early in the year, when students are likely to be more eager to study, they repeat what they have seen before. Later on, when they are sufficiently bored, they see new material—if they get to the end of the book. (1987, p. 22).

He elaborates, "There should be little wonder why good students get bored: they do the same thing year after year" (1987, p. 23).

Usiskin (1987) indicates that not only have textbooks decreased in difficulty, but they also incorporate a large percentage of repetition to facilitate learning. Usiskin argues that even average eighth-grade students should study algebra because only 25% of the pages in typical seventh- and eighth-grade mathematics texts contain new content. Usiskin points out that the current practice of spending a great deal of time reviewing work taught in earlier grades is counterproductive:

> For the student who does not know the material, the review is simply repeating what they are bad at. We find out what some students do not know and give them little else. It is not the spiral approach winding its way up the helix of understanding; it is the circular approach going round and round and back to the same place. (1987, p. 432)

Because so much content can be eliminated, we must assume that the textbooks and materials are not providing the type of challenge that gifted students need. Therefore, it also seems safe to conclude that many able students spend a great deal of their school year reviewing material that they have already mastered and that alternative instructional materials and instructional techniques should be used with these students.

Intentions About Future Use of Compacting

Although the majority of teachers in this study indicated that they would continue to use curriculum compacting in the future, it is clear that many classroom teachers throughout the United States do not make the modifications necessary to ensure an appropriate challenge level for gifted students (Archambault et al., 1993; Westberg et al., 1993). With the current movement in our country to eliminate most forms of ability grouping (Oakes & Lipton, 1992) and the practice of mainstreaming students with various handicapping conditions into regular classrooms, the skills needed by a classroom teacher to modify instruction to meet the needs of a diverse population become more demanding. Research indicates that the most difficult task in the compacting process is the replacement of what has been eliminated with appropriately challenging content and activities (Reis & Purcell, 1993). Although the vast majority of teachers in this study were able to implement curriculum compacting for the targeted student(s) they selected, many indicated frustration over the following issues: lack of expertise in knowing what to substitute for high-ability students, lack of time needed to plan to meet individual differences, the logistics of teaching different topics to different groups of students, the support staff needed to implement replacement activities (reading and math specialists, gifted and talented program staff), and other concerns relating to classroom management. Although curriculum compacting seems to be a viable process for meeting the needs of high-ability students in the regular classroom, it does take time, effort, and planning on the part of classroom teachers.

A follow-up of the teachers involved in the compacting study will be conducted to determine whether teachers continue to use curriculum compacting in their classrooms. Presumably, many factors will contribute to this decision, including administrative support and encouragement, availability of materials and resources for substitution of the regular curriculum, and teachers' continued ease with compacting. It is interesting to note that an increasing but statistically insignificant number of teachers in each treatment group expressed unsure or negative responses about the future use of compacting. As teachers learn more about the compacting process and work with each other to learn how to compact curriculum, they may become more hesitant about their own success in being able to implement compacting effectively. In any event, the very high percentage of teachers who expressed positive reactions about their future use of compacting is certainly an encouraging indication that this process may be useful in addressing the needs of able students in the classroom.

In addition to implementing curriculum compacting for the targeted students in their classrooms, a substantial number of teachers involved in the study indicated in anecdotal records that they were able to extend the service to other students, many of whom were not identified and involved in the gifted program. This finding may indicate the usefulness of extending the types of technology so often reserved for high-ability students to a larger segment of the population, as has been previously suggested by researchers (Renzulli & Reis, 1991). The compacting process has been recommended as a service that should be provided to any student who has mastered or is capable of mastering regular curriculum at a different pace from his/her peers (Reis et al., 1992; Renzulli et al., 1982).

The Impact of Staff Development on the Compacting Process

Teachers in Group 3 created compactor forms of significantly higher quality than did those in Groups 1 and 2. Reis and Purcell (1993) also found that they used more replacement strategies and more diverse options for targeted students. This would seem to lend support to the work of both Joyce and Showers (1982, 1983) and Guskey (1986, 1990). The staff development opportunities provided to Group 3 included peer coaching as suggested by Joyce and Showers (1983). Guskey's (1986) model provides insight into this study since teachers' practices seemed to change and develop as they observed their students' positive responses to the elimination of previously mastered work and substitution of more appropriately challenging material. This, in turn, affected teachers' beliefs and attitudes. The staff development program provided to each group included increased levels of training culminating in peer coaching. The anecdotal records and responses to questions on the Classroom Practices Questionnaire indicated that as classroom teachers observed students benefiting from compacting, they become more committed to implementing the procedure. This confirms Guskey's findings about teaching practices that are sustained.

A key factor in the endurance of any change in instructional practices is demonstrable results in terms of the learning success of a teacher's students. Activities that are successful tend to be repeated while those that are not successful, or for which there is not tangible evidence of success, are generally avoided. (Guskey, 1986, p. 7)

What remains to be seen is how much time and effort teachers will expend in implementing a practice, such as compacting, if considerable obstacles exist, such as larger class sizes and the inclusion of more students with a wide range of abilities and special needs in the classroom. However, in this study, the positive response of teachers and their ability to eliminate content and replace it with various activities and content provides an optimistic view of the impact of staff development on teachers' ability to modify curriculum for students who need and can benefit from this service.

REFERENCES

Archambault, F. X. Jr., Westberg, K. L., Brown, S., Hallmark, B. W., Zhang, W., & Emmons, C. (1993). Regular classroom practices with gifted students: Findings from the classroom practices survey. *Journal for the Education of the Gifted, 16,* 103–119.

Betts, G. T. (1986). The autonomous learner model. In J. S. Renzulli (Ed.), *Systems and models for developing programs for the gifted and talented* (pp. 27–56). Mansfield Center, CT: Creative Learning Press.

Clifford, J. A., Runions, T., & Smythe, E. (1986). The learning enrichment service (LES): A participatory model for gifted adolescents. In J. S. Renzulli (Ed.), *Systems and models for developing programs for the gifted and talented* (pp. 92–125). Mansfield Center, CT: Creative Learning Press.

Cuban, L. (1982). *How teachers taught: Constancy and change in American classrooms, 1890–1980*. New York: Longman.

Educational Products Information Exchange Institute (EPIE). (1980–1981). *Educational research and development report, 3*(4).

Farr, R., & Tulley, M. (1985). Do adoption committees perpetuate mediocre textbooks? *Phi Delta Kappan, 66*, 467–471.

Feldhusen, J. F., & Kolloff, M. B. (1986). The Purdue three-stage enrichment model for gifted education at the elementary level. In J. S. Renzulli (Ed.), *Systems and models for developing programs for the gifted and talented* (pp 126–152). Mansfield Center, CT: Creative Learning Press.

Flanders, J. R. (1987). How much of the content in mathematics textbooks is new? *Arithmetic Teacher, 35*, 18–23.

Goodlad, J. (1983). A study of schooling: Some findings and hypotheses. *Phi Delta Kappan, 64*, 465–470.

Goodlad, J. (1984). *A place called school: Prospects for the future*. New York: McGraw Hill.

Good, T. L., & Brophy, J. E. (1987). *Looking in classrooms* (4th ed.). New York: Harper & Row.

Guskey, T. R. (1986). Staff development and the process of teacher change. *Educational Researcher, 15*, 5–12.

Guskey, T. R. (1990). Integrating innovations. *Educational Leadership, 47*(5), 11–15.

Guskey, T. R., & Sparks, D. (1991). What to consider when evaluating staff development. *Educational Leadership, 49*(3), 73–76.

Imbeau, M. B. (1991). *Teacher attitudes toward curriculum compacting: A comparison of different inservice strategies*. Unpublished doctoral dissertation. The University of Connecticut, Storrs.

Joyce, B., & Showers, B. (1982). The coaching of teaching. *Educational Leadership, 40*(1), 4–10.

Joyce, B., & Showers, B. (1983). *Power in staff development through research in training*. Alexandria, VA: Association for Supervision and Curriculum Development.

Joyce, B., & Showers, B. (1987). *Student achievement through staff development*. New York: Longman.

Kirst, M. W. (1982). How to improve schools without spending more money. *Phi Delta Kappan, 64*, 6–8.

Knowles, M. S. (1978). *The adult learner: A neglected species*. Houston, TX: Gulf Publishing.

Kolb, D. A. (1976). *Experiential learning: Experience as the source of learning and development*. Englewood Cliffs, NJ: Prentice Hall.

Kulik, J. A., & Kulik, C. L. (1984). Synthesis of research on effects of accelerated instruction. *Educational Leadership, 42*(2), 84–90.

Oakes, J., & Lipton, M. (1992). Detracking schools: Early lessons from the field. *Phi Delta Kappan, 73*, 448–454.

Reed, S. E. (1987). *Effects of curriculum compacting on student attitudes in reading*. Unpublished specialist's thesis. College of St. Thomas. St. Paul, MN.

Reis, S. M., Burns, D. E., & Renzulli, J. S. (1992). *Curriculum compacting: The complete guide to modifying the regular curriculum for high-ability students.* Mansfield Center, CT: Creative Learning Press.

Reis, S. M., & Purcell, J. H. (1993). An analysis of content elimination and strategies used by elementary classroom teachers and the curriculum compacting process. *Journal for the Education of the Gifted, 16,* 147–170.

Reis, S. M., Westberg, K. L., Kulikowich, J., Caillard, F., Hébert, T., Purcell, J. H., Rogers, J., Smist, J., & Plucker, J. (1993). *Why not let high-ability students start school in January?* Technical report on the curriculum compacting study. Storrs. CT: The National Research Center on the Gifted and Talented.

Renzulli, J. S. (1977). *The enrichment triad model: A guide for developing defensible programs for the gifted and talented.* Mansfield Center, CT: Creative Learning Press.

Renzulli, J. S., & Reis, S. M. (1985). *The schoolwide enrichment model A comprehensive plan for educational excellence.* Mansfield Center, CT: Creative Learning Press.

Renzulli, J. S., & Reis, S. M. (1991). The reform movement and the quiet crisis in gifted education. *Gifted Child Quarterly, 35,* 26–35.

Renzulli, J. S., & Smith, L. H. (1978). *The compactor.* Mansfield Center, CT: Creative Learning Press.

Renzulli, J. S., Smith, L. H., & Reis, S. M. (1982). Curriculum compacting: An essential strategy for working with gifted students. *The Elementary School Journal, 82*(3), 185–194.

Showers, B., Joyce, B., & Bennett, B. (1987). Synthesis of research on staff development: A framework for future study and a state-of-the-art analysis. *Educational Leadership, 45*(1), 77–87.

Slavin, R. E. (1984). Meta-analysis in education: How has it been used? *Educational Researcher, 13*(8), 24–27.

Slavin, R. E. (1986) Best-evidence synthesis: An alternative to meta-analytic and traditional reviews. *Educational Researcher, 15*(9), 5–11.

Slavin, R. E., Karweit, N. L., & Madden, N. A. (1989). *Effective programs for students at risk.* Needham Heights, MA: Allyn and Bacon.

Sparks, G. M. (1986). The effectiveness of alternative training activities in changing teacher practices. *American Educational Research Journal, 23,* 217–225.

Starko, A. J. (1986). *It is about time: Inservice strategies for curriculum compacting.* Mansfield Center, CT: Creative Learning Press.

Steen, L. A. (1989). *Everybody counts: A report to the nation on the future of mathematics education.* Washington, DC: National Academy Press.

Tannenbaum, A. J. (1986). The enrichment matrix model. In J. S. Renzulli (Ed.), *Systems and models for developing programs for the gifted and talented* (pp. 126–152). Mansfield Center, CT: Creative Learning Press.

Taylor, B. M., & Frye, B. J. (1988). Pretesting: Minimizing time spent on skill work of intermediated readers. *The Reading Teacher, 47*(2). 100–103.

Treffinger, D. J. (1986). Fostering effective, independent learning through individualized programming. In J. S. Renzulli (Ed.), *Systems and models for developing programs for the gifted and talented* (pp. 429–460). Mansfield Center, CT: Creative Learning Press.

Tyson-Bernstein, H., & Woodward, A. (1989). Nineteenth-century policies for 21st-century practice: The textbook reform dilemma. *Educational Policy, 3*(2), 95–106.

Usiskin, Z. (1987). Why elementary algebra can, should, and must be an eighth-grade course for average students. *Mathematics Teacher, 80,* 428–438.

Van Tassel-Baska, J. (1985). Appropriate curriculum for the gifted. In J. Feldhusen (Ed.), *Toward excellence in gifted education* (pp. 175–189). Denver, CO: Love.

Westberg, K. L., Archambault, F. X., Dobyns, S. M., & Salvin, T. J. (1993). An observational study of classroom practices used with third- and fourth-grade students. *Journal for the Education of the Gifted, 16,* 120–146.

4

A Multi-Site Case Study of Successful Classroom Practices for High Ability Students

Karen L. Westberg and Francis X. Archambault, Jr.

University of Connecticut

A multi-site case study was conducted to describe 10 elementary schools and classrooms with a reputation for implementing differentiated practices to meet the needs of high ability students. The researchers found that classroom teachers at some sites employed flexible grouping practices or provided opportunities for advanced level projects to accommodate students' differing academic needs. At other sites, teachers collaborated with other teachers at their grade level or with district curriculum specialists to provide more academic challenge for talented students. And in some situations, the leadership of school principals or superintendents

Editor's Note: From Westberg, K. L., & Archambault, F. X. (1997). A multi-site case study of successful classroom practices for high ability students. *Gifted Child Quarterly, 41*(1), 42-51. © 1997 National Association for Gifted Children. Reprinted with permission.

appeared to have a strong impact on teachers' instructional practices. The themes that emerged across the sites include: (at) teachers' advanced knowledge and training, (b) teachers' willingness and readiness to embrace change, (c) collaboration, (d) teachers' beliefs and strategies for differentiating the curriculum, (e) leadership, and (f) autonomy and support.

C an you name an elementary school that has a reputation for meeting the individual needs of students, and specifically, the needs of high ability students? If you can name one, are you able to describe the classroom practices or explain why they occur at this particular site? These were among the questions that guided The Successful Practices Study, an in-depth investigation of schools and regular classrooms with a reputation for effective implementation of curriculum differentiation practices to meet the needs of high ability students. This article presents an overview of the findings and a synthesis of the themes across the sites in the study.

REVIEW OF RELATED LITERATURE

The Successful Practices Study was undertaken to extend the information gained from previous studies of regular classrooms conducted by the University of Connecticut site of The National Research Center on the Gifted and Talented (NRC/GT). After conducting these studies and reviewing the literature on instructional and curricular adaptations for developing the talent of capable students, we believed it would be beneficial to conduct an in-depth investigation of elementary schools and classrooms with a reputation for effectiveness in meeting students' individual needs.

NRC/GT Studies on Regular Classroom Practices

The National Research Center on the Gifted and Talented conducted three studies of regular classroom practices during 1990–1991. The Classroom Practices Survey solicited information from a stratified random sample of over 7000 third and fourth grade teachers about the practices they used with gifted and average students in their classrooms (Archambault et al., 1993). The most salient finding from the survey was that classroom teachers reported making only minor modifications in the regular curriculum to meet the needs of gifted students. The few teachers who did make modifications indicated that they provided for the capable students in their classrooms by assigning advanced readings, enrichment worksheets, and reports of various kinds. A very small number of teachers also indicated that they attempt to eliminate materials that students have already mastered, provide opportunities for students to do more advanced work, or expose students to higher level thinking skill materials. It should be noted that the teachers themselves reported these practices on a confidential survey.

Putting the Research to Use

This in-depth study provides a description of a variety of strategies teachers and schools use to develop the talents of high ability students in regular classrooms. The six general themes identified across sites—teachers' advanced training and knowledge, teachers' willingness and readiness to embrace change, collaboration, teachers' beliefs and strategies for differentiating instruction, leadership, and autonomy and support—have implications for classroom teachers, gifted education specialists, curriculum specialists, administrators, parents, and policy makers. The study contributes to our understanding of what can be done to improve the classroom practices for high ability students and how these improvements might be achieved.

For The Classroom Practices Observation Study, semi-structured observations were conducted in 46 third or fourth grade classrooms (Westberg, Archambault, Dobyns, & Salvin, 1993). An observation instrument entitled *The Classroom Practices Record (CPR)* was used by trained observers to document the extent to which gifted and talented students receive modifications in curricular activities, materials, and teacher-student verbal interactions in the classroom. The results indicated that the gifted and talented students received a limited amount of differentiation in reading, language, mathematics, science, and social studies instruction. Across all five subject areas, the gifted and talented students received no differentiated experiences in 84 percent of the activities in which they were involved. The conclusion from both The Classroom Practices Survey Study and The Classroom Practices Observation Study was that instructional and curricular differentiation for high ability students occurred only to a limited degree in the majority of the regular classrooms throughout the country.

The Curriculum Compacting Study was an experimental study that investigated the effects of a curriculum modification technique, curriculum compacting (Reis et al., 1993). Curriculum compacting is a procedure for streamlining the regular curriculum and replacing it with material at an appropriate challenge level for high ability students. Teachers from 27 school districts throughout the country were assigned to one of four groups, three treatment groups that received different levels of staff development or a control group. When the teachers in the treatment groups eliminated 40 to 50 percent of the regular curriculum for one or two high ability students in their classrooms, there was no significant decrease in students' pre and post standardized achievement test scores, and the teachers provided students with more enriching and appropriate curricular experiences.

Adapting Instruction for Individual Students

Educators recognize that students learn in different ways. For example, Wang and Walberg (1985) said:

> Every class contains students with different interests, problems, and talents; and most educators realize that whole-group instruction lessons geared to the "average" student are bound to be too difficult for some learners in the class and too easy for others. (p. 325)

Despite this recognition, several studies indicate that a "one size fits all" instructional method is the predominant practice in the majority of classrooms throughout the country (Archambault et al., 1993; Goodlad, 1984; Westberg et al., 1993). In a recent, four-year study (Morocco, Riley, Gordon, & Howard, 1996) that examined elementary teachers' planning for individual students with unique needs, the researchers concluded:

> Teachers generally focused their planning on the class as a whole. When they did think about individuals, their focus was mainly on the students' social and emotional needs, or on global and unconditional traits. The implication was that such traits and social/emotional issues were beyond the boundaries of the teachers' influence. (p. 164)

Emmer, Evertson, and Anderson (1980) investigated the instructional strategies that distinguish effective elementary teachers from ineffective elementary teachers as measured by students' achievement. They found that the effective teachers adapted their instruction to students' interests, skill levels, and attention span. When Evertson, Sanford, and Emmer (1981) focused on the ways that junior high teachers adapt their instruction in heterogeneous classrooms, they found that a few teachers used appropriate techniques for managing the classroom and for providing differentiated instruction, but that implementing these modifications required a high degree of teachers' energy, commitment, and determination.

Adapting instruction to accommodate differences demonstrated by students whose skills and capabilities are more advanced is particularly challenging. Unfortunately, most classroom teachers have had little, if any, professional preparation for adapting instruction to meet the needs of capable students and for managing the classrooms in which these students learn (Archambault et al., 1993; Westberg, Archambault, & Brown, in press; Westberg et al., 1993). For example, in the Classroom Practices Survey Study, 61% percent of the third and fourth grade public school teachers reported that they had no hours of inservice training or formal coursework that addressed any gifted education topics (Archambault et al., 1993).

Throughout the past thirty to forty years, advocates have called for a differentiated education for high ability students. The earliest definition of differential education for the gifted was offered by Virgil Ward who stated that gifted students comprise " . . . a potential for recognizably different experiences— some say categorically different" (1961, p. 79). Ward called for a differentiated curriculum in the areas of humanities, mathematics, social sciences, natural sciences, dance, drama, music, and painting. The Marland Report, a national study on the gifted commissioned by the U. S. Congress in 1971, stated that gifted and talented children "require differentiated educational programs and/or services beyond those normally provided by the regular school program" if they are "to realize their contribution to self and society" (p. ix). Thus, a rationale for providing differentiated education is grounded in the recognition of students' differing learning characteristics and behaviors. Passow (1982) stated, "The philosophy which underlies differentiated education is one which asserts that gifted/talented individuals, like all others, possess unique needs which can only be addressed through appropriately designed curricula" (p. 5). Like all students, gifted students need learning experiences appropriate to their "individual abilities, interests, and learning styles. Individual uniqueness should be respected and provided for, and every effort should be made to adapt learning experiences to the wide variety of student needs" (Passow, p. 5).

Experts concur that differentiation of instruction and the curriculum is necessary to accommodate the different learning needs and maximize the education of gifted students. For example, The United States Department of Education recently concluded in a report entitled *National Excellence: A Case for Developing America's Talent* (1993) that: "Schools also must assess students' levels of competence in the regular school curriculum in each of the core subjects and provide alternative learning opportunities for students who have mastered them" (p. 27). VanTassel-Baska (1989) identified four aspects of curriculum modification that should be addressed in the curriculum: deleting or compressing basic curriculum that has already been mastered or that can be mastered quickly; concentrating on higher level thinking skills to provide tools for the production rather than the consumption of knowledge; providing depth to the curriculum by concentrating on the interrelationships among bodies of knowledge; and encouraging self-directed learning so that the students can utilize more program options of an independent nature. In a recent video and guidebook for teachers (ASCD, 1994), Tomlinson presents several specific instructional and management strategies for providing differentiated experiences appropriate for advanced learners: curriculum compacting, independent projects, interest centers or interest groups, tiered assignments, flexible skills grouping, high-level questions, mentorships/apprenticeships, learning centers, and contracts/management plans.

Effective Schools and Practices

Several different variables and a variety of criteria have been used to examine or to recognize effective schools in this country. For example, the 1985–1986 school year was designated the Year of the Elementary School by then Secretary of Education William Bennett, and schools throughout the country were encouraged to apply for recognition (Hostrop, 1989). A total of 212 public and 60 private elementary schools were given awards based on how well the schools used resources, how they met students' academic needs, or how they overcame obstacles. None of the schools that received awards, however, were recognized specifically for their efforts to address students' individual needs. In fact, no mention is made in the literature about an award program that has addressed schools' effectiveness or success in addressing students' individual needs and, in particular, the needs of high ability students. Instead, schools are recognized usually as "effective" or "successful" for improving their governance practices.

The literature informs us about what could and what should be done to accommodate students' needs of advanced needs; however, these practices are not employed on a widespread basis. Nevertheless, these practices are employed in some classrooms, and The Successful Practices Study was conducted to learn more about the specific ways in which teachers make accommodations for students and the factors that influence them.

RESEARCH DESIGN

This study is based on the premise that immersion in classrooms using curricular differentiation practices would provide the best means for acquiring data about the complexities and processes that have an impact on successful school practices for high ability students. Therefore, a qualitative research design was adopted, and because we were interested in describing these practices, a multi-site case study approach was selected to conduct observations in classrooms and interviews with teachers, administrators, students, and others. The research questions that guided the study were: (1) What factors contribute to classroom teachers' effective use of differentiated teaching strategies? (2) What environmental factors within the classroom and school contribute to the effective use of differentiated teaching strategies? (3) How does the existence of a gifted education program, if one exists, affect the instructional strategies and materials used in the regular classroom and the students' need for instructional and curricular differentiation?

PROCEDURES

Sampling

Purposive sampling was used to select 10 elementary school sites for the study (2 urban, 6 rural, and 2 suburban.) To select the sites, telephone calls were made to individuals familiar with a large number of school districts within a state or region including, for example, state directors of gifted education, state curriculum specialists, university instructors, supervisors of student teaching, and regional educational service directors. These individuals were asked to name school districts in their state or area that had a reputation for meeting students' individual needs, particularly the needs of capable students. Districts that had received national or state awards for excellence were added to the list. When a district had been named by at least three sources, discussions were held with appropriate administrators to obtain permission for conducting the study in one elementary school within the district and, more specifically, in one third, fourth, or fifth grade classroom. Some of the districts had formal gifted education programs or services. All classrooms contained students who were formally identified as gifted or informally identified by their teachers as being eligible for gifted education services.

Data Collection and Analysis

The on-site researchers who gathered data for the study are: Linda Emerick, Thomas Hays, Thomas Hébert, Marcia Imbeau, Jann Leppien, Marian Matthews, Stuart Omdal, and Karen Westberg. These researchers, all of whom have training and experience in general education, gifted education, and research methodology, gathered data at the 10 elementary schools and wrote case studies that are individual chapters in the full research monograph on the study (Westberg & Archambault, 1995).

The major data-gathering techniques included "passive participant observation," which refers to a researchers' role as a "participant as observer" (Fraenkel & Wallen, 1993), and open-ended interviews with classroom teachers and other individuals, such as curriculum coordinators, gifted education specialists, parents, students, and community members. "Grand tour questions" (Spradley, 1979, p. 86) such as, "Can you explain the modifications you use to meet the needs of your high ability students?" or "Can you explain to me how your teacher determines what you already know?" elicited responses that enabled the researchers to obtain an understanding of participants' views.

The researchers spent several months observing in classrooms and kept detailed field notes and field logs to keep inferences to a low level. In addition to gathering data through observations and interviews, school documents, such as policy statements, administrative memos, faculty meeting minutes, curriculum guides, enrichment materials, and curriculum compacting records were reviewed. The triangulation of data through observations, interviews and documents from various sources provides reliability support for the findings (Lincoln & Guba, 1985). The researchers coded and analyzed field notes, interview protocols, and document data for topics, patterns, and themes. The coding process involved inductive analysis to uncover patterns to provide a description of the findings and themes at each site.

OVERVIEW OF SITE PROFILES

An overview of the sites in The Successful Practices Study, including selected findings, is presented in Figure 1. Assurances of confidentiality were provided to school districts, schools, and individuals at the various sites; therefore, pseudonyms are used instead of actual names.

Linda Emerick conducted a case study at East Meadow Elementary, a school located in an economically disadvantaged, urban city. This city is faced with the difficulties and problems that plague most cities in this country, including poverty and crime. Despite these challenges, however, the staff at East Meadow has created an exciting and challenging learning environment for its students. The strategies used by the teachers, the leadership provided by the principal, and the efforts of the parents have resulted in unique opportunities for students, such as "Enrichment Wednesdays," days when special enrichment classes are offered to students.

A different picture is provided by Tom Hays who studied three rural schools in the Midwest, and his case studies include a discussion about the relationship between the communities and the education provided in these small towns. Although the findings from all three sites are not identical, Hays found similarities among them, such as collaboration between the gifted education coordinators and the classroom teachers.

Jann Leppien conducted a case study at Forest Hills Elementary, a school located in a rural New England community considered an "emerging suburban area." Although the school is small (320 students), the district employs several teaching specialists and classroom teachers. In fact, the effects of the collaboration between the curriculum specialists and classroom teachers is one of the major findings from the site.

More than two thousand miles away in another small school, Marian Matthews conducted a case study at Homer Elementary School. Homer School is located in a very rural area in the Southwest and has an enrollment of only 160 students. Despite its small size and limited resources, this school offers a gifted program, and the Superintendent of Schools is its greatest advocate. Schoolwide enrichment opportunities are among the innovations that occur at this school.

Tom Hébert conducted research at Maple Grove School which borders a large urban area. Although technically located in a suburban school district, the school is located in a neighborhood faced with challenges that are associated with urban areas. He focuses on a teacher whom he calls "a visionary." Because of her training in special education, this teacher is especially aware of how students learn at different rates, and she knows how to adapt instruction to meet students' differing needs.

Stuart Omdal presents a case study of Salisbury, a small school in New England. This school uses the Schoolwide Enrichment Model (Renzulli and Reis, 1985) to provide enrichment teaching and learning, and many of the findings from this site are related to the enrichment program coordinator's effective implementation of the model. Omdal describes several successful practices at this rural school.

Marcia Imbeau presents a site profile of a suburban school district in the South Central region of the United States. She discusses the findings from two elementary schools in the Sutton School District, Rogers Elementary and Franklin Elementary. The successful practices that she describes include (a) the collaboration between the gifted education teachers and the classroom teachers, and (b) the teachers' strategies for adapting instruction for high ability students.

Another profile of a suburban school district is presented in the case study at Woodland Elementary. Karen Westberg focuses on a fifth grade teacher who provided curriculum compacting services to students in three fifth grade classrooms through a departmentalized teaching arrangement at the school.

As indicated in the brief overview of the sites, the findings were varied. Detailed descriptions of the settings, informants, findings, and themes for each site are presented in the researchers' case studies reported in the full research monograph on the study (Westberg & Archambault, 1995).

THEMES ACROSS SITES

We conducted this study to describe how teachers implement curriculum differentiation practices to accommodate the needs of their high ability students and describe the factors that influence these practices. While some of the findings are unique to individual sites, the following themes emerged across the sites: teachers' advanced training and knowledge; teachers' willingness and readiness to embrace change; teachers' beliefs and strategies for instructing individual students; collaboration (within grade levels, between gifted education specialists and classroom teachers, between curriculum specialists and classroom teachers); teachers' beliefs and strategies for differentiating curriculum; administrative leadership; and autonomy and support.

Teachers' Advanced Training and Knowledge

After reading the case studies, we noted that several researchers discussed the advanced training and knowledge of the classroom teachers who were the focus of the investigations. The majority of the teachers had graduate degrees, often in areas of special education or reading. For example, the fifth grade teacher at Forest Hills had a degree in reading; the fourth grade teacher at Maple Grove had a degree in special education; the teacher at Woodland had graduate degrees in reading and gifted education; and the entire team of fifth grade teachers at East Meadow had degrees in learning disabilities or gifted education. We believe it is not coincidental that these teachers—teachers with a reputation for effectiveness in dealing with high ability students—had training in various areas of special education, a field in which teachers focus on students as individuals.

Figure 1   Overview of the Sites in the Successful Practices Study

School Site	Community Type/Region	Selected Findings
1. East Meadow	Urban North Central	Grade Level Team Teaching Curricular Modifications Wednesday Enrichment
2. Eastville	Rural Midwest	Advanced Level Content Collaboration Between G/T Coordinator and Teachers Community Support for Education
3. Forest Hills	Rural New England	Collaboration Between Teachers and Curriculum Coordinators Flexible Grouping Practices Administrative Advocacy of the G/T Program
4. Homer	Rural Southwest	Flexible Identification for Gifted Education Services Superintendent's Involvement in the Educational Program Schoolwide Theme-Based Projects
5. Maple Grove	Urban-Suburban New England	Classroom Teacher's Special Education Training University Mentorship Program Talents Unlimited Program
6. Northtown	Rural Midwest	Students' Advanced Level Products Higher Order Questioning Strategies Curriculum Compacting
7. Salisbury	Rural New England	Flexible Grouping Practices Curricular Modifications Schoolwide Enrichment Model
8. Springdale	Rural Midwest	Curriculum Compacting in Student's Strength Areas Curriculum "Extensions," i.e., Breadth & Depth Collaboration Between G/T Teacher & Classroom Teachers
9. Sutton	Suburban South Central	Collaboration Between G/T Teacher & Classroom Teachers Teacher's Concern About Meeting Individual Differences
10. Woodland	Suburban New England	Curriculum Compacting in Mathematics & Spelling Departmentalized Teaching Integrated Language Arts Curriculum

Although every teacher did not have a graduate degree, all teachers had been involved in a variety of professional development experiences over the years. For example, several teachers had received training from their school districts on thinking skills instruction, whole language instruction, questioning strategies, and curriculum modification techniques. Inservice training was used by districts quite frequently to provide opportunities for teachers to learn new strategies, but the teachers reported that they learned new techniques through a variety of professional development experiences. Some teachers indicated that they learned about specific instructional strategies from mentors and co-workers. For example, the new fourth grade teacher at Maple Grove School indicated that he learned new techniques from his more experienced colleague, and a fourth grade teacher at Adams School said she worked closely with her co-worker to plan curriculum. Whether the training was formal or informal, the teachers applied what they learned through various professional development opportunities to increase their repertoire of teaching strategies.

In recent years, educational leaders and reformers have argued that the improvement of education depends on teachers' professional growth. In fact, the National Education Goals 2000, adopted by the nation's governors and the President in 1989, was modified in 1994 to include a new goal—the professional growth of teachers (Lewis, 1996). In discussing why professional growth is so essential, Barth (1990) said, "When teachers observe, examine, question, and reflect on their ideas and develop new practices that lead toward their ideals, students are alive. When teachers stop growing, so do their students" (p. 50). School districts are increasingly making a commitment to the professional growth of teachers; they recognize that it doesn't occur in a couple of staff development days held each year. Instead, school districts are using a variety of formats to develop long term professional development plans, such as peer coaching and collaborative action research. Furthermore, some school districts are using the content, process, context standards developed recently by the National Staff Development Council (1995) to guide school improvement efforts. For example, the process standard: "Effective elementary staff development uses a variety of staff development approaches to accomplish the goals of improving instruction and student success" (p. 23) may motivate schools to experiment with new forms of staff development.

In addition to being knowledgeable about various practices, the teachers in the study appeared to be life-long learners who expressed curiosity about new topics, issues, and skills. Most of the teachers had been teaching for several years, and they continued to be interested in improving their practices. A teacher at one of the sites had twenty years' experience, not one year of experience repeated twenty times. Educational leaders recognize that teachers who continue to grow are effective teachers. The importance of personal and professional growth was expressed by Barth:

> Just as potters cannot teach others to craft in clay without setting their own hands to work at the wheel, so teachers cannot fully teach others the excitement, the difficulty, the patience, and the satisfaction that accompany learning without themselves engaging in the messy, frustrating and rewarding "clay" of learning. (p. 49)

The teachers in this study continued to learn and grow. Anderson noted, "Reform efforts should focus on teachers' learning-in terms of values, beliefs, and competencies—for these are at the heart of reform" (p. 35). The importance of teachers' learning was underscored recently by Sergiovanni (1996) who said, " . . . making classrooms into learning communities for students will remain more rhetoric than real unless schools become learning communities for teachers too" (p. 139).

An aspect of professional development that has received attention recently is the need to provide different types of professional development experiences to different teachers. As teachers, we advocate providing differentiated learning opportunities to meet the unique needs and interests of students, but do school districts likewise provide differentiated professional development opportunities to meet the needs and interests of teachers? According to Barth:

> The conditions under which each teacher learns are probably as varied as those under which students learn. We hear talk of matching learning styles of students with teaching styles of adults. It would be well to also contemplate the implications of different adult learning styles. (p. 54)

If more differentiated professional development experiences had been found at the sites in this study, perhaps even more "successful practices" would have been reported by the researchers.

Teachers' Willingness and Readiness to Embrace Change

The researchers also found that the teachers were willing to make changes in their practices. They did not teach as they were taught when they were students (at least we don't think they did), and they probably don't teach as they did when they were novice teachers. Several teachers indicated that when experimenting with new strategies, they realized that they will not be successful every time. The teachers may not all be risk-takers by nature; therefore, other factors influenced their willingness to experiment with new practices, such as the culture of the school, an effective leader, or administrative support. Regardless of the factors, however, it is important to note that the teachers felt comfortable experimenting with new techniques, strategies, or materials. For example, the fourth grade teacher in the Sutton School District was comfortable taking on the challenge of participating in a national economics competition, and the fifth grade teacher at Woodland Elementary was confident about her ability to provide curriculum compacting services for students in three classes.

Because the teachers were *willing* to spend extra time and effort to make changes in their practices, they had the *requisite readiness* to make it happen. Fullan (1993) says, "If there is one cardinal rule of change in human condition, it is that you cannot *make* people change" (p. 23). The case studies indicate that several teachers spent many extra hours each week planning voluntarily with their colleagues and preparing instructional lessons and materials. The teachers' psychological and intellectual readiness for making changes appears to have influenced their practices.

Collaboration

Three different forms of collaboration were reported in the case studies. One form of collaboration was observed at sites where the teachers attributed their successful practices to collaboration with grade-level colleagues, such as at Adams School and East Meadow Elementary. A second form of collaboration was reported at sites where classroom teachers collaborated a great deal with the gifted education specialists in their buildings, such as at Franklin and Rogers Elementary Schools, Salisbury School, and Westhills School. A third form of collaboration was observed at Forest Hills Elementary School where the classroom teachers collaborated with the curriculum specialists to plan differentiated instruction for high ability students. The literature indicates that collaboration among teachers has a major influence on teachers' willingness to change their practices (Bennett, 1986; Dantonio, 1995; Hord, Rutherford, Huling-Austin, & Hall, 1987). Schmoker, who believes that teacher collaboration is essential for school improvement, states: "Teachers, like other professionals, perform more effectively—even exponentially—if they collaborate. Although collaboration represents a significant change in how most teachers work, it should become an expectation" (1996, p. 7).

Most educators recognize that collaboration among teachers has a major impact on practices, however, having the *time* for collaboration is often a barrier. The teachers in the study who were involved in collaborative efforts were either *provided the time* or they *made the time* to collaborate with colleagues. Most of the teachers did not have sufficient time during the school day to plan with their colleagues. To remedy this problem, the teachers at East Meadow created Ol' Mexico nights, Wednesday evenings when they went out for dinner at a Mexican restaurant to debrief, discuss, and plan. Dantonio (1995) said, "Time for teacher collaboration must be important enough to be included in the school schedule" (p. 44). While not among the findings in this study, time for collaboration during the school day can be obtained through various ways, such as by having (a) substitute teachers rotate to release classroom teachers during the day, (b) a principal take over teachers' classes, or (c) special programs scheduled for combined classrooms.

It should be noted that the collaboration practices among colleagues in this study were self-initiated and voluntary. Some authors refer to the type of collaboration described in this study as collegial coaching, which Dantonio (1995) defines "a collaborative, self-initiated, egalitarian way for teachers to develop professionally" (p. 3). According to Friend and Cook (1992), collaboration includes: voluntary participation, parity among participants, mutual goals, shared responsibility for participation and decision making, shared resources, and shared accountability. Although collaboration was not found at every site, these characteristics describe the types of collaborations observed in this study.

Teachers' Beliefs and Strategies for Differentiating Instruction

The researchers described a variety of strategies used by teachers to differentiate instruction for high ability students in the study. Although differentiation is defined in many different ways, it generally refers to the various approaches that teachers use for accommodating students' academic differences by determining what students will learn, how students will learn, and how students will demonstrate what they have learned (Tomlinson, 1995). The majority of the teachers had an awareness of students' academic differences. They did not view students in their classrooms as a large mass; rather, they saw students as individuals with different skills, interests, styles, and talents. In addition, they were aware of students' strengths, not just their weaknesses.

Because the teachers had an awareness of the academic diversity among students, they tailored their instruction to meet students' individual needs. They did not expect all of their students to complete all of the same pages in a textbook, at exactly the same times throughout the year, with the same readiness, and with the same outcomes. They did not believe it was important to "keep them all together." Instead, the teachers established high standards, made curriculum modifications, found mentors, encouraged independent investigations and projects, or created flexible instructional groups to develop the talents of their more capable students. Like the U.S. Army motto, they wanted their students to "be all they could be." And as masterful teachers, they knew how to select appropriate strategies for meeting unique needs.

In describing what differentiation is and is not, Tomlinson (1995) states that a paradigm shift is necessary to understand the role of a teacher in a differentiated classroom. In this paradigm, teachers are not dispensers of knowledge, but "organizers of learning opportunities." This is an apt description of the teachers in this study. For example, the fourth grade teacher at Maple Grove School organized a mentorship program for her students, the fourth grade teacher at Salisbury Elementary used learning contracts with students, and the teachers at Springdale School described the degree to which students had choices in their curriculum.

Although the teachers used various strategies to "organize learning opportunities" for meeting students' needs, they provided "challenges and choices" to students. Some teachers discussed their high expectations for advanced learners and their attempts to provide challenging material. Many teachers provided opportunities for students to pursue individual projects on topics of their choice. "Challenges and choices" may be a succinct, but clear explanation of differentiation. To illustrate this, we have asked adults to recall, first of all, their favorite subject in high school or favorite course in college and, secondly, to name why these were their favorite subjects or courses. Invariably, we have found that their reasons have something to do with "challenges and choices." In fact, the provision of challenges and choices appear to be associated with people's most meaningful educational experiences. Many of the teachers in the study provided challenges and choices to their students.

By providing choices to students, the teachers stimulated students' interests and recognized the influence of interests on students' learning. Although educators have long advocated accommodating students' interests, it is not often put into practice in classrooms throughout the country (Goodlad, 1984;

Westberg, Archambault, Dobyns, & Salvin, 1993). Phenix (1964), an expert in curriculum development, said: "Students learn best what they most profoundly want to know. Their learning efficiency is in direct relation to their motivation. Hence, the materials of instruction should be selected in the light of students' real interests" (pp. 345–346). Some teachers in this study strived to provide instruction and curriculum to accommodate students' interests, which is a major strategy for differentiating the curriculum for advanced learners.

Leadership

The researchers discussed the role of significant leaders in some of the case studies. The influence of school superintendents was described, in particular, at Homer Elementary and Forest Hills Elementary. The superintendents at these two rural schools spoke publicly about the importance of providing programming for high ability students and were strong advocates of their schoolwide enrichment programs. The influence of a school principal was particularly significant at East Meadow, where the principal was viewed by the teachers as a highly effective leader who influenced their classroom practices.

In recent years, educational reformers have been advocating a different role for principals within learning organizations. Bechtol and Sorenson (1993) point to one of the changes frequently cited: "Good principals are willing to collaborate with teachers to experiment with new strategies" (p. 363). While not observed at all sites in the study, some of the principals had an impact on what the teachers were attempting to do to provide differentiated instruction for the high ability students in their classrooms.

Autonomy and Support

Teachers discussed the autonomy and support they felt for implementing new practices. Some teachers were allowed to experiment with flexible staffing patterns. For example, the Woodland teacher and her colleagues were allowed to departmentalize their instruction, and they did not have school district policies that prevented them from engaging in various practices. Other teachers described the support they had for implementing new curriculum. For example, the teachers at East Meadow spoke about the principal's support for experimenting with "Enrichment Wednesdays." Their principal stated that she "gets out of the teacher's way" when they want to try out new ideas.

Many researchers discussed the supportive atmosphere or collaborative culture of the schools. In some cases, a special atmosphere was readily apparent, as at East Meadow where visitors to the school are provided with a brochure entitled "A Year of Excellence: It Takes All Three," which reflects how teachers, students, and parents work toward common goals. A particular culture was observed in the three midwestern, rural schools and communities: Springfield, Eastville, and Westhills. Individuals in all three towns were strong supporters of education and the schools, and the schools' activities were the central focus of the communities. Peterson and Brietzken (as cited in "Collaborative Culture Supports Improvement," 1996) describe collaborative cultures as the following:

> The school culture is a complex web of norms, values, beliefs and assumptions, and tradition and rituals that have been built up over time as teachers, students, parents, and administrators work together, deal with crises, and develop unstated expectations for interacting and working together. (p. 1).

It appears that most sites in this study, if not all, had collaborative cultures that supported teachers as they worked to improve their practices and develop students' talent. Dantonio (1995) said, "In order to obtain competence in newly introduced instructional actions, teachers need extended opportunities to practice them in a safe environment before they can use them successfully with learners" (p. 12). Many teachers in the study worked in an environment that supported their students' as well as their own professional and personal learning, which brings us back to where we started this section, namely, with teachers' advanced knowledge and training.

We have discussed the following themes as being relatively common across sites: (a) teachers' advanced knowledge and training, (b) teachers' willingness and readiness to embrace change, (c) collaboration, (d) teachers' beliefs and strategies for differentiating curriculum, (e) leadership, and (f) autonomy and support. These factors may be somewhat linear; namely, the implementation of successful classroom practices begins with teachers' advanced knowledge and training, which impacts teachers' willingness and readiness to embrace change. When teachers collaborate with others in their efforts to affect change, they implement various strategies for differentiating the curriculum. Furthermore, teachers are successful if they have strong administrative leaders who provide them with autonomy and support, which results in a belief system and school culture that supports the development of students' talent.

Many of the on-site researchers noted a special atmosphere at the sites in the study. In general, they found that the atmosphere in these schools was pleasant and comfortable. Furthermore, they discovered a supportive attitude toward capable students. The following statement made by John F. Kennedy exemplifies this attitude: "Not every child has an equal talent or an equal ability or equal motivation, but children have the equal right to develop their talent, their ability and their motivation" (cited in Ravitch, 1985, p. 141).

Teaching is a very isolated activity. Most teachers have the freedom to close their classroom doors; we don't know specifically what happens within those classrooms. The Successful Practices Study permitted a peek into classrooms to describe what was occurring. As with all research, we must admit that this "peek" was limited. Time and scope are among the limitations in this study. An in-depth examination of classrooms limited the number of sites that could be studied. The potential existence of observer effects, which may have influenced teachers' and students' actions, is another limitation. And finally, we realize that a degree of observer bias exists in all qualitative investigations. We acknowledge all of these potential limitations.

We believe this study served a useful purpose and its findings contribute to our collective understanding of the practices that teachers use to accommodate the needs of talented students in regular classrooms. We maintain that *typical* teachers tailor instruction to students' *similarities;* but truly *effective* teachers tailor instruction to students' *differences* as well as their similarities. The case studies reported in this article shed some light on how effective teachers and schools accomplish this challenging task.

REFERENCES

Archambault, F. X., Jr., Westberg, K. L., Brown, S. W., Hallmark, B. W., Emmons, C. L., & Zhang, W. (1993). *Regular classroom practices with gifted students: Results of a national survey of classroom teachers* (Research Monograph 93102). Storrs, CT: University of Connecticut, The National Research Center on the Gifted and Talented.

Association for Supervision and Curriculum Development. (1994). *Challenge the gifted in the regular classroom: Facilitator's guide.* Alexandria, VA: Author.

Barth, R. S. (1990). *Improving schools from within.* San Francisco: Jossey-Bass.

Bechtol, W. M., & Sorenson, J. S. (1993). *Restructuring schooling for individual students.* Boston: Allyn & Bacon.

Bennett, W. J. (1986). *What works: Research about teaching and learning.* Washington, DC: U.S. Department of Education.

Collaborative culture supports improvement. (1996, April). *School team innovator, 1,* 5.

Dantonio, M. (1995). *Collegial coaching. Inquiry into the teaching self.* Bloomington, IN: Phi Delta Kappa.

Emmer, E. T., Evertson, C. M., & Anderson, L. M. (1980). Effective classroom management at the beginning of the school year. *Elementary School Journal, 80,* 219–231.

Evertson, C., Sanford, J., & Emmet, E. (1981). Effects of class heterogeneity in junior high school. *American Educational Research Journal, 18,* 219–222.

Fraenkel, J. R., & Wallen, N. E. (1993). *How to design and evaluate research in education* (2nd ed.). New York: McGraw-Hill.

Friend, M., & Cook, L. (1992). *Interactions: Collaboration skills for school professionals.* White Plains, NY: Longman.

Fullan, M. (1993). *Change forces: Probing the depths of educational reform.* Bristol, PA: Falmer Press.

Goodlad, J. I. (1984). *A place called school: Prospects for the future.* New York: McGraw-Hill Book Company.

Hord, S. M., Rutherford, W. L., Huling-Austin, L., & Hall, G. E. (1987). *Taking charge of change.* Alexandria, VA: Association for Supervision and Curriculum Development.

Hostrop, R. W. (1989). *Outstanding elementary schools.* Palm Springs, CA: ETC Publications.

Lewis, A. C. (1996). Questions and answers about school leadership. *Phi Delta Kappan, 77,* 525.

Lincoln, Y. S., & Guba, E. G. (1985). *Naturalistic inquiry.* Newbury Park, CA: Sage Publications.

Marland, S. P., Jr. (1971). *Education of the gifted and talented, 1.* Washington, DC: U.S. Government Printing Office.

Morocco, C. C., Riley, M. K., Gordon, S. M., & Howard, C. L. (1996). The elusive individual in teachers' planning. In G. G. Brannigan (Ed.), *The enlightened educator* (pp. 154–176). New York: McGraw-Hill.

National Staff Development Council, (1995). *NSDC's standards for staff development.* Oxford, OH: National Staff Development Council.

Passow, A. H. (1982). Differentiated curricula for the gifted/talented: A point of view. In S. Kaplan, A. H. Passow, P. H. Phenix, S. Reis, J. S. Renzulli, I. Sato, L. Smith, E. P. Torrance, & V. S. Ward. *Curricula for the gifted.* (pp. 4–20). Ventura, CA: National/State Leadership Training Institute on the Gifted/Talented.

Ravitch, D. (1985). *The troubled crusade: American education 1945–1980.* New York: Basic Books.

Reis, S. M., Westberg, K. L., Kulikowich, J., Caillard, E, Hébert, T., Plucker, J., Purcell, J., Rogers, J., & Smist, J. (1993). *Why not let high ability students start school in January? The curriculum compacting study* (Research Monograph 93106). Storrs, CT: The National Research Center on the Gifted and Talented.

Renzulli, J. S., & Reis, S. M. (1985). *The schoolwide enrichment model: A comprehensive plan for educational excellence.* Mansfield Center, CT: Creative Learning Press, Inc.

Schmoker, M. (1996). *Results: The key to continuous school improvement.* Alexandria VA: The Association for Supervision and Curriculum Development.

Sergiovanni, T. (1996). *Leadership in the schoolhouse.* San Francisco: Jossey-Bass.

Spradley, J. P. (1979). *The ethnographic interview.* New York: Holt, Rinehart & Winston.

Strauss, A., & Corbin, J. (1990). *Basics of qualitative research.* Newbury Park, CA: Sage.

Tomlinson, C. A. (1995). *How to differentiate instruction in mixed-ability classrooms.* Alexandria, VA: Association for Supervision and Curriculum Development.

U.S. Department of Education. (1993). *National excellence: A case for developing America's talent.* Washington, DC: U.S. Government Printing Office.

VanTassel-Baska, J. (1989). Appropriate curriculum for the gifted. In J. Feldhusen, J. VanTassel-Baska, & K. Seeley. *Excellence in educating the gifted* (pp. 175–192). Denver; CO: Love.

Wang, M. C., & Walberg, H. J. (1985). Adaptive education in retrospect and prospect. In M. C. Wang & H. J. Walberg (Eds.), *Adapting instruction to individual differences* (pp. 325–329). Berkeley, CA: McCutchan Publishing Corp.

Ward, V. (1961). *Educating the gifted: An axiomatic approach.* Columbus, OH: Charles E. Merrill.

Westberg, K. L., & Archambault, F. X., Jr. (Eds.). (1995). Profiles of successful practices for high ability students in elementary classrooms (Research Monograph 95122). Storrs, CT: University of Connecticut, The National Research Center on the Gifted and Talented.

Westberg, K. L., Archambault, F. X., Jr., & Brown, S. B. (1995). *Profiles of successful practices for high ability students in elementary classrooms* (Research Monograph 95122). Storrs, CT: University of Connecticut, The National Research Center on the Gifted and Talented.

Westberg, K. L., Archambault, F. X., Jr., & Brown, S. B. (in press). A survey of classroom practices with third and fourth grade students in the United States. *Gifted Education International.*

Westberg, K. L., Archambault, F. X., Jr., Dobyns, S. M., & Salvin T. J. (1993). *An observational study of instructional and curricular practices used with gifted and talented students in regular classrooms* (Research Monograph 93104). Storrs, CT: University of Connecticut, The National Research Center on the Gifted and Talented.

5

Open-Ended Activities: Differentiation Through Learner Responses

Nancy B. Hertzog

University of Illinois at Urbana-Champaign

This article explores the meaning of curricular differentiation for identified gifted students by examining learner responses to open-ended activities. Very little research supports or describes how open-ended activities— which have been advocated as a strategy to allow students to work in their own interest areas, in their own learning styles, and at their own ability level—serve to differentiate the curriculum. This paper sets curriculum differentiation in an historical perspective, reviews a comprehensive investigation into the nature of open-ended activities, and focuses on how and in what ways the responses to open-ended activities of children identified as gifted differed from responses of children who were not identified as gifted in a third-grade and a fourth-grade heterogeneously grouped classroom. The study also focuses on teacher perceptions of classroom activities and learner responses. Data sources included observations over

Editor's Note: From Hertzog, N. B. (1998). Open-ended activities: Differentiation through learner responses. *Gifted Child Quarterly*, 42(4), 212-227. © 1998 National Association for Gifted Children. Reprinted with permission.

the course of one academic year, interviews with teachers and students, learning style and interest assessment instruments, and documents related to over 33 open-ended activities. Based on the findings reported here, the author proposes a reexamination of the meaning of curricular differentiation with a renewed emphasis on determining how an instructional strategy, for example, providing open-ended activities, maximizes student's capabilities.

A t 10 a.m. Monday through Friday, all 24 students in Keith's third-grade classroom open their writing notebooks and begin their 30 minutes of writing time. They may write anything, in whatever genre they choose (fiction, non-fiction, poetry), and they may take as long as they'd like to finish a story that they have begun. For some children, one written piece may take weeks. When students finish their first drafts, they get help from the teacher to edit their work. Then they copy their story into a final form and bind it to be displayed on a rack of finished stories.

Would all children want to be involved in such a learning experience? Could all children participate in such a learning experience? Should all children be expected to succeed in such a learning experience? If the answer is "yes" to all of those questions, then this is not differentiated instruction for students identified as gifted as defined by Passow (1982). Open-ended activities, such as Keith's writing instructional time period, defy the criteria of differentiation suggested by these three questions. Open-ended activities embody instead the potential to differentiate the curriculum through learner responses. Differentiating learning experiences through learner responses, as opposed to offering different learning experiences, means to differentiate instruction by allowing students to work at their own rates, use their preferred learning styles, investigate their own interests, and produce work commensurate with their abilities. Research examining how learner responses can differentiate instruction is limited.

Putting the Research to Use

The findings presented in this paper have practical as well as theoretical implications. In most classrooms, teachers assume responsibility for differentiating the curriculum to address a diverse array of educational needs. Open-ended activities are an often-advocated, but ambiguous strategy for differentiating the curriculum in a heterogeneous setting. The teachers in this study demonstrated that they used a variety of open-ended activities for different instructional goals. Articulating openness as a continuum of choices in the content, process, and product domains provides a conceptual framework for empowering teachers and students in their instructional decision making. Teachers may become more aware of how the design and implementation of open-ended activities affect the quality and variability of learner responses.

For researchers, this discussion of quality and variability suggests moving beyond the accepted theoretical framework of differentiation to a more individualized notion of maximizing student capabilities. Whether or not students identified as gifted responded in a way that was "qualitatively different" from their peers who were not identified as gifted was perhaps not as relevant as whether or not students responded in ways that maximized their performance. This paper ignites discourse about the meaning of curricular differentiation in heterogeneously grouped classrooms, and suggests a redefinition of "differentiation through learner response."

The application of curricular differentiation—providing different learning experiences to a selected group of children, one critical component of gifted education—is perhaps the most debatable issue in the field. Yet, it is the least understood for practitioners. It is no coincidence that Robinson (1995) noted that papers on curriculum study are the least selected for outstanding papers in *Gifted Child Quarterly* over the last 10 years. Delving into the complexities of the term *curricular differentiation* is a challenge for all researchers pursuing curricular studies. The purpose of this paper is to examine open-ended activities as an instructional strategy to differentiate instruction in a general educational setting. The meaning of curricular differentiation will be thoroughly explored first, because it is necessary to understand this concept before applying it to open-ended activities.

DIFFERENTIATION: AN HISTORICAL PERSPECTIVE

When the headlines from the *Boston Globe* read "Dull Work for Bright Students: Survey Finds Their Studies Repetitive" (McCarthy, 1992) and an article in the *Chicago Tribune* is titled "The Educational Mainstream Drowns Gifted Children," (Beck, 1992), the public is being made aware that education should be different for students with exceptional abilities. These headlines were generated after findings from a study conducted by The National Research Center on the Gifted and Talented, University of Connecticut, were made public (Westberg, Archambault, Dobyns, & Salvin, 1993). The study found that, although "nearly all gifted and talented students in this country spend most of their school day in the regular classroom" (p. 3), "target gifted and talented students experienced no instructional or curricular differentiation in 84% of the instructional activities in which they participated" (p. 1).

In order to address curricular differentiation in the general education setting, the meaning of differentiation must be clear. Over the last two decades, the ambiguity of what is meant by curricular differentiation or the misapplication of differentiation principles has created hostilities that have brought charges of elitism to the entire field of gifted education. Sapon-Shevin (1993) not only criticized the notion of providing different learning experiences, but also faulted the basic principles which underlie the rationale for gifted education. Gifted programs, she argued, are not democratic. She stated:

> Declaring that there is something undemocratic about gifted education, something fundamentally wrong with labeling a small group of children in a way that entitles them to a highly differentiated, almost always superior, education is a bit like saying that the emperor has no clothes—it is both patently obvious to many and yet not something we talk about. (p. 26)

The major finding of the Classroom Practices Survey, that classroom teachers make only minor modifications in the regular curriculum to meet the needs of identified gifted students, was criticized by Delisle (1994):

> In a classic case of being damned if you do and damned if you don't, teachers who claimed they treated their gifted and 'average' students differently could be accused of giving preferential treatment, while those who did not distinguish between students as regards resources and instruction might be chided as being boring. Go figure." (p. 226)

At the 1995 annual convention of the National Association for Gifted Children, the meaning and history of curricular differentiation was revisited with a panel discussion entitled, "Beyond the Leadership Training Institute (LTI) Principles—What Is Appropriate Curriculum for the Gifted?" (Callahan, 1995). Most significantly, this discussion was to heighten an awareness of the distinguishing features of curriculum for identified gifted students and to question, perhaps intellectually, how it is different from best practices in curriculum and instruction for all learners. Panel members were asked specifically to address the relevancy of the founding principles of curricular differentiation within the context of the 1990s curriculum reform movements. I present the reader now with an overview of the historical perspective of differentiation as it came to be defined in the field of gifted education. In order to understand what is meant by differentiation through "learner responses" and to comprehend the significance of this strategy, it is necessary to see how the meaning of curricular differentiation has evolved.

Ward's Theory

In 1961, Virgil Ward wrote a theoretical book entitled *Education for the Gifted: An Axiomatic Approach*. Although gifted education was advanced by the events surrounding Soviet competition and Sputnik in the 1950s, Ward's book was one of the first to conceptualize characteristics of gifted education as different from education for all students. He has often been referred to as the "grandfather" of Differential Education for the Gifted (DEG). His theory consisted of propositions and corollaries based upon learning characteristics, social and historical context of school and society, and pedagogical principles. Though they were developed over 30 years ago, they still remain the theoretical framework from which many practitioners have developed their curricular models. While many references in the literature credit other authors for principles of differentiated instruction, it can clearly be seen in Ward's work that he advocated differences in process, product, and content domains. One of his propositions stated: "The education of the gifted child and youth should emphasize enduring methods and sources of learning, as opposed to a terminal emphasis upon present states of knowledge" (p. 156). Long before creative problem solving programs became prevalent, Ward advocated that "learning should be conceived as the continuous, ongoing acquisition of data pertinent to problem situations, not as a set of given facts which, it is hoped, will apply to problems that arise subsequently in the life career" (p. 156). One of the major criticisms of Ward's theoretical framework is that he based all of his propositions on the characteristics of gifted children whom he defined as those with exceptional intellectual ability. His theories were based on a narrow definition of giftedness (children who scored at least two standard deviations above the mean on a test of intellectual ability).

Definitions and National Guidelines

In 1976, the Office of the Gifted and Talented defined differentiated education or services as

> that process of instruction which is capable of being integrated into the school program and is adaptable to varying levels of individual learning response in the education of the gifted and talented and includes but is not limited to:

1. A differentiated curriculum embodying a high level of cognitive and affective concepts and processes beyond those normally provided in the regular curriculum of the local educational agency;

2. Instructional strategies which accommodate the unique learning styles of the gifted and talented; and

3. Flexible administrative arrangements for instruction both in and out of school, such as special classes, seminars, resource rooms, independent

study, student internships, mentorships, research field trips, library media research centers and other appropriate arrangements. (North Carolina State Department, 1988, p. 24)

In 1981, The National/State Leadership Training Institute on the Gifted/Talented sponsored the First National Curriculum Conference for the Gifted and Talented in Baltimore, Maryland. The mission of the participants was to clarify the questions raised by the Marland Report (Marland, 1972), which listed three characteristics for a differentiated educational program for gifted students:

1. a differentiated curriculum that promotes higher cognitive processes;

2. instructional strategies that accommodate both curriculum content and the learning styles of gifted and talented children; and

3. special grouping arrangements appropriate to particular children (i.e., special classes, honor classes, seminars, resource rooms, and the like).

Out of this First National Curriculum Conference came Passow's frequently quoted seven guiding principles to differentiation:

1. The content of curricula for the gifted/talented should focus on and be organized to include more elaborate, complex, and in-depth study of major ideas, problems, and themes that integrate knowledge with and across systems of thought;

2. Curricula for the gifted should allow for the development and application of productive thinking skills to enable students to reconceptualize existing knowledge and/or generate new knowledge;

3. Curricula for the gifted/talented should enable them to explore constantly changing knowledge and information and develop the attitude that knowledge is worth pursuing in an open world;

4. Curricula for the gifted/talented should encourage exposure to, selection, and use of appropriate and specialized resources;

5. Curricula for the gifted/talented should promote self-initiated and self-directed learning and growth;

6. Curricula for the gifted/talented should provide for the development of self-understandings and the understanding of one's relationship to persons, societal institutions, nature, and culture; and

7. Evaluations of curricula for the gifted/talented should be conducted in accordance with prior stated principles, stressing higher-level thinking skills, creativity, and excellence in performance and products. (Passow, 1982, pp. 7–10).

Passow maintained that differentiation was relative to what was being taught in the regular curriculum. In a paper prepared by Passow (1982), the Curriculum Council put forth the following definition of differentiated curriculum:

> Differentiating curricula for the gifted/talented is essentially a process of individualizing curricula to better match individual and group learning needs, abilities, and styles. For the gifted/talented, "differentiated curriculum" denotes sets of specialized learning experiences which develop the unique abilities of students identified as "gifted/talented." A differentiated curriculum embodies recognition of differing learning rates, styles, interests, and abilities. Curriculum differentiation aims at *eliciting learner responses* [italics added] commensurate with gifts or talents. (p. 6)

Passow pointed out, "We are concerned with eliciting what might be called a 'gifted response,' the result of interactions between the predispositions the student brings to the learning situation and the richness of the situation itself" (1982, p. 7).

CURRICULAR IMPLICATIONS

Thus, even though Passow stated the importance of the "gifted response," most of the curricular implications have focused on "should" statements about the type of instruction which should be given to students identified as gifted (Kaplan, 1974; Maker, 1982; Passow, 1982). For example, Renzulli (1977a) emphasized the following modifications:

1. teachers must move above and beyond the regular curriculum;

2. teachers must take into account specific content interests of students;

3. teachers must accommodate students' preferred styles of learning; and

4. teachers must give gifted/talented students opportunities to pursue topic areas to unlimited areas of inquiry.

Maker's (1982) list of suggestions for curricular modifications included the following:

1. it must be more accelerated or advanced;

2. it must be more complex;

3. it must move beyond the regular curriculum;

4. it must be selected by the students according to their interests; and

5. it must be concerned with the more abstract concepts in each content area.

Although the authors are unlikely to have intended it, the nature of a differentiated curriculum, as embodied above, has relied historically on practices advocated for identified gifted children, but has been deemed inappropriate for children not identified as gifted. Research supporting most of those strategies, particularly in the area of curriculum, is lacking (Shore, Cornell, Robinson, & Ward, 1991).

Maker maintained that many of the "curricular principles advocated for gifted children were appropriate for all children because they were designed to allow participation at the student level and encourage responses at the highest level possible" (1986, p. 63). It cannot be supported that these teaching strategies need to be both "appropriate for the gifted and inappropriate for other students" (Maker, p. 63).

Expanding definitions of giftedness have compounded the problem of determining what is appropriate for gifted children and inappropriate for all children. Giftedness is no longer defined by a score on a standardized test of intelligence. Rather, the construct of giftedness is variable and does not define a homogeneous population (e.g., IQ over 130). A child may be labeled gifted in one school district and not gifted in another within the same city or state, depending upon the criteria used for the selection process. This variability in who is labeled gifted and who is not, changes the way identified gifted children can be grouped. Students identified as gifted do not all have the same learning characteristics. Therefore, curricula cannot be prescribed for their characteristics as a whole group. Some children not identified as gifted by the arbitrary criteria set forth in a particular school district's definition have indeed benefited from curriculum and teaching strategies designed for gifted students (Reis et al., 1993).

Returning, then, to the notion that curriculum differentiation aims at "eliciting learner responses commensurate with gifts or talents" (Passow, 1982, p. 6), we must examine those activities that allow for differentiated responses. Open-ended activities have the potential to allow for differentiated responses, but there has been little discussion in the literature of this strategy for curricular differentiation. If the most basic principle underlying curriculum development for the gifted is that the "experiences for these children must be qualitatively different from the basic program provided for all children" (Maker, 1982, p. 3), then responses to learning activities must be examined to determine if and how they are qualitatively different. Thus, although the investigation into the nature of open-ended activities (Hertzog, 1995) delved into all aspects of the teaching strategy including design, characteristics, and interactions among the students and teachers, this paper focuses on the learner responses to those activities. It is necessary now to define open-ended activities as they were conceptualized for this study.

DEFINITION OF OPEN-ENDED ACTIVITIES

In the literature on creativity, open-ended activities referred specifically to those activities with multiple responses (enhance fluency), rather than one correct answer. Maker (1982) expanded the meaning of open-ended activities to include not only variety in the end product (i.e., the response), but also in the process. Her definition of open-ended activities involved choices.

Expanding the definition of open-ended activities from being open only in the product domain to those that provided the learner with choices in the content, process, or product domain enhanced their potential use as a strategy to modify curriculum. Using the conceptual framework of curricular differentiation to examine open-ended activities, I articulated differences between the activities, and specifically looked to see in what ways the curriculum was modified for students who pursued open-ended activities.

By examining the ways that curriculum was differentiated, a broad rather than narrow definition of curriculum was used. This broad definition of curriculum includes "all of the experiences, both planned and unplanned, that occur under the auspices of the school" (Jackson, 1992, p. 8). Situating open-ended activities into the larger framework of classroom research, they can be described as an instructional strategy or instructional format, the third of six components of instruction as defined by Anderson and Burns (1989), "patterns of teacher behavior that are recurrent, applicable to various subject matters, characteristic of more than one teacher, and relevant to learning" (Gage, 1969, as cited in Anderson & Burns, 1989, p. 11).

The research question guiding the study was how open-ended activities provided curricular differentiation in a general education setting. Responses to open-ended activities included the interactions that students had with the subject matter, the teacher, their peers, curricular materials, and their classroom environment. Responses included the products of these interactions as well as the processes of completing the products. A qualitative design was needed to appreciate the complexity of the relationships between the teacher, the curriculum, implementation of the instructional strategy, and the classroom dynamics which influenced the students' learning experiences.

METHOD

Using a naturalistic, qualitative design, I observed how open-ended activities were designed across curricular areas, and focused on the way students who were identified as gifted responded to them in one third- and one fourth-grade classroom throughout one academic year (Hertzog, 1995). No attempt to alter the patterns or methods in which the teacher implemented them were made. Thus, they were observed with all of the complexities of classroom life, including last minute or on-the-spot changes in implementation, as well as ritualistic (same day, same activity) implementation. The phenomenon under study was the relationship of open-ended activities to curricular differentiation.

Setting and Participants

Purposeful sampling (Patton, 1980) was used to select the setting and participants. The school district was selected because there were no formal pull-out programs or special classes for identified gifted and talented children in this district. Curricular differentiation for students identified as gifted was the responsibility of every classroom teacher. Therefore, I expected that all teachers would be using strategies to differentiate curriculum and instruction. The selection of teachers Keith and Becky represented extreme case sampling because I chose them for their interest in meeting the needs of identified gifted students. Both teachers were building representatives on the district wide committee for gifted education. Both teachers self-reported that they used open-ended activities on a regular basis. They provided opportunities for me to observe open-ended activities over an extensive time period.

The school district was situated near a large state university in the midwest. The district reported a population of 4,703 students with a 92.9% graduation rate. Demographics for the 1995 school year were reported in the Annual School Report Card: 65% Caucasian, 24.9% African American, 2.1% Hispanic, 7.7% Asian/Pacific Islander, and .2% Native American.

Teachers. Keith, the third grade teacher, was the building coordinator for gifted programs for several years. He had a Ph.D. in education, an administrative certificate and nearly 20 years of teaching experience. His classroom had 14 boys and 10 girls. Eleven were identified gifted students, four were receiving special education services for their learning disabilities (LD), and one was labeled behavior disordered (BD).

Becky, the fourth grade teacher, had a B.A. in education and more than 25 years of teaching experience. Becky had a total of 28 students, 15 boys and 13 girls, in her class. Many of her students received special education services. Four students were labeled learning disabled (LD), four students received speech therapy, two went to the Chapter 1 reading program, five saw a social worker, and two were referred for special education for exhibiting evidence of behavior disorders. Because of her experience and her interest in gifted education, Becky had all of the identified gifted students from the fourth grade, a total of nine, in her class.

Students. Eleven out of 20 students identified as gifted in both classrooms were selected to be the target students for the study (see Figure 1). The primary criteria for selection was parental consent for students' responses of open-ended activities to be copied and collected for the study. In Keith's room, I chose 6 students out of 11. Of the five that I did not target, one parent refused permission, two parents did not return permission slips, one child was away from the country the first semester, and the last student was the child of my faculty advisor. Out of a pool of nine in Becky's classroom, I targeted five students whose parents also consented. Of the four whom I did not choose, one parent refused permission, and the other three failed to return consent forms. Four out of five of the target students from Becky's room were female because only one out of five identified male students returned the consent form. Figure 1 summarizes their gender, ethnicity, and areas of giftedness identified.

Figure 1   Target Children and Their Identified Area of Giftedness

					Areas of Giftedness					
Student	GE	ET	C/HL	LA	LS	MA	RE	SC	SO	V/PA
Keith's Third Grade										
Terrance	M	C	X	X	X	X	X	X	X	
Mickey	M	C			X		X	X	X	
Sandy	F	C	X	X	X	X	X	X	X	X
Mali*	M	M					X			
Jennifer	F	C			X					
Elaine	F	C			X					
Becky's Fourth Grade										
Gene	M	M	X	X	X	X	X	X		
Annie	F	C	X	X	X	X	X		X	
Roxanne	F	C	X	X	X	X	X			
Deanna	F	C		X	X	X	X		X	X
May	F	C	X	X	X		X	X	X	X

*Identified in math by previous school district.
Note: GE = Gender, M = Male, F = Female, ET = Ethnicity, C = Caucasian, M = Minority
C/HL = Creative/Higher Level Thinking, LA = Language Arts, LS = Leadership, MA = Mathematics,
RE = Reading, SC = Science, SO = Social Studies, V/PA = Visual/Performing Arts

Children in the district were identified as gifted in the areas of leadership, creative/higher level thinking, visual/performing arts, language arts, mathematics (concepts or applications), science, and social studies. The State Comprehensive Plan for Gifted Education (School District 116, 1990) stated,

> Although the identification is an ongoing process, students will be evaluated at the beginning of the kindergarten year, the fourth grade year, the seventh grade year, and the ninth grade year. With the exception of the kindergarten year, these are years which follow achievement testing. In addition to these objective measures, one or more subjective measures are used to confirm identification of talents. Subjective measures may be a checklist nomination completed by teachers, peers or parents, past grades and performance, or products, auditions or portfolios. (p. 4)

Approximately 15–20% of the students were identified as gifted in this school district. Third-graders were identified based on their kindergarten screening test scores from the Peabody Picture Vocabulary Test and a recommendation from their classroom teacher. Fourth-graders were screened by using the third-grade scores resulting from the Iowa Test of Basic Skills (ITBS). Cut-off scores for the various subject areas included 70th percentile in vocabulary, reading comprehension or language skills; 95th percentile in math; 90th percentile in science; and 80th percentile in all other areas.

Data Sources and Analysis

Data sources included observations, interviews with participating teachers and target students, and documents related to the activities or the classrooms of the participating teachers involved. Over 100 hours were spent observing in the classrooms from October 1993 to May 1994. Thirty-three different open-ended activities were analyzed.

Observational data were triangulated with students' responses on the Interest-a-lyzer (Renzulli, 1977b), and the Learning Styles Inventory (Renzulli & Smith, 1978). These instruments were used to determine whether responses to open-ended activities were in students' preferred learning styles, interest areas, or both. Two formal interviews and ongoing informal interviews with each classroom teacher, as well as informal interviews with target students, were also used to triangulate observational data.

Data analysis was inductive, allowing categories, themes, and patterns to emerge (Janesick, 1994). To analyze how open-ended activities were designed and implemented, I developed the Open-Ended Activity Profile, adapted from Kaplan's Grid (Kaplan, 1986). Using a matrix as a form of data display is a recommended strategy for analyzing qualitative data (Huberman & Miles, 1994). Operational definitions of content, process, and product were generated for the purposes of categorizing the choices in the open-ended activities. Content referred to the topic or area of study. The process category included choices in how the children would proceed during the open-ended activity. Examples of choices in the process domain include sequence, materials, selecting work partner(s), working at school or at home, or choosing from processes specific to a discipline such as editing before doing a final draft, predicting before calculating, or working backwards to solve a math problem. The product domain was defined as the tangible response to the activity. The activities were described by examining whether students had unlimited, many, few, or no choices within those domains.

Establishing Trustworthiness

Three methods were used to enhance the credibility of the study: prolonged engagement, persistent observation, and triangulation (Lincoln & Guba, 1985). In addition, member checks were an integral part of the study. Engaging participating teachers in constant dialogue about the activities, interviews, and observations provided ongoing member checks for the analysis and writing stages of the study. Transcripts were routinely shared with participating teachers for their edits and comments. This ongoing communication gave insight and credence to interpreting the findings.

A variety of data sources, data triangulation described by Denzin (1978), were used to verify observational data. For example, to verify that students' responses reflected their ability levels, multiple student responses were collected over time, teachers were interviewed to ascertain their assessment, and informal interviews with the students were documented in the field notes. To determine whether the students made choices according to their preferred learning styles, observational data was triangulated with the Learning Styles Inventory (Renzulli & Smith, 1978), teacher interviews, and informal student interviews which were documented on a daily basis in the field notes.

Other methods to enhance the credibility of the study included peer reviews, interim and progress reports, and prolonged engagement in the field. Peer reviews occurred during the data collection, analysis, and writing processes of the study.

Reflections of Personal Bias Toward Open-Ended Activities

The biases within the researcher must be examined in qualitative studies, as bias must be examined in instruments of measurement for quantitative studies. To examine emerging subjectivities, I kept a reflective journal. In the journal, I kept track of my thoughts about my research, my decisions along the way, and my biases toward open-ended activities and my participants. Reflective journals have been advocated in the literature (Van Manen, 1990).

Throughout the study, peer reviewers questioned me about my biases toward open-ended activities. Prior to the study, I highly valued them. I suspected strongly that (a) responses from open-ended activities revealed more about the students than responses from close-ended activities; (b) it is good to know as much as possible about the students; (c) the more teachers know about their students, the more teachers can personalize instruction, and (d) the more personalized instruction teachers give to students, the more engaged students will be in their learning. Ultimately, I wanted to make it easier for teachers to develop open-ended activities. As the study progressed, and I examined the complexities of their design and use, I became more cautious in my advocacy. This cautious stance will be described more fully when I present the implications of this research in the discussion section of this paper.

Open-Ended Activities Across the Curriculum

Open-ended activities were observed in nearly every curricular area, although they were designed and implemented differently across the two classroom settings. Briefly, I will describe some of those differences and the types of activities which I observed in each setting. Space is too limited here for a thorough description of all 33 activities. For a more thorough discussion of all of the activities, see Hertzog (1995).

In Keith's third grade classroom, I observed mostly writing, reading, discussion periods, and "free time" because these were the areas in which he told me I would have the most opportunities to see children engaged in open-ended activities. As explained earlier, writing was routinely an open-ended activity time period where children had approximately 30 minutes to write whatever they wanted in their notebooks. They could write with a partner or by themselves, at their seats or somewhere else in the room. They had many choices in the content and process domain, but their choices in the product domain were limited. Students were expected to write a first draft of a story, get help from a teacher to edit it, copy it over in final form, and bind it with a book binder that was located in the room. Students had the choice of sharing stories orally with the class or leaving it on a book rack to be read by other children.

Reading in Keith's room was a time for children to read any book of their choice silently at their seats or somewhere else in the room. Keith held private book conferences with the children to enhance understanding of what they read and to share information about their chosen books with him.

In Keith's room, discussion periods took place regularly every morning and every afternoon at group meeting times. Keith often let children discuss what was on their minds. Children had free time when they finished their work and the teacher was not ready to move on to the next subject. Keith valued free time. Most days Keith built a free time period into their schedule. Children could choose to do anything during free time, including playing games, drawing pictures, listening to music with ear phones, or working on plays together. Keith's free time had unlimited options in every domain: content, process, and product.

Whereas Keith's open-ended activities were built into the pattern and construction of his schedule and subject areas, Becky routinely varied the design of her open-ended activities across the disciplines. In Becky's room, I observed math, science, language arts, French, and discussion periods. Becky constructed open-ended activities for writing on some days by giving students a theme or title to write about, or asking students for a specific genre within which they could choose the topic. Becky frequently varied the number of choices and types of domains in which the activities were open. Becky's math, however, focused on problem solving skills and nearly always had unlimited options in the process domain. Examples of how some of these activities were analyzed graphically on the Open-Ended Activity Profile are given in Figure 2.

The Open-Ended Activity Profile provided an analysis tool to examine the differences in design of the open-ended activities. They also enhanced the analysis of the student's responses in terms of their variability. In other words, when students had few or no options within one domain, were responses more similar than when students had unlimited options within one domain? If students had unlimited options within the product domain, were their responses more varied than if they had unlimited options within the content domain? Thus, variability (differentiation) was explored not only among students' responses, but also in relation to the type of open-ended activity that was presented.

RESULTS

How Responses to Open-Ended Activities Differed

To examine how open-ended activities differentiated instruction through learner responses, it was necessary to apply the principles of differentiation as

Figure 2   Activities Categorized on the Open-Ended Activity Profile

	Domains		
Choices	Content	Process	Product
Unlimited	KW, KFT	KFT, BMPS	KFT
Many			
Few	BW	KW	KW
None	BMPS	BW	BW, BMPS

Note: KW = Keith's Writing Period, BW = Becky's Writing Activity-Title Given, KFT = Keith's Free Time Period, BMPS = Becky's Math Problem-Solving Time

stated earlier. I explicitly asked the two teachers how responses from identified gifted children differed, in general, from responses of other children on open-ended activities. Keith explained:

> One thing that surprises me is that most often times my high achieving students or the students who are traditionally A students don't tend to just do the assignment and quit and do something else. They tend to also elaborate, take more time, be more personally involved, and it's certainly encouraged.

Becky described how her students identified as gifted performed differently from her other students in open-ended activities:

> If I ask them, if we're studying other cultures or something, they can select an easier or a more difficult level. Usually, the children who aren't very gifted perhaps will write about things that they see in the films and things that we do in class, but don't do a lot of research to find out more things to go into depth. And the children who are the real thinkers and the readers will go in and read through encyclopedias, books and all kinds of wonderful things.

Note that Becky and Keith perceived differences in the students' process of learning and in the products. Becky and Keith described evidence of students taking on self-initiative to make more elaborate and better products. They also described how students became more involved in the process of learning, and sought external resources according to their interests. My observational data and copies of students' responses verified the teachers' perceptions. This level of personal involvement was especially seen in the writing instruction in Keith's room, and in the project activities in Becky's room. Targeted students in Keith's room were self-motivated to create elaborate stories, and they often planned ahead for other stories. In Becky's room, targeted students raced to tell me about the projects, how and with whom they planned them, where they met after school, and all of the materials and resources they used, including a child's home computer. Most of the other children in her room, doing the same projects, did not seek outside help or materials, or meet after school to work on their projects.

The teachers saw variability in terms of interest and going beyond what other children did. Going "above and beyond" what other children do is supported in the gifted education literature as a means of differentiating instruction. In this sense, open-ended activities were a means of providing opportunities for students to go beyond what was required. However, to examine whether responses were in other ways qualitatively different, I looked at other dimensions of variability. Specifically, I questioned teachers about whether the quality of students' products or responses differed, and whether students were working at their ability levels.

Judgments of Quality

Becky and Keith did not compare responses of targeted students to other students. Rather, they individualized their evaluation criteria and evaluated students' responses based on their perceptions of the students' capabilities. This factor may have been instrumental in facilitating the environment for the activities to occur. Students were not threatened by unfair comparisons of their products.

When the products were in written form, such as Keith's writing or stories in Becky's class that focused on a given topic, the quality of writing reflected students' writing abilities. The district writing expert scored writing samples holistically according to quality of content, organization, style, and mechanics. Without knowing who the identified gifted students were, she was able to name all but two of the targeted students by examining their writing samples. This demonstrated that most of the targeted students performed better than their peers on these activities. The open-ended writing activities provided an opportunity for children to produce qualitatively different responses which demonstrated their strength in the language arts area.

Some of the responses to open-ended activities involved drawing. Elements of drawing ability were never part of the teacher's evaluation criteria. Some of the students who were not target students demonstrated exceptional drawing skills with elaborate details, unusual uses of space and color, and original ideas. The drawing samples serve to illustrate that targeted students, no matter how motivated, how capable, or how organized they were, did not perform necessarily better as a group than their peers on activities which involved drawing. This was totally dependent on students' interests and strengths in the art discipline. In fact, responses in this format gave students who were not identified as gifted an opportunity to demonstrate their strengths and creative imagination through their drawing.

Quality of responses seemed relatively unimportant to the teachers in some of the open-ended activities. Becky used the math and science journals for her own information and for class discussion. When she asked the students to write down the hardest math fact they knew, or some scientific event that they had heard about over the weekend, the purpose was to share information, not to judge the quality of their work. For example, in the science journals, it was evident that some of the students understood the science concepts they wrote about while others did not. In our interview, I talked with Becky about the science journal responses. She said that she just wanted to know if they could relate some of the things they see to science. I asked her if it was important for them to get the scientific principle correct. She replied, "Since I never talked to them about that, or explained to them that they had to understand it, I certainly wouldn't have evaluated them on that."

Thus, although quality of responses in the science journal was not an issue to the teacher, quality differed in the criteria that I developed for analysis purposes: writing clarity, sophistication, understanding of the assignment, and the students' abilities to relate what they saw to science. Referring back to Passow's three questions: All children participated in their science journals (whether they wanted to or not), all children were able to participate at their own ability level, and all children were expected to succeed in this activity, because it was designed to provide the teacher with information. To further allow the reader to judge how quality differed between targeted and non-target students, four examples of science journal responses (what they saw in the last week that related to science) are given below. The first two (R1, R2) are from target students, and the second two (R3, R4) were chosen randomly from Becky's other students. They are quoted with their original spelling:

R1: Dec. 14, 1993
Last week in Science, I liked it when the student teacher did a sort of science experiment with us with the eggbeaters. We had to find out how many times the beater goes around when you turn the wheel around once. Then twice, and so on.
R2: My mom blew up our baked potatoes. When she forget to fork them she opened the microwave and pop, bang, we had mashed potatoes. It's scientific because it had to [do] with machines and electricity.
R3: On Saterday moring tuck apurt my toy car. Thin I let it go and I sall how the lechtrysoty run throe it.
R4: I saw my mom makeing hameburgres.

After discussing all of the science responses with Becky, she commented, "It's really interesting, you know, when you give these kinds of assignments, you give it for one reason and maybe, you know, you learn so much more." These responses, although brief, were indicative of writing, spelling, organization, and thinking abilities. They revealed students' awareness and interest in science. The emphasis on the journal activities was on what the children knew, not on how well they expressed it. Thus, although the quality of responses differed, this appeared to be irrelevant to the goal or the instructional design of the activity. For Becky, a high quality response was not a goal in the science journal. Instead, her goal was simply to learn about the students' abilities to connect an event to science. In reviewing the students' responses with me, she admitted that she learned more about the students than she had expected. Judgments of quality in open-ended activities that are primarily designed for self-expression may not be important to the teacher, even though these types of activities may reveal vast differences in abilities and interests.

In summary, the quality of responses was based on arbitrary criteria, contextual for each open-ended activity. The quality of responses was indicative of differences in students' abilities. In most cases where the products were written, responses required language skills such as spelling, use of capital letters, sentence structure, and organization. Targeted students' written responses most often could be discerned from the written responses of their peers who were not identified as gifted in the language arts area. This finding, although not surprising because most of the students were identified as gifted in the language arts area, demonstrated that open-ended activities such as journal writing provided those students an opportunity to express themselves in their strength areas (e.g., language arts).

Comparing quality of responses between targeted and other students was not the whole issue. Specifically, I wanted to know if the quality of response matched students' ability levels, because this would be an indicator that the activity served to differentiate instruction according to the characteristics of the learners.

Relationship of Response to Structure of the Activity

I examined whether the design of the open-ended activities gave students the option of performing in a way that either was or was not commensurate with their abilities. I believed that attitudes as well as the instructional design factored into whether students worked at their ability levels. Because the teachers knew the students' ability levels better than I did, I questioned the teachers, "Does the quality of response match their ability level?" Keith responded, "Generally yes . . . There are rare exceptions, and that is a student who has a particular aversion to a discipline area and they tend to do minimal work." Keith gave me the example of one of the target students in his room whom he felt was not writing to his potential. Keith felt that the student needed to get used to the writing instruction, and then he would perform at his ability level.

Where I expected the most visible differences to occur in students' responses were those activities where students had the most choices in the product domain, the traditional open-ended view. In all of these types of open-ended activities, students had an opportunity to work in groups or with a partner. Interestingly enough, I found that when there were unlimited choices within the product domains, more similarities in responses existed than differences. Giving students unlimited choices within the product domain did not necessarily result in vast differences in their products. Other factors worked to enhance the similarity of their products, including group dynamics, peer pressure, and spontaneous examples being given to the students by the teachers during the activity. For example, in describing the noun presentations to the class, Becky simply suggested a game show idea and every group but one proceeded to do a game show. The original intent or design of the activity was for the students to review a particular section of their language books on nouns, and make a presentation about what they learned in that section. The French teacher asked the students to design their own menu and dramatize being at a French restaurant. When she introduced the activity, she told Becky's students how another class had used paper for their food items in the restaurant presentations. She did not tell Becky's class to do the same, but they did. Because these activities were shared with classmates, other students had the opportunity to use the same ideas and shape their responses similarly.

It is important to note the distinction between the structure of the activity and its implementation. The teacher designed the noun presentation activity to have unlimited options in the product domain. Becky's suggestions during the implementation phase of the noun presentation activity may have altered the choices that students made, but her suggestions did not alter the original design of the activity. As in all matters pertaining to instructional design, the method of implementation has the potential to change the experiences of the students. In analyzing the relationship of students' responses to the design of the activity, it is important to understand the factors during implementation that impacted the intended design.

In terms of ideas, the greatest differences in responses seemed to emerge when there were few or no options within the product domain. In other words, the children had to have the same product, but had options within the content and process domains. It is significant for teachers to be aware that offering options within the content and process domains (and not just in the product domain) provides students with opportunities to demonstrate creative thinking.

The ABC story activity is a good example to illustrate differences in children's ideas within the confines of the same product. The children were asked to write a story with each sentence beginning with the next letter of the alphabet. Differences occurred in the content domain, even though the product was quite structured. The stories resulted in very creative responses. In general, children seemed to enjoy having choices in the content domain. Differences in students' interests were most prevalent when activities provided unlimited choices within the content domain, such as writing in Keith's room, silent reading, free time, and discussion periods.

The data suggested that responses to open-ended activities that had virtually no options in the product domain were still differentiated. These activities revealed students' academic abilities, creative thinking, and personal interests. In contrast, when there were unlimited choices in the product domain, the activities were most often group-oriented, and it was difficult to see differences according to individuals' abilities, interests, or preferred learning styles.

Differences Related to Making Choices

An unexpected finding was that in some types of open-ended activities where unlimited choices were provided in the process domain, students consistently chose to pursue these activities with peers of similar abilities and with peers of the same ethnicity. In this respect, at times, the social and learning structure of the room became grouped along lines of ability and ethnicity. This differs from traditional instruction where teachers make intentional decisions about grouping children in their classrooms. Open-ended activities allowed students to make decisions about grouping in their class, often resulting in self-selected grouping patterns. Open-ended activities also provided an outlet for students to express their preferences for working with students of similar abilities. Thus, by working together consistently and over time, students with high abilities were experiencing different learning opportunities than those children of low abilities who consistently chose to work together.

Students, when given the opportunity, made other choices consistently in addition to their work partners. These patterns of consistency, described through five case studies (Hertzog, 1997), allowed students to work predominately in their preferred learning style and with their preferred peers, which contributed toward their making choices to work at their level of comfort rather than challenge. Thus, although their responses to open-ended activities were differentiated, and they provided a vehicle for curricular differentiation to occur, they did not represent necessarily the maximum capabilities of the children.

Summary

In summary, the findings suggested that targeted students' responses to open-ended activities were qualitatively different from those of students not identified as gifted. The fact that the quality differed between targeted and non-targeted learner responses was not necessarily seen by the teachers as the intention for using them. Differences in the content, process, and product domains of "general" curriculum were manifest through student choices as opposed to teacher choices. Differentiation occurred by students responding in more depth, with higher level skills, and in ways which were guided by their learning style preferences, and not from the teacher offering something different, more complex, or more abstract.

DISCUSSION

The notion that all children can be *doing* the same thing (i.e., be given the same assignment) at the same time, and yet yield variability in responses, implores us to look beyond the previous standards for defining differentiation in gifted education: would, could, and should statements. This examination into the nature of students' responses compels us in the field of gifted education to examine more in depth the meaning and nature of curricular differentiation.

To be qualitatively different, with whom should the quality be compared and how should that quality be assessed? In this study, I was more interested than the teachers in the relationship of targeted students' responses to non-targeted students' responses. Both of the teachers in this study evaluated the students' responses to open-ended activities according to their beliefs about the individual student's abilities and not on criteria that was standard for all children. In interviews, the teachers told me that they had different expectations for their students and evaluated their work according to those expectations. It could be inferred from this that providing standard criteria for evaluation of open-ended activities may not have been important to the teachers, and differentiation might not occur where standard criteria for evaluation are applied. Keith, referring to his observation that targeted students take more time, elaborate, and get more involved with the open-ended activities, commented in an interview:

> I think I encourage some of that because I don't sit and say this is the standard that I want you to perform. Do this and you should be satisfied. It's more as though this is what the task is, what are you going to do?

His concerns about stating standard criteria and having students do the minimum to accomplish those criteria are echoed in the debates over the effects of minimum competencies on the performance of students identified as gifted. Also, the notion that the teachers individualize their expectations and evaluations for their students brings back the continuing difficulty to articulate the difference between individualized and differentiated instruction. By referring again to Passow's definition—"differentiating curricula for the gifted/talented is essentially a process of individualizing curricula to better match individual and group learning needs, abilities, and styles" (1982, p. 6)—one can see individualized expectations for learners were applied to responses from open-ended activities. The individualization occurred by evaluating responses individually, and not by offering a different type of assignment to a particular child.

The findings raised another issue quite unexpectedly. Open-ended activities, which allowed students options in the process domain, may have contributed to grouped learning experiences in the classroom by allowing children to self-select their work partners. In other words, the quality and variability of group work was directly related to the range of abilities in the group. No attempt will be made here to reiterate all the findings of the massive studies of ability grouping. However, one finding which is especially appropriate to mention is that "Ability grouping for enrichment, especially when enrichment is part of a within class ability grouping practice or as a pullout program, produces substantial academic gains in general achievement, critical thinking, and creativity for the gifted and talented learner" (Vaughn, 1990, as cited in Rogers, 1991, p. 2). In the context of these classrooms, children identified as gifted varied the quality of their work by working in groups with children of similar abilities. Therefore, open-ended activities that allowed for a self-selected grouping process provided a vehicle for the quality of responses to be differentiated. On the other hand, segregated groupings may have violated democratic principles in the classroom by altering the quality of learning opportunities for some portion of the student population. Thus, inclusive environments do not preclude ability grouping from taking place within the context of classroom instructional activities.

IMPLICATIONS AND LIMITATIONS

Implications of the Study

Implications of this study for practitioners are numerous. To determine how the responses to open-ended activities are qualitatively different, they must be assessed by using criteria contextual to the goal of the activity. The assessment issue is critical for practitioners. How identified gifted children should be graded, assessed, or evaluated has been questioned previously by VanTassel-Baska (1994):

> Should the gifted be expected to do more as well as do it better? Or should they be judged according to an entirely different standard—one that gives them credit for being high achievers in a general context, and therefore does not shift its stringency pattern based on the population? (p. 69)

Teachers' value systems and assumptions about how children learn play a large role in determining the criteria and the manner in which learner responses are evaluated. The two teachers in this study evaluated students' responses relative to their expectations of the students. Although this seems to be an individualized method, questions should be raised about the role that relative assessments of some children may play in lowering the ceiling on some students' performances. Differentiation should then reflect not only whether the quality of responses are different from other responses, but whether or not the maximum amount of student performance is exhibited. Differentiation should have an explicit conceptual meaning of maximizing a student's performance. This eliminates the need for comparing instruction or responses to other individuals. Differentiation, as it relates to maximum performance, is individual in nature. As the teachers in this study intuitively believed, the quality of the response must be judged in relationship to the student's own abilities.

To suggest that differentiation of curriculum and instruction occurs when teachers use open-ended activities, and when students' responses match students' ability levels, does not imply that curricular differentiation would not occur by using other means of differentiation, such as accelerated classes, described in the literature. It does however, challenge the belief that "When educators differentiate the curriculum, they make different knowledge available to different groups of students" (Oakes, Gamoran, & Page, 1992, p. 570). Teachers in this study facilitated differentiation, not by making different knowledge available, but by making choices available for students to pursue different content areas in different ways. Thus, educators using open-ended activities can make the same knowledge available to a heterogeneous group of students by providing choices for students to interact with that body of knowledge in ways that enable them to maximize their performances.

The emphasis on the word "different" has placed those of us in the field of gifted education in defensive positions. The belief that differentiation is synonymous with tracking or purposeful offering of "better" curriculum (Oakes et al., 1992) does not allow for the concept of differentiation to be operationalized within the context of instructional strategies within heterogeneously grouped classrooms.

Limitations to the Study

Examining the concept of qualitatively different as it related to open-ended activities provided new lenses for examining the nature of curricular differentiation. As a naturalistic study, I did not compare open-ended activities to other methods or instructional strategies of providing curricular differentiation. I do not infer from this study that open-ended activities provide a "better" means of differentiating instruction than other strategies that are thoroughly described in the literature (e.g., advanced content, accelerated classes, curriculum compacting).

Nor do I mean to infer that differentiation of learner responses would occur in any classroom with any teacher designing open-ended activities. These teachers were highly motivated and skilled to meet the needs of their students and to apply principles of curricular differentiation in their classroom. The teachers were selected to provide the "best case scenario." Their differences in implementing open-ended activities illuminated the complexities involved in using this strategy to differentiate instruction.

The naturalistic design of the study allowed me to see the ways that teachers used open-ended activities according to their own beliefs, patterns and styles of teaching. Designing open-ended activities was a part of these teachers' methodologies for providing interaction and engagement with various disciplines, subjects, and content areas. As was noted, when choices were provided within the content domain, some of the greatest differences in responses occurred, thus supporting the notion that the content of the activity plays a key role in individualizing and differentiating curriculum.

I agree with one reviewer who noted that this investigation did not address learning that occurred during segments of time used for journal writing, story writing, and so forth. Although learning "occurs gradually over time and is largely unobservable" (Anderson & Burns, 1989, p. 16), I believe this study implicitly addressed the contemporary view of student learning that "recognizes the interplay between the ways in which students organize their existing knowledge and the changes in that organization that are necessary to accommodate new information and experiences" (p. 42) by examining learner responses over time and relating those responses to students' abilities. I am intrigued to pursue the reviewer's insightful question, "How do we know that these forms of self-expression actually reflect learning?" (anonymous reviewer, 1996). I would urge continued studies related to the role that open-ended activities play in the teaching and learning process.

Studies that further explored to what extent open-ended activities provided teachers with knowledge about their students would be complementary to this study. In addition, it would be interesting to examine open-ended activities in relation to students with learning characteristics other than giftedness. Based on the findings, I questioned the belief that "less successful students may prefer rather than be alienated by individual worksheets, which allow them to work privately, at their own pace, on unambiguous questions with one right answer" (Metz, 1978). Although I targeted identified gifted students, many of the students that I did not target or who were not identified as gifted seemed to enjoy activities which enabled them to work with partners, choose drawing or acting over writing, or simply express themselves in unusual ways. In this study, I did not compare whether identified gifted students enjoyed or benefited from open-ended activities more than other students.

SUMMARY AND CONCLUSIONS: CURRICULAR DIFFERENTIATION AND BEYOND

I began this paper with a comprehensive review of curricular differentiation. I used the data from an investigation into the nature of open-ended activities (Hertzog, 1995) to demonstrate how responses of children identified as gifted were qualitatively different than responses to the same activities from children who were not identified by the school district as gifted. Examining student responses to open-ended activities ignites discourse about the meaning of "qualitatively different," a term that Maker (1982) suggested was value-laden and ambiguous.

In addition, the broadened conception of open-ended activities provided a basis to compare and discuss different types of open-ended activities. Findings revealed that differentiation of learner responses occurred even when the product involved limited student choices and was quite defined, not "open." The notion that teachers may structure open-ended activities in many ways for different instructional goals is worthy of continued exploration. Teachers may wish to vary the format of the products to allow for both nonverbal and verbal responses. This would give all students more opportunities to demonstrate their strengths and to promote opportunities for these strengths to be shared. It would be interesting to study how teacher training or awareness could enhance the ability of teachers to develop and implement open-ended activities for various instructional purposes.

Gifted programs have traditionally provided opportunities for students to work in their own learning styles and to pursue their own interests. About students in gifted programs, Renzulli stated:

> An almost universal finding in the evaluation work I have done in numerous programs for the gifted has been that the greatest source of student satisfaction almost always resulted from the students' freedom to pursue topics of their own choosing in a manner with which they themselves felt most comfortable. (cited in Shore et al., 1991, p. 107)

As a result of this study, I would advocate open-ended activities as a powerful teaching strategy to provide such freedom in a general education setting. I would advocate that teachers design open-ended activities for students to reveal their interests, their learning styles, and their capabilities. In that role, I believe open-ended activities have value for all learners, as well as identified gifted learners. On a more cautious note, I would urge teachers to pay attention to the choices they provide, and to the ways in which their implementation of the activity impacts student choices and responses.

In closing, I urge a continuation of the dialogue about the meaning of curricular differentiation. In the field, we must move beyond should statements and comparisons between what we give to gifted students that is different than what we provide for all students. We must better inform practitioners how the articulation of differentiation as "eliciting learner responses commensurate with gifts and talents" (Passow, 1982, p. 6) can be applied in all classrooms. We must continue to make systematic inquiries into curricular strategies that maximize students' performances.

REFERENCES

Anderson, L. W., & Burns, R. B. (1989). *Research in classrooms. The study of teachers, teaching and instruction.* Oxford: Pergamon Press.

Beck, J. (1992, February 6). The educational mainstream drowns gifted children. *Chicago Tribune*, p. 23.

Callahan, C. M. (November, 1995). (Moderator). *Beyond the LTI principles—What is appropriate curriculum for the gifted?* Symposium at the 42nd Annual Convention of the National Association for Gifted Children, Tampa, Florida.

Delisle, J. R. (1994). Perhaps I know the wrong teachers. *Roeper Review, 16*, 225–226.

Denzin, N. K. (1978). *The research act: A theoretical introduction to sociological methods.* (2nd ed). New York: McGraw-Hill.

Hertzog, N. B. (1995). *Investigating the nature of open-ended activities.* Unpublished doctoral dissertation, University of Illinois, Champaign-Urbana.

Hertzog, N. B. (1997). Open-ended activities and their role in maintaining challenge. *Journal for the Education of the Gifted, 21*, 54–81.

Huberman, A. M., & Miles, M. B. (1994). Data management and analysis methods. In N. K. Denzin & Y. S. Lincoln (Eds.), *Handbook of qualitative research* (pp. 428–444). London: Sage Publications.

Jackson, P. W. (Ed.). (1992) *Handbook of Research on Curriculum*, NY: Macmillan Publishing.

Janesick, V. J. (1994). The dance of qualitative research design: Metaphor, methodolatry, and meaning. In N. K. Denzin & Y. S. Lincoln (Eds.), *Handbook of qualitative research* (pp. 209–219). London: Sage Publications.

Kaplan, S. (1974). *Providing programs for the gifted and talented: A handbook.* Ventura, CA: Office of the Ventura County Superintendent of Schools.

Kaplan, S. (1986). The grid: A model to construct differentiated curriculum for the gifted. In J. S. Renzulli (Ed.), *Systems and models for developing programs for the gifted and talented* (pp. 180–193). Mansfield Center, CT: Creative Learning Press.

Lincoln, Y. S., & Guba, E. G. (1985). *Naturalistic inquiry.* Beverly Hills, CA: Sage.

Maker, C. J. (1982). *Curriculum development for the gifted.* Rockville, MD: Aspen Systems Corporation.

Maker, C. J. (1986). Suggested principles for gifted preschool curricula. *Topics in Early Childhood Special Education, 6,* 62–73.

Marland, S., Jr. (1972). *Education of the gifted and talented* (Report to the Congress of the United States). Washington, DC: U.S. Department of Education.

McCarthy, P. (1992, January 28). Dull work for bright students. *The Boston Globe,* p. 1.

Metz, K. E. (1978). Children's thinking in primary social studies curricula. *Elementary School Journal, 79*(2), 115–121.

North Carolina State Department (1988). *Program options for the academically gifted.* (1988). North Carolina State Department of Public Instruction. Raleigh Division for Exceptional Children.

Oakes, J., Gamoran, A., & Page, R. N. (1992). Curriculum differentiation: Opportunities, outcomes, and meanings. In P. W. Jackson (Ed.), *Handbook of Research and Curriculum* (pp. 570–608).

Passow, H. A. (1982). *Differentiated curricula for the gifted/talented.* Ventura, CA: Ventura County Superintendent of Schools Office.

Patton, M. Q. (1980). *Qualitative evaluation methods.* Beverly Hills, CA: Sage.

Reis, S. M., Westberg, K. L., Kulikowich, J., Caillard, F., Hébert, T., Plucker, J., Purcell, J. H., Rogers, J. B., & Smist, J. M. (1993). *Why not let high ability students start school in January? The curriculum compacting study* (Research Monograph No. 93106). Storrs: University of Connecticut, The National Research Center on the Gifted and Talented.

Renzulli, J. S. (1977a). *The enrichment triad model: A guide for developing defensible programs for the gifted and talented.* Mansfield Center, CT: Creative Learning Press.

Renzulli, J. S. (1977b). *The interest-a-lyzer.* Mansfield Center, CT: Creative Learning Press.

Renzulli, J. S., & Smith, L. H. (1978). *Learning styles inventory: A measure of student preference for instructional techniques.* Mansfield Center, CT: Creative Learning Press.

Robinson, A. (1995). A decade of scholarship: The Gifted Child Quarterly Paper of the Year. *The Gifted Child Quarterly, 39*(4), 193–194.

Rogers, K. B. (1991). *The relationship of grouping practices to the education of the gifted and talented learner.* Storrs, CT: The National Research Center on the Gifted and Talented.

Sapon-Shevin, M. (1993). Gifted education and the protection of privilege: Breaking the silence, opening the discourse. In L. Weiss & M. Fine (Eds.), *Beyond silenced voices* (pp. 25–44). Albany, NY: State University of New York Press.

School District 116. (1990). *State mandated gifted comprehensive plan.* Urbana, IL: Author.

Shore, B. M., Cornell, D. G., Robinson, A., & Ward, V. S. (1991). *Recommended practices in gifted education.* New York: Teachers College Press.

Van Manen, M. (1990). *Researching lived experience. Human science for an action sensitive pedagogy.* Albany, NY: The State University of New York.

VanTassel-Baska, J. (1994). *Comprehensive curriculum for gifted learners.* (2nd ed.). Boston: Allyn & Bacon.

Ward, V. (1961). *Education for the gifted: An axiomatic approach.* Columbus, OH: Charles E. Merrill Books.

Westberg, K. L., Archambault, F. X., Jr., Dobyns, S. M., & Salvin, T. J. (July, 1993). *An observational study of instructional and curricular practices used with gifted and talented students in regular classrooms. Executive Summary.* Storrs, CT: National Research Center on Gifted and Talented, The University of Connecticut. Research Monograph 93103.

6

Curriculum Compacting and Achievement Test Scores: What Does the Research Say?

Sally M. Reis, Karen L. Westberg, Jonna M. Kulikowich, and Jeanne H. Purcell

University of Connecticut

This study examined the effects of curriculum compacting on the achievement test scores of a national sample of 336 high ability students from second through sixth grade heterogeneous classrooms in rural, suburban, and urban settings. Curriculum compacting is a strategy for eliminating curricular material that students have already mastered and replacing it with more appropriate learning activities. Teachers from three treatment and control groups in this experimental study selected one to

Editor's Note: From Reis, S. M., Westberg, K. L., Kulikowich, J. M., & Purcell, J. H. (1998). Curriculum compacting and achievement test scores: What does the research say? *Gifted Child Quarterly, 42*(2), 123-129. © 1998 National Association for Gifted Children. Reprinted with permission.

two students from their classes who demonstrated superior ability and advanced content knowledge prior to instruction. They were able to eliminate between 40%–50% of curricula for these students across content areas. Pre and post student achievement was examined using the *Iowa Test of Basic Skills*, and out-of-grade-level (one grade higher) tests were used to guard against ceiling effects. The results indicated that the achievement test scores of students whose curriculum was compacted did not differ significantly from students whose curriculum was not compacted. These findings from a national study minimize teachers' fears about declines in students' achievement test scores due to compacting.

Recent research seems to indicate that increasing numbers of high ability and high achieving students spend large proportions of their time in regular classrooms and that few curricular modifications are made for high ability students in regular classrooms (Archambault et al., 1993; Purcell, 1993; Renzulli & Reis, 1991; U.S. Department of Education, 1993; Westberg, Archambault, Dobyns, & Salvin, 1993). The minimal use of differentiation strategies persists even though a variety of instructional strategies are recommended to better meet the academic needs of high ability and high achieving students.

Several strategies can be used to differentiate curricula and instruction for high ability students including the use of advanced content, higher level questioning skills, curriculum compacting, independent study, tiered assignments, flexible grouping, and others. Little empirical research has examined the use of these strategies and this study of curriculum compacting was an attempt to address this area. Curriculum compacting (Reis, Burns, & Renzulli, 1992; Renzulli & Reis, 1985; Renzulli & Smith, 1978) is an instructional strategy that has been used to streamline the learning activities for students who demonstrate proficiency on curricular objectives prior to teaching. It has been widely recognized and suggested by educational experts as a method to address the needs of high ability and high achieving students (Barbour & Kiernan, 1994; George, 1995; Winebrenner, 1992). The curriculum compacting process uses a document called The Compactor (Renzulli & Smith), which enables record-keeping. The Compactor form includes three columns which parallel the steps of the curriculum compacting process. In the first column, teachers document what a student knows prior to beginning a curricular unit or area of study. The second column provides space for teachers to indicate the concepts or material a student has yet to master, and in the third column, teachers list appropriate replacement activities which are usually enrichment or acceleration options for a student whose curriculum has been compacted. The following case study provides an example of the use of curriculum compacting.

Putting the Research to Use

Although most educators believe that curricular adaptations should be provided to students who have demonstrated mastery of the regular curriculum, previous research indicates that actual adaptations are minor or even nonexistent in most classrooms throughout the country. Curriculum compacting is one adaptation that has been recommended for meeting the needs of high achieving students, and the research reported in this article supports its use. The results should alleviate concerns of both teachers and administrators who may have been hesitant about the use of curricular adaptations because of testing issues. This study indicates that teachers can implement curriculum compacting with capable students, without fears that normative national test scores will decline when 40%–50% of the regular curriculum content is eliminated for students who display content mastery.

Shanoah is a 9-year-old attending fourth grade in a large, urban setting. Within the first two weeks of the school year, her teacher noted that she was a voracious reader. He subsequently checked the scores she received on statewide mastery tests and discovered that she scored above the 90th percentile in all subtests related to reading and writing. Shanoah scored 100% in literal understanding and inference making and at the 90th percentile on evaluation skills. With respect to writing, she had mastered 100% of the skills required at her grade level.

Shanoah appeared restless in class, frequently asked for more challenging assignments, and, on occasion, began to disturb other students around her. It was clear that her classroom work in reading and writing needed to be compacted. Her teacher eliminated the workbook assignments related to the reading skills she had mastered, as well as basic writing assignments. To extend Shanoah's understanding in reading and writing, he substituted advanced-level reading in a subject of Shanoah's choice and provided her with choices for creative writing assignments. Through the time that was gained with compacting, he and Shanoah pursued several enrichment options. She had choices including: reading for pleasure, working on monthly reading projects of her choice, pursuing her interest in African American history, and working as co-editor on the school newspaper. Shanoah chose to work on all of these enrichment options during fourth grade.

Research about curriculum compacting has indicated that high achieving students may already know between 40%–50% of their lessons before they are taught (Reis et al., 1993). This research and other studies about curriculum compacting also indicated that teachers discuss several reasons when asked why curriculum compacting is not widely adopted, including: lack of sufficient teacher preparation to initiate pre-assessment and differentiation, limited time during the school day and year to prepare supplemental lessons, and financial exigencies that preclude the purchase of enrichment material necessary for replacement learning activities (Imbeau, 1991; Westberg, Archambault, & Brown, 1997). One of the reasons frequently cited by teachers is their fear that students whose curriculum is compacted may not score as well on state mastery tests and other standardized measures of achievement. Many teachers indicate that their administrators do not want teachers to eliminate any skills, even for high ability students, for fear of lower standardized achievement tests or state mastery scores.

Little empirical research exists to address teachers' questions related to the effect of compacting on elementary students' academic achievement. Schultz (1991) conducted one study in which she examined the effect of curriculum compacting on the mathematics achievement of fourth grade mathematics students in a midwestern school district. One hundred and thirty-two students participated in Schultz' research, in which achievement was measured in both October and May of one school year using the Mathematics Concepts, Mathematics Problem Solving, and Mathematics Computation subtests of the *Iowa Tests of Basic Skills*. Schultz reported no significant differences between control and treatment groups with respect to scores on any of the mathematics subtests; students whose curriculum was compacted achieved equally as well as their agemates whose curriculum had not been compacted.

This article describes the results of a national research study that examined the academic achievement of elementary students whose curriculum was compacted. Three research questions guided the study.

1. Do students whose curriculum was compacted in one or more content areas perform differently on measures of achievement than students whose curriculum was not compacted?

2. Do students whose curriculum was compacted in mathematics perform differently than their control counterparts on measures of achievement?

3. Do students whose curriculum was compacted in language arts perform differently than their control counterparts on measures of achievement?

The findings related to these research questions can be used to address questions related to the academic achievement of students who have sections of curriculum eliminated from their curricula, and the diverse replacement strategies employed by their classroom teachers.

THE CURRICULUM COMPACTING STUDY

Sample

A sample of 27 school districts and 436 second through sixth grade classroom teachers throughout the country from collaborative school districts that are a part of The National Research Center on the Gifted and Talented (NRC/GT) was selected for this study. The achievement data of 336 students are reported here. These data represent complete sets of pretest and posttest scores on all subscales of the *Iowa Tests of Basic Skills*. To participate, districts had to meet two criteria: no previous training or implementation of curriculum compacting and a willingness to accept random assignment to one of three treatment groups or a control group. Efforts were made to recruit districts with widely varying demographics including elementary school populations that included economically disadvantaged, limited English proficient, and students with disabilities. The districts participating in the study represented elementary schools from across the country, ranging from a small rural school in Wyoming to a magnet school for Hispanic students in California. Districts were randomly assigned to a control group or to one of three treatment groups in which teachers received increasing amounts of inservice about curriculum compacting.

After receiving staff development about curriculum compacting and the characteristics of students who need their curricula modified, the teachers selected one or two students from their classrooms. These students had either been identified as gifted and talented and participated in a district's program or had demonstrated high achievement in a content area which indicated that they would benefit from curriculum compacting. Students were used as the unit of analysis because the treatment, curriculum compacting, was provided to individual students rather than to the class as a whole.

Several out-of-level (one grade higher) *Iowa Tests of Basic Skills* subtests were given to the students in the fall (pre-achievement test), and again at the end of May or beginning of June (post-achievement test). The median percentile for all students on the out-of-grade-level reading and math concepts subtests was 93. The median percentile in the out-of-level math computation subtest was 90. These data indicate that teachers selected students for whom compacting was appropriate.

Procedure

Three treatment groups of teachers who received increasing levels of staff development were used to examine the most efficient but effective method for training teachers to modify curricula. All treatment group teachers received the first staff development session which provided two half-hour videotapes and a book about the compacting process. After receiving the first staff inservice session in October, teachers were asked to select one or two qualified students from their classroom. Teachers in Treatment Group 2 received the videotape training and book, as well as approximately two hours of group compacting simulations (Starko, 1986) conducted by the local gifted and talented resource teacher or consultant. The simulations developed by Starko have been a standard resource in this type of training. Treatment Group 3 received the same training as Treatment Group 2, with the addition of local peer coaching or consultant services. Local consultants provided informal peer coaching throughout the year and provided 6–10 hours of organized peer coaching between March and June. All treatment group teachers completed the Compactor form detailing the amount of content eliminated or compacted, as well as replacement strategies used.

Instrumentation

Three instruments were used to address the research questions stated earlier in this article: the Classroom Practices Questionnaire, the Compactor form, and the *Iowa Tests of Basic Skills*.

The Classroom Practices Questionnaire (CPQ) and the Compactor form were used to assess classroom teachers' practices related to the curriculum compacting procedure. At the end of the treatment period, teachers were asked to indicate the content areas in which curriculum compacting had been completed and to estimate the percentage of curricula that had been eliminated for each selected student. The Compactor was used to identify the amount of content eliminated or streamlined as well as the type of replacement strategies used by classroom teachers. Teachers in all treatment groups provided curriculum compacting most frequently in mathematics in which 39%–49% of content was eliminated. The next most frequently compacted content area was language arts in which 36%–54% of the content was eliminated. Research about these replacement strategies indicated that many diverse strategies were used and that teachers who had higher levels of professional development (Treatment Group 3) used more enrichment strategies within content areas than did the other treatment groups (Reis & Purcell, 1993). Replacement strategies included: independent study, projects, alternative assignments, advanced content, interdisciplinary units and studies, learning games, self-selected study topics, technology opportunities, and a variety of other choices. Replacement strategies were not necessarily provided in the same content area as the one in which curriculum compacting occurred.

Pre and post student achievement was assessed by the *Iowa Tests of Basic Skills* (ITBS), which was administered to students in the control and experimental groups. The reading, mathematical concepts, mathematical computation, science, social studies, and spelling subscales of Form 3 of the ITBS were administered. Tests designed for students one grade level above each student's current grade level were administered to guard against potential ceiling effects.

Validity and reliability information on the ITBS is well documented as is additional technical support. Detailed information is reported in *The Tenth Mental Measurement Yearbook* in which Willson (1989) concludes, "the ITBS is not a perfect battery, but it represents the best that modern educational measurement can produce" (p. 398). The reliability coefficients for the various subscales range from .85 to .95 (see Iowa Tests of Basic Skills, Form J, 1990).

Data Analysis

Multivariate analysis of covariance procedures were conducted to address the research questions in this study. For these analyses, all subscale scores of the *Iowa Test of Basic Skills* (i.e., reading, spelling, mathematical concepts, mathematical computations, social studies, and science) which were administered as posttest measures were the dependent variables. All subscale pretest measures were covariates, and treatment (i.e., three treatment levels and control) was the independent variable. Multivariate analysis of covariance was selected for the analyses because we anticipated strong correlations among the set of dependent variables and the multivariate covariate vector (Stevens, 1986). The results of these analyses follow.

RESULTS

Question 1: Do students whose curriculum was compacted in one or more content areas perform differently on measures of achievement than students whose curriculum was not compacted?

To address research question one, the complete data sets of 336 students were submitted to a multivariate analysis of covariance procedure. The results demonstrated that all covariates were significant. Wilks' Lambda (Λ) values, corresponding F-ratios, and levels of significance were us follows: a) Reading Pretest, ($\Lambda = .73$, $F[6, 321] = 20.12$, $p < .0001$); b) Spelling Pretest, ($\Lambda = .50$, $F[6, 321] = 54.50$, $p < .0001$); c) Mathematical Concepts Pretest, ($\Lambda = .72$, $F[6, 321] = 21.15$, $p < .0001$); d) Mathematical Computation Pretest, ($\Lambda = .67$, $F[6, 321] = 26.90$, $p < .0001$); e) Social Studies Pretest, ($\Lambda = .87$, $F[6, 321] = 8.35$, $p < .0001$); and, f) Science Pretest, ($\Lambda = .79$, $F[6, 321] = 14.06$, $p < .0001$). The main effect for treatment was also significant, ($\Lambda = .85$, $F[18, 908.41] = 2.98$, $p < .0001$).

Table 1 displays the overall means and standard deviations for the dependent variables and covariates. Means, standard deviations, and adjusted means are reported by treatment groups.

Interpretations of the adjusted means at the univariate level should be made with care as the significant effect for treatment is a multivariate effect. Upon examination of the adjusted posttest means, descriptively, Treatment Group 2 had the highest means for three of the six subscales (i.e., reading, mathematical concepts, and social studies). Treatment Group 1 had the highest adjusted mean for science. In spelling and mathematical computations, the control group outperformed all curriculum compacting groups. While these mean comparisons should be made with care, we determined that for Treatment Group 2, 86% of the students in the group had curriculum that was compacted in language arts, mathematics, or both areas simultaneously. By comparison, we determined that 71% of the students assigned to Treatment Group 1 had their curriculum compacted in language arts, mathematics, or both areas. Finally, the lower results observed for Treatment Group 3 may be in part due to the fact that only 67% of the students' curriculum was compacted in the areas of language arts, mathematics, or a combination of both content areas.

Table 1 ITBS Means, Adjusted Means, and Standard Deviations by Levels of Treatment

	Pretests						Posttests					
	Read M (SD)	Spell M (SD)	MathC M (SD)	Comp M (SD)	SS M (SD)	Science M (SD)	Read Adj. M (SD)	Spell Adj. M (SD)	MathC Adj. M (SD)	Comp Adj. M (SD)	SS Adj. M (SD)	Science Adj. M (SD)
Treatment Group 1 (n = 72)	139.17 (25.16)	135.60 (28.98)	132.68 (21.80)	125.88 (22.88)	136.44 (30.02)	147.26 (28.74)	141.64 (25.71)	135.02 (28.96)	137.26 (24.97)	130.75 (23.95)	140.44 (32.70)	153.28 (27.22)
Treatment Group 2 (n = 57)	135.98 (24.11)	129.14 (27.66)	128.07 (24.78)	119.07 (17.78)	134.18 (27.18)	146.91 (23.25)	144.45 (22.65)	136.92 (25.45)	137.42 (23.87)	127.70 (19.87)	144.63 (30.10)	151.12 (23.68)
Treatment Group 3 (n = 66)	139.73 (24.47)	131.36 (27.92)	132.97 (24.48)	127.70 (19.79)	135.08 (27.73)	147.71 (26.40)	142.05 (24.45)	133.90 (24.63)	134.08 (24.32)	127.28 (21.25)	136.40 (26.03)	146.08 (27.36)
Control (n = 141)	131.61 (25.21)	127.09 (28.36)	123.41 (21.88)	117.86 (20.37)	127.01 (34.93)	135.08 (30.36)	143.59 (24.68)	138.85 (27.49)	136.67 (23.33)	132.03 (21.44)	141.18 (30.77)	149.15 (28.13)
Total (n = 336)	135.57 (25.20)	130.09 (28.36)	128.06 (23.20)	121.71 (20.77)	131.71 (31.48)	142.18 (28.68)	143.01 (24.62)	136.73 (26.88)	136.42 (24.21)	130.09 (21.86)	140.67 (30.37)	149.76 (27.53)

Question 2: Do students whose curriculum was compacted in mathematics perform differently than their control counterparts on measures of achievement?

Question 3: Do students whose curriculum was compacted in language arts perform differently than their control counterparts on measures of achievement?

To address the effects of the content area (i.e., mathematics or language arts) in which one's curriculum was compacted on achievement scores, two multivariate analyses of covariance (MANCOVAs) were performed on two randomly selected subsamples of the students' data. The random selection of subsamples was considered necessary in order to examine the effects of content area curriculum compacting given specific subscales of the ITBS instead of the full battery of scores. Because the full battery of subscales is highly correlated, we anticipated that the random subsample selections would eliminate some of the problems associated with the variance inflation attributable to the strong intercorrelations among dependent variables and covariates.

For research question two, two levels of curriculum compacting (i.e., those students in Treatment Groups 1, 2, or 3 whose curriculum was compacted specifically in mathematics versus control) made up the independent variable. The dependent variables were scores on the ITBS mathematics concepts and computation subscales. Pretest scores for these two measures served as covariates. While covariates were significant (Λs > .66, Fs > 47.57, ps < .0001), there were no significant differences between treatment levels.

For research question three, a parallel analysis to the one described above was performed for language arts. A random subsample was selected to examine the effects of curriculum compacting in language arts on achievement scores. For this analysis, reading scores, spelling scores, and social science scores of the posttests were the dependent variables and the pretest scores of these scales were covariates. As with the analysis for mathematics curriculum compacting, treatment had two levels: students in any of the three treatment groups with curriculum compacting in language arts and the control group. Results were similar to those observed for the mathematics analysis. While all covariates were significant, (Λs > .45, Fs > 16.51, ps < .0001), there was no main effect for treatment.

A discriminant function analysis was run as a follow-up procedure to the MANCOVA. This analysis was conducted to identify whether partial correlations among the subscales would have discriminated among the groups. The discriminant function coefficients were comparable across groups, which indicates that each treatment group made similar pretest to posttest gains.

DISCUSSION

Three research questions were addressed in this study: Do students whose curriculum was compacted in one or more content areas perform differently on measures of achievement than students whose curriculum was not compacted? Do students whose curriculum was compacted in mathematics perform differently than their control counterparts on measures of achievement? Do students whose curriculum was compacted in language arts perform differently than their control counterparts on measures of achievement? To answer these three questions, students' achievement test scores were examined by three multivariate analyses of covariance. Results of these multivariate analyses supported that there were no significant differences in favor of the control group over the treatment groups.

The findings related to these questions provide empirical support for concerned practitioners who want to 1) provide alternative learning activities for high achieving students in heterogeneous classrooms, and 2) ensure that highly able students continue to score well on standardized tests. Three findings from this research are particularly salient. First, as mentioned above, the achievement test scores of gifted students whose curriculum was compacted did not differ significantly from gifted students whose curriculum was not compacted. Even when as much as 40%–50% of content was eliminated for some students, they still scored as well as their counterparts who did not have their curricula eliminated or streamlined. These results are based on out-of-level tests scores which were used to increase the sensitivity to gains and declines at the upper end of the scale. The median percentile performance on all post subscales of the ITBS was greater than 90. Using one year beyond grade level tests may still not have been sufficient to prevent ceiling effects, however. If ceiling effects had an impact, a Type II error occurred; namely, gains in post scores, not declines, would have been masked.

Second, the descriptive findings, as shown in Table 1, suggest that students in some of the treatment groups performed better than the control group on some of the subscales. For example, students in Treatment Group 1 had higher adjusted posttest scores in science than all other groups. Similarly for Treatment Group 2, students had higher adjusted posttest social studies scores than the other groups. We did note two trends which suggested that students in the control group performed slightly better than students in the treatment groups in mathematical computation and spelling. This probably reflects that they experienced more drill practice in these areas. All differences are minimal, however, and should not be interpreted as having practical significance.

Third, the findings in the Compacting Research Study support the beliefs of many classroom teachers who maintain that high ability and high achieving students need curriculum differentiation. The median pretest achievement test scores of students selected by teachers for curriculum compacting were high; selected children scored above the 90th percentile on one year above grade level tests in reading and mathematics. This clearly indicated classroom teachers' ability to identify high achieving students who would benefit from curriculum compacting. The scores of these children support the opinions of teachers and underscore the critical need for practitioners to identify advanced students and provide appropriate instruction for young people who know a great deal of the curriculum before it is taught.

Finally, the findings prompt questions related to the use of curriculum compacting over long periods of time and at the secondary level. Specifically, what are the effects of compacting students' curricula over several years? Would the continuous use of this instructional strategy be associated with long-term achievement and attitudinal gains? In addition, new research should focus on eliminating basic skill instruction for gifted students in favor of complex, faster paced, problem-based learning and the effects of this change on future achievement test scores. Empirical research must also examine the achievement effects of compacting at the secondary level. Can substantial portions of secondary students' curriculum be eliminated without affecting students' scores on standardized achievement tests? Answers to these research questions will provide classroom practitioners with the additional empirical data necessary to make well-grounded decisions about students' learning opportunities at all grade levels.

CONCLUSION

Our research began with a question that teachers have wrestled with for some time: What effect will compacting elementary school students' curricula have on standardized measures of academic achievement? As demands for accountability grow, the question is a critical one for professionals who want students to perform at high levels on standardized achievement tests. The results of this study may provide support for elementary teachers who seek empirical evidence for eliminating content which students have already mastered. Curriculum compacting provides documentation of students' knowledge of the regular curriculum covered in class, and it enables teachers to provide many types of differentiated replacement learning opportunities. The research presented in this article suggests that elementary teachers can preassess students' prior knowledge of content, eliminate portions of the curriculum that students already know, replace those portions with various types of interdisciplinary learning activities, and remain reasonably confident that students' achievement test scores will not decline. Furthermore, it should be noted that students' scores did not decline, even when the replacement material is not within the same content area, rather in students' interest areas.

REFERENCES

Archambault, F. X., Jr., Westberg, K. L., Brown, S., Hallmark, B.W., Zhang, W., & Emmons, C. (1993). Classroom practices used with gifted third and fourth grade students. *Journal for the Education of the Gifted, 16*(2), 103–119.

Barbour, C. M. (Director and Writer) & Kiernan, L. J. (Writer). (1994). *Challenging the gifted in the regular classroom.* [Videotape] (Available from Association for Supervision and Curriculum Development, Alexandria, VA)

George, P. S. (1995). Talent development and grouping in the middle grades: Challenging the brightest without sacrificing the rest. *Middle School Journal, 26*(4), 12–17.

Imbeau, M. B. (1991). *Teachers' attitudes toward curriculum compacting: A comparison of different inservice strategies.* Unpublished doctoral dissertation, University of Connecticut, Storrs.

Iowa Tests of Basic Skills. (1990). *Manual for school administrators supplement.* Chicago: Riverside Publishing.

Purcell, J. H. (1993). The effects of the elimination of gifted and talented programs on participating students and their parents. *Gifted Child Quarterly, 37*(4), 177–187.

Reis, S. M., Burns, D. E., & Renzulli, J. S. (1992). *Curriculum compacting: The complete guide to modifying the curriculum for high ability students.* Mansfield Center, CT: Creative Learning Press.

Reis, S. M., & Purcell, J. H. (1993). An analysis of content elimination and strategies used by elementary classroom teachers in the curriculum compacting process. *Journal for the Education of the Gifted, 16*(2), 147–170.

Reis, S. M., Westberg, K. L., Kulikowich, J., Caillard, F., Hébert, T., Plucker, J., Purcell, J. H., Rogers, J. B., & Smist, J. M. (1993). *Why not let high ability students start school in January? The curriculum compacting study* (Research Monograph 93106). Storrs, CT: University of Connecticut, The National Research Center on the Gifted and Talented.

Renzulli, J. S., & Reis, S. M. (1985). *The schoolwide enrichment model: A comprehensive plan for educational excellence.* Mansfield Center, CT: Creative Learning Press.

Renzulli, J. S., & Reis, S. M. (1991). The reform movement and the quiet crisis in gifted education. *Gifted Child Quarterly, 35*(1), 26–35.

Renzulli, J. S., & Smith, L. H. (1978). *A guidebook for developing individualized educational programs for gifted and talented students.* Mansfield Center, CT: Creative Learning Press.

Schultz, C. B. (1991). *The effects of curriculum compacting upon student achievement in fourth grade mathematics.* Unpublished master's thesis, University Northern Iowa.

Starko, A. J. (1986). *It's about time: Inservice strategies for curriculum compacting.* Mansfield Center, CT: Creative Learning Press.

Stevens, J. (1986). *Applied multivariate statistics for the social sciences.* Hillsdale, NJ: Lawrence Erlbaum Associates.

U.S. Department of Education. (1993). *National excellence: A case for developing America's talent.* Washington, DC: Author.

Westberg, K. L., Archambault, F. X., Jr., & Brown, S. W. (1997). A survey of classroom practices with third and fourth grade students in the United States. *Gifted Education International, 12*, 29–33.

Westberg, K. L., Archambault, F. X., Dobyns, S. M., & Salvin, T. J. (1993). The classroom practices observation study. *Journal for the Education of the Gifted, 16*(2), 120–146.

Willson, V. L. (1989). Review of the Iowa Tests of Basic Skills, forms G & H. In J. C. Conoley and J. J. Kramer (Eds.), *The tenth mental measurements yearbook* (pp. 395–398). Lincoln, NE: Buros Institute of Mental Measurements.

Winebrenner, S. (1992). *Teaching gifted kids in the regular classroom: Strategies and techniques every teacher can use to meet the academic needs of the gifted and talented.* Minneapolis, MN: Free Spirit Press.

7

Building Bridges Between General Practitioners and Educators of the Gifted: A Study of Collaboration

Jeanne H. Purcell

University of Connecticut

Jann H. Leppien

University of Great Falls

The Collaboration Research Study examined the incidence of collaboration, as well as the assumptions of those who entered collaborative alliances. Collaboration was defined as "dialogue and planning between professionals in which the goal is to provide differentiated services for high achieving

Editor's Note: From Purcell, J. H., & Leppien, J. H. (1998). Building bridges between general practitioners and educators of the gifted: A study of collaboration. *Gifted Child Quarterly*, 42(3), 172-181. © 1998 National Association for Gifted Children. Reprinted with permission.

students." Two hundred and eighty-nine enrichment specialists, classroom teachers, and administrators, selected purposefully, took part in this national, descriptive, ex post facto research. The response rate from the three groups was 61%, 55%, and 51%, respectively. Results indicate that more than 80% of those sampled engage in collaboration. Data suggest that classroom teachers and enrichment specialists enter the collaborative relationship with different, and sometimes conflicting, sets of assumptions about the skills and attitudes of their collaborative partners. These empirical findings suggest that collaboration is a complex, interpersonal process. Implications of the study are twofold. First, collaboration depends upon highly developed interpersonal skills. Second, successful collaborative relationships rest upon the match between the assumptions that each party holds about the other. In order to ensure collaborative alliances that can produce high quality, differentiated learning options, the assumptions of each party need to be understood and, if necessary, bridges need to be built when gaps exist between the assumptions and the actual skills and attitudes of collaborative partners.

The investigation explained in this article is based upon three research findings and several unanswered questions. The first research finding, is that the roles and responsibilities of those who educate students are changing (Donaldson, 1993: Fullan, 1992; Holcomb, 1993; Monson & Monson, 1993). Teaming, collegiality, site-based management, and collaboration are words that describe some of the new roles for educators, and these words are heard in teachers' rooms and board of education meetings, and are written about in educational journals and books. Practitioners at all levels are taking on new roles and forming new kinds of relationships to improve the academic performance of America's youth.

Putting the Research to Use

The data from this study indicate that classroom teachers and general practitioners enter collaborative alliances with a common goal: to provide high quality, differentiated learning activities for all students. While collaborative partners undertake alliances with the same goal in mind, the research reported here suggests that collaborative partners embark upon alliances with different, yet complementary, sets of expectations about the competencies and attitudes of their partner. These results can be used by classroom teachers and enrichment specialists to deepen our understanding about the interpersonal dynamics upon which collaborative alliances are built and, thereby, help to ensure the success of these vital alliances for all students who require modified and differentiated curricula and instruction. Enrichment specialists can use the data to provide support services in the areas mentioned by classroom teachers and to create alliances with classroom teachers to adapt existing curricula for students needing differentiated learning opportunities. The results can also be used by school administrators who seek to enhance the capacity of school personnel to deliver high quality services to young people. Through sustained inservice about the nature of collaboration and the interpersonal skills required to facilitate such educational partnerships, administrators may be able to increase the effectiveness of instruction for all students, including those with high abilities. Finally, these results can be used by researchers to investigate, more fully, the extent of collaborative alliances in our nation's schools, the conditions under which these alliances flourish, and the benefits of the alliances, as perceived by practitioners, administrators, students, and parents.

This investigation is also based upon the research finding that systems for delivering services to high achieving students are changing (Debuse & Shoemaker, 1993; Purcell, 1995; Renzulli, 1994; Schack, 1996). Purcell reported that pull-out programs for high achieving students in a large proportion of states were being eliminated and reduced. As a result, high achieving students returned to the regular classroom in large numbers. Debuse and Shoemaker addressed the role of the teacher of the gifted within the context of educational reform in Oregon. They predicted that the job of the teacher of the gifted would move away from providing direct services to students to providing more direct services to classroom teachers. Like Debuse and Shoemaker, Renzulli also concludes that the role of the enrichment specialist is changing. He calls the reconfigured role of the enrichment specialist the "three-fifths solution" (p. 254). Under this new plan, specialists may spend 60% of their time providing direct services to students and 40% of their time providing resource services to classroom teachers. Schack discusses how enrichment specialists can assist teachers in implementing reforms in ways that maximize the promise and minimize the problems of those reforms for gifted students.

Fueled by changes in roles and changes in the delivery system of services for high achieving students, classroom teachers and many in the field of gifted education call increasingly for collaboration between general practitioners and those who educate the academically able (Council for Exceptional Children, 1994; Dettmer, 1993; Hanninen, 1994; Tomlinson, Coleman, Allan, Udall, & Landrum, 1996; Treffinger, 1991; VanTassel-Baska, 1991). Tomlinson et al. recently reported the results of a national study in which they examined the beliefs of educators and parents regarding the need for linkages between general and gifted education. They concluded that "broad consensus" existed about the "merit and urgency" (Tomlinson et al., p. 171) for collaboration between the two fields of education.

In spite of reform initiatives based upon new roles and relationships for educators, changes in delivery systems for high achieving students, and increasing support and calls for collaboration between classroom teachers and teachers of the gifted, no systematic research exists that examines the nature of these collaborative alliances. The purpose of this research was to investigate two questions: "What events triggered collaboration among classroom teachers and enrichment specialists?" and "What are the assumptions of each party as he or she enters collaborative alliances to deliver differentiated learning opportunities to high achieving young people?"

METHOD

Qualitative procedures were used to examine the data in this ex post facto, descriptive research study.

Sampling Procedure

Purposeful sampling was used to collect data about the scope and nature of successful collaborative practices. An initial pool of 173 graduates from a three-year degree program in gifted education was selected for participation in the research. The targeted graduates from the University of Connecticut had completed a graduate degree within the last four years and the majority of graduates were employed as enrichment specialists within their respective schools or school districts. The most recent graduates were selected because researchers believed they would be the ones most likely to be employed in enrichment specialist positions.

To ensure the highest possible response rate, procedures in a meta-analysis of factors which positively influenced response rates (Fox, Crask, & Kim, 1988) were followed. Accordingly, notification letters preceded the mailing of the Collaboration Survey. Additionally, surveys were printed on colored stationery and transmittal letters were printed on letter-head. A follow-up to non-respondents was mailed approximately two weeks after the mailing of the first survey. Finally, phone calls were made to non-respondents to the second mailing approximately two weeks after the mailing of the second survey.

To triangulate data from graduates, two additional sources of data were collected using snowball sampling procedures (Lincoln & Guba, 1985). Snowball sampling is a naturalistic sampling process which is utilized to achieve maximum sampling variation. The first respondent is the gatekeeper to successive respondents who are queried to extend the information already obtained. Thus, in the notification letter for this research, respondents were asked to identify a classroom teacher and administrator in their school or district willing to complete a parallel form of the Collaboration Survey. Respondents for the Collaboration Research Study consisted of triads of educators from the same schools/districts: enrichment specialists, classroom teachers, and administrators. Data from the triads were not matched; rather, data were matched by respondent group, that is, enrichment specialist, classroom teacher, and administrator.

Instrumentation

A five-part survey was developed for this study. Part I contained questions related to demographics including questions about the respondent's training in gifted education, number of professional staff members within the school, and number of years experience with collaboration, defined as "dialogue and planning between professionals in which the goal is to provide differentiated services for high achieving students." Part II contained open- and close-ended questions designed to obtain information about the origin of collaboration. The third part, related to the nature of collaboration—such as the topics discussed during collaboration—contained nine open- and close-ended questions. Part IV, the most lengthy section of the questionnaire, concerned the continuing use of collaboration. Examples of questions in this section include: "What interpersonal skills have you seen demonstrated by those most successful at collaboration?" and "What skills are most needed by classroom teachers/teachers of the gifted to ensure successful collaboration?" The last part of the survey contained questions related to the outcomes of collaboration.

Data Coding and Analysis

Qualitative procedures were used to analyze the data in this study. Three different types of coding were used to analyze the data from the open-ended responses provided by the different groups of respondents in this study: open, axial, and selective coding (Strauss & Corbin, 1990). Open coding, the initial form of coding, involved unrestricted analyses of data. All open-ended survey responses were reproduced verbatim in type, color coded by respondent (i.e., enrichment specialists' responses were reproduced on blue paper, classroom teachers' responses were reproduced on yellow paper, and administrators' data were reproduced on green paper), and then separated by respondent and question number. Then, each typed response was analyzed for blocks of data-words, phrases, clauses, and sentences. These blocks or "chunks" of verbatim data were then cut into single units. Frequently, several chunks of data occurred within one written response.

Axial coding, the next phase of analysis, involved the iterative comparing and contrasting of chunks of coded data, by respondent, in order to establish clusters of data. These data clusters or patterns acted to pull the seemingly disparate chunks of data into meaningful categories or units. In order to construct these categories, the typed data chunks for each question, by respondent, were placed on blank pieces of paper. Single chunks were compared and contrasted with initial categories that emerged quickly. As all data were examined in turn, new categories emerged because data chunks did not fit into the existing category structures.

In this way, loose families of categorized data for each respondent group were formed which shared critical attributes. Each family of data was then named by asking the questions: "What are these data chunks an instance of?" and "To what more general class do these data chunks belong?" The grouping and naming of the data into more abstract, conceptual categories helped researchers make connections between categories and subcategories of data. Categories of data were then pasted onto the blank pieces of paper. Finally, all coded pages were arranged by research question and respondent.

In the final phase of data analysis, selective coding, loose families of data were refined, and core categories of data were selected. Core categories were determined by the researchers to be the central phenomenon around which all subcategories were integrated.

RESULTS

Response Rate and Extent of Collaboration

The response rate for the survey varied by population samples. Sixty-one percent ($n = 105$) of the enrichment specialists returned the survey. Fifty-five percent ($n = 95$) of classroom teachers responded, as did 51% ($n = 88$) of the administrators. Although the three populations sampled varied slightly, all groups indicated that collaboration was practiced extensively to service the educational needs of high achieving students. Eighty-two percent of the enrichment specialists indicated that collaboration was utilized to personalize curricula for these students, 80% of classroom teachers reported that they used collaboration, and 88% of administrators perceived that this strategy was used by practitioners to meet the learning needs of young people.

What person, event, or set of circumstances "triggered" collaboration? Data reveal that people and events triggered collaboration (see Figure 1). First, all respondent groups reported that collaboration had been teacher driven and arose, in large part, from teachers' perceptions that high achieving students' needs were not being met in classrooms. Second, the teacher of the gifted or the enrichment specialist played a major role in initiating the collaborative process. Finally, respondents also observed that collaborative efforts were fueled by "outside pressures."

Who triggered collaboration?: Enrichment Specialists and Classroom Teachers. Enrichment specialists and classroom practitioners reported that teachers, either in groups or individually, triggered the process. "Teaming led to discussion about individual students," "the closeness of the entire staff resulted in

Figure I   Perceptions, by Group, of the People and Events that Triggered
Collaboration

Respondent	People	Events
Enrichment Specialists	Practitioners' perceptions that high achieving students had unmet learning needs	• Parents' concerns about their children's unchallenging academic program • Diminished funding for gifted and talented programs • Site visits to other places • Dissatisfaction with the current system to deliver quality services to high achieving young people
Classroom Teachers	Practitioners' perceptions that high achieving students had unmet learning needs	• Implications arising from pull-out programs • Poor SAT scores • The time involved with developing IEPs
Administrators	Practitioners' perceptions that high achieving students had unmet learning needs	• The move toward inclusion • Inservice training • Parental pressure • Increasing student participation in other high level programs • Board of Education concerns about the need for challenging curricula and instruction

group discussions about student needs," and "a committee of elementary teachers got together to talk about students." Individual teachers were also reported to have triggered collaboration. "One teacher began splitting her class to have the advanced students together to meet their needs." "[A pair of teachers] traded kids for certain activities to increase the challenge level for them." One enrichment specialist reported that she observed a teacher share the student of a former colleague with another teacher who had a small group of high achieving students.

Who triggered collaboration?: Administrators. Administrators echoed the data reported by classroom teachers and enrichment specialists regarding the triggering mechanism for collaboration. "[It] emerged from a sense of professional sharing," "teacher teams working together," "concerns from teachers," "teacher inquiry," "just a willingness to work together," and "mutual interest" typify the comments reported by this group of respondents.

Mutual Interest: Enrichment Specialists, Classroom Teachers and Administrators. The "mutual interest" that was reported by classroom teachers, enrichment specialists, and administrators was the recognition that high achieving students' learning needs were not being met in the classroom. Enrichment specialists reported that "Students were not challenged, especially in the area of math," "students needed a differentiated curriculum," "student need," and "kids even told me that they knew the stuff in their books." Classroom practitioners commented, "Some of my students displayed great skills in math, communication, problem solving, art, and music," "[Some of my students] needed more stimulation in the classroom," "[I saw] boredom, as well as no motivation displayed by some of my students," and "students with high abilities wanted to know more than the typical topics covered in the classroom." Administrators, too, reported that the unmet needs of gifted students was the mutual interest of practitioners: "[They see] children whose academic needs are not being met in the classroom," "teachers realize that gifted students' needs are not met in the heterogeneous classroom," and "we realize we need to improve instruction for bright students."

Enrichment specialists were key people in the development of the collaborative process. Seventy percent of enrichment teachers reported they had initiated the collaborative process. Sixty-seven percent of classroom teachers identified the enrichment specialist as the one who had initiated collaboration. Similarly, 69% of administrators identified the enrichment specialist as the person who had "led the way" toward collaborative planning for students with high abilities. Classroom teachers made many unsolicited written comments that elaborated on the role of the enrichment specialist: "Our enrichment coordinator held meetings with us to let us know what services were available," "Our teacher of the gifted met with the primary teachers and taught us how to compact curricula," and "I made end-of-the-year math tests with our TAG teacher and began a program for my gifted math students."

The unmet needs of high achieving students were not the only catalysts for collaboration among practitioners. Outside pressure was another category that emerged from the data related to this research question. Each group of respondents reported different outside pressures that fueled the move toward collaboration.

Outside forces: Enrichment specialists. Enrichment specialists reported the following outside pressures: parents' concerns about their children's academic program, diminished funding for gifted and talented programs, site visits to other places, and dissatisfaction with the current system to deliver quality services to high achieving young people. Most of the data reported by enrichment specialists focused on parental pressures. "Parental pressure" and "parental complaints about boredom" were the most frequently cited outside pressures that encouraged collaboration.

Outside forces: Classroom teachers. Classroom teachers reported a different list of outside pressures that heightened the need for collaboration, including: the implications arising from pull-out programs, poor SAT scores, and the time involved with developing IEPs. The most frequently cited outside pressure from this group of respondents was "concern about missing skills and class work while at the gifted program."

Outside forces: Administrators. Administrators indicated that outside pressures included the move toward inclusion, inservice training, parental pressure to provide more quality services for high achieving students, increasing student participation in other high level programs (e.g., Invention Convention, Math Olympiad), and board of education concerns.

What are the assumptions of collaborative partners as they enter alliances to deliver differentiated learning opportunities to high achieving young people?

Separate survey questions for enrichment specialists and classroom teachers were designed to elicit information about this research question. Classroom teachers were asked to respond to the following: What skills/attitudes/dispositions do you believe are most required of enrichment specialists to ensure successful collaboration with classroom practitioners? Likewise, enrichment specialists were asked this question: What skills/attitudes/dispositions do you believe are most required of classroom teachers to ensure successful collaboration with teachers of the gifted?

Respondents indicated that skills and attitudes of participants contributed most to the success of collaboration. Classroom teachers assumed that enrichment specialists would possess certain skills and attitudes as they entered the collaborative relationship. Likewise, enrichment specialists assumed classroom teachers would possess certain skills and attitudes. Data from classroom teachers will be presented first, followed by the results collected from enrichment specialists. The findings are also illustrated in Table 2.

Classroom Teachers

Classroom teachers expected enrichment specialists to possess two important skills: resourcefulness and the ability to communicate. Classroom teachers defined resourcefulness in terms of several factors. First, they expected specialists to be knowledgeable about curricular materials. They also expected enrichment specialists to have a broad knowledge base of experience and wisdom related to teaching and learning and to keep them informed about important curricular issues related to high achieving young people. Second, they expected specialists to understand tacit knowledge related to schooling, specifically the classroom and the school schedule. Classroom teachers indicated they needed a specialist who "understood the goals of the classroom teacher," who understood "all the difficulties [encountered by teachers] in the classroom," and who was "aware of the pressures and schedules" of the classroom practitioner. Third, they expected specialists to be problem solvers and creative. They expected specialists to be able to provide them with "new" ideas for teaching,

Table 2   Assumptions Held by Parterns Entering a Collaborative Alliance

Respondent	Skills	Attitudes

Classroom teachers expected enrichment specialists/teachers of the gifted to be:	• Resourceful
	  – Knowledge-about curricula, instruction, assessment and curricular materials
	  – Able to understand the tacit knowledge related to schools and schooling
	  – Can problem solve; be creative
	• Able to communicate effectively orally and in writing
		• Flexible
		• Willing to give of his/her time
		• Tolerant
		• Respectful
		• Patient

Enrichment specialists/teachers of the gifted expected classroom teachers to be:	• Able to perceive and diagnose differences among students • Able to adapt and monitor curriculum for individual students	• Respectful of individual differences among students • Willing to try new ideas • Excited about learning • Positive about collaboration

provide them with "concrete examples of materials or resources to use," help them "find solutions" to problems with high achieving learners, "come up with many options for teaching young people," and be able to "find answers quickly."

Classroom teachers expected enrichment specialists to be able to communicate consistently and effectively. They wanted specialists to provide "ongoing communication about student progress," and "insightful information about the student to all classroom teachers" with whom the student worked. Classroom teachers expected specialists to be able to communicate effectively, "to possess the verbal skills [needed] to give teachers directions about where they [the classroom teachers] were going." Furthermore, classroom teachers expected specialists to have the communication skills necessary to be "respected by other teachers."

In addition to expecting specialists to have a set of skills, classroom teachers expected specialists to demonstrate a disposition characterized by flexibility, a willingness to give of his or her time, tolerance, and supportiveness. Teachers expected specialists to be adaptable to any classroom situation and demonstrate a willingness to adjust to "any teaching or learning style." Not only did classroom teachers expect specialists to give of their time, but they also expected that specialists would provide teachers with time "to assimilate new things." Classroom teachers repeatedly stated that they needed specialists who would be tolerant "of ignorance (on my part)," who could perceive a teacher's "strengths and stretch gently," and who "would use a teacher's strengths to develop a plan of action."

Classroom teachers were wary of specialists who demonstrated "attitudes that they were better than classroom teachers." They reported that they needed a specialist who: was "respectful of other people's turf and personal limitations," possessed "keen observational powers," "was analytical, but not judgmental," "was encouraging," "provided praise," and "provided support for independent learning."

Enrichment Specialists

Like their counterparts, enrichment specialists also held expectations about the skills and attitudes of classroom teachers. Data from the specialists indicated that their expectations regarding hoped-for skills and attitudes differed from those held by classroom teachers. With respect to skills, specialists expected that teachers would know how to be flexible and that they would have the ability to "adapt," "monitor," and "adjust" curricula and instruction. Specifically, the data suggest that specialists expected classroom teachers to be able to modify learning activities based upon the needs of the students.

In addition to having the skill to adapt and monitor the curriculum, specialists also expected classroom teachers to have certain dispositions about the teaching and learning process, including an understanding of the needs of all students, a willingness to try new ideas, an excitement for learning, and a collaborative spirit. They hoped teachers would have "an authentic concern for each child" and an "understanding and appreciation for the differences among children." Toward that end, they hoped classroom teachers would "empathize with bright children" and have a "desire to challenge bright, quick learners," even if it meant placing bright children outside the classroom for periods of time. Specialists hoped that classroom teachers would recognize the need to let go of some children, and be able to "share the students for the year with the school, the specialist, and community."

Specialists expected classroom teachers to enter the collaborative relationship with an open mind, that they would be willing "to try new ideas," such as "pre-assessment" and "subject acceleration." The data also indicate that specialists hoped teachers would be willing to change "teaching styles" to accommodate learners who learned best with simulations or peer tutoring, for example. Specialists hoped teachers would be risk-takers, and willing to "break out of traditional ways of doing things."

Specialists hoped that classroom teachers would be excited about learning. They hoped classroom teachers would be "filled with curiosity" and a desire to "create." Furthermore, they assumed that teachers would have an "interest in learning about themselves," and "desire to grow professionally."

They also hoped classroom teachers would enter the collaborative relationship with a "cooperative attitude" and a "deep sense of responsibility." They wanted classroom teachers to demonstrate "a willingness to work hard," and be willing "to put in the extra time and effort to meet." Finally, they hoped classroom teachers would be "tolerant" and "patient," and give the new collaborative relationship the "time it needed to develop and succeed."

DISCUSSION

This study includes two major findings which have implications for those involved with graduate-level training programs, preservice programs, and staff development. These findings and implications are explained below.

Extent of Collaboration

The first finding is that collaboration between classroom practitioners and enrichment specialists or teachers of the gifted is being practiced successfully in some schools across the country. This is encouraging news in light of the fact that many educators from all levels have called urgently for collaboration among general and gifted education. Data from this research also suggest that educators of the gifted frequently initiated the partnership. It is satisfying to know that some in gifted education realize how important it is to risk "taking the first step." There are, of course, limitations to these data. The sample is small and all respondents attended the same graduate-level program in gifted education where the role of the enrichment specialist was emphasized. Accordingly, collaboration may not be as common as indicated in this study because gifted education specialists may not have received the pre-requisite training to initiate and sustain educational partnerships.

Expectations of Collaborative Partners

The heart of the research, however, is the second major finding: the expectations that collaborators from general education and gifted education hold for one another. The finding is compelling for two reasons. First, it underscores the importance of the interpersonal dynamics of the collaborative process. Collaboration is, first and foremost, about people and the skills they bring to the relationship. Second, the finding pinpoints the expectations that enrichment specialists and classroom teachers hold for one another as they enter the collaborative alliance. These expectations or assumptions have, heretofore, not been explicit. Knowing the different, yet seemingly complementary sets of expectations that collaborative partners hold for each other, we can now build important bridges to increase the likelihood of successful collaboration.

Building bridges: Resourcefulness. How do we, in gifted education, build such bridges? By extracting and carefully examining the meaning of each skill and attitude the general practitioners in this research believed was necessary for effective collaboration and then identifying ways to enhance our aptitude related to the identified skill or attitude. For example, the overwhelming majority of classroom teachers in this research expected teachers of the gifted to be resourceful. Data from this research study indicate that resourceful means a variety of different things, including: having a broad knowledge base of experience and wisdom related to teaching and learning, being able to come up with many options for teaching gifted students, and being able to locate answers quickly. How, then, do we nurture our resourcefulness? Answers include, but are not limited to: joining professional organizations related to education, reading content area journals; volunteering to serve on curriculum review committees, reading gifted education journals, spending time reading at children's book stores, copying and sharing noteworthy articles with colleagues, sharing materials freely, writing mini-grants to send classroom teachers to professional development opportunities, networking with other practitioners including those at the university level and state departments of education, attending conferences and bringing back materials, developing a lending library, talking with professionals in other areas to learn about representative topics related to content area studies, reading newspapers and news magazines, and responding to requests from classroom teachers as quickly as possible.

Building bridges: Demonstrating effective communication skills. How can we nurture our communication skills to ensure that we communicate "consistently" and "effectively" so that "we are respected by other teachers?" The literature from special education is replete with information about effective communication. Friend and Cook (1992) elaborate about the characteristics of effective verbal feedback. It is descriptive, rather than evaluative; specific, rather than general; directed toward a situation over which the teacher can change; concise; and checked to ensure clear communication (pp. 94–97). With respect to nonverbal communication, Friend and Cook ask collaborators to be mindful of different body movements, vocal cues, spatial relations, and the use of encouragers (pp. 73–75). Salend (1994) defines the characteristics of effective team members. Among other skills, individual team members "listen without interrupting, consider the perspective of others, avoid making judgments, reflect upon a speaker's message, expand ideas of others, take notes, wait before speaking, refrain from anger, and use humor" (p. 120). As enrichment specialists, it is important to note that it is not the job of the classroom teacher to listen to us. It is our job to find a way to communicate effectively so that classroom teachers will want to listen to what we have to offer.

Building bridges: Demonstrating understanding. What can teachers of the gifted do to meet the expectations general practitioners hold about attitudes required for successful collaboration? For example, how can we ensure that we are perceived as understanding? Among other things, we can listen; be keenly observant; be patient; provide modeling or offer to coteach, if necessary; avoid being judgmental; use praise and encouragement; and acknowledge the schedules and pressures of the classroom teacher.

Building bridges: Checking our own perceptions. So far, we have looked at how we can build bridges between classroom practitioners' assumptions and the skills and attitudes we, as enrichment specialists, possess. This analysis represents only half of the story, however. It is essential to look at the assumptions we, as enrichment specialists, hold for classroom teachers. Are our assumptions about their skills and attitudes consistent with the skills and attitudes they actually possess and hold? Our research indicates that we expect classroom teachers to be able to diagnose individual learning differences among children and then be able to adapt and monitor learning activities to meet their needs. Quite simply, our expectations regarding their skills may be too high (Tomlinson et al., 1994). In light of the increasing diversity among students in today's classroom, teachers face enormous pressures and demands.

Nor can we expect teachers to have the attitudes we expect of them. The research in this article indicates that we expect classroom teachers to "be filled with curiosity," possess "a desire to create," "be interested in learning about themselves," "have a desire to grow professionally," "be cooperative," have a "deep sense of responsibility," "be willing to work hard," and "put in the extra time and effort." Fullan (1997) reports, "Anyone who spends time in public schools can feel the growing and deepening malaise among educators, whether it stems from a sense on the part of teachers that the public and the government do not care about them, or from an overwhelming sense of despair that the problems are insurmountable and worsening. . . . For large numbers of the teaching profession, the pressure of the job has taken the joy out of teaching" (pp. 217–218). To summarize, the research presented here suggests that we, as teachers of the gifted, may unwittingly hold romantic notions that may increase the gap between classroom practitioners and teachers of the gifted and may even create more alienation and cynicism than heretofore has existed.

To effectively build bridges between our own expectations about the skills and attitudes of classroom teachers and their actual skills and attitudes requires a realignment on our part. We must sense deeply the enormity of problems and challenges facing classroom teachers and be willing to take on a part of their burden. To unwittingly overlook, disregard, or dismiss the realities—even paralysis—of some classroom teachers ensures the failure of collaboration and the successful delivery of differentiated learning opportunities for high achieving students. An understanding and acknowledgment of the complexity of problems faced by teachers and the concomitant emotional side of their daily dilemmas will provide us with a much firmer ground upon which to build successful collaborative alliances.

Implications of the Research for Those in Education

Finally, this research has implications for those involved with preservice, graduate-level, and inservice programs. The results reported here suggest preservice teachers and graduate-level students need exposure to a variety of topics including the nature of teaming and collaboration; the assumptions of partners as they enter collaborative alliances; differences among students; the characteristics and needs of all learners, including those who are gifted and talented; methods and materials, K-12; the principles of differentiation; and classroom management in the differentiated classroom. Specifically, this research suggests that preservice teachers and graduate students need to understand the nature of collaborative alliances and the prerequisite skills and attitudes that support educational partnerships. Additionally, they need to practice initiating and sustaining collaborative alliances. Both groups of future teachers and specialists also need sustained exposure to course work that requires them to learn about the many types of learners in today's classrooms. Equally important, they need to spend several semesters becoming well-versed in methods and materials, K-12. Without a thorough mastery of curricular objectives, instructional strategies, and educational materials, future classroom teachers will be unable to differentiate learning activities for diverse learners. Without a thorough mastery of curriculum objectives, instructional strategies, and educational materials across all content areas, K-12, future enrichment specialists will be unable to be the "resourceful partner" that classroom teachers in this study said they desperately needed.

This research also has implications for school administrators who are responsible for implementing inservice programs for those currently practicing in the field. Put simply, our ability to deliver high quality, challenging learning opportunities for all learners, including those who are gifted and talented, rests upon our ability to form and sustain productive educational partnerships. Accordingly, public school inservice programs need to address the roles of professionals in collaborative partnerships; the expectations held by partners entering collaborative alliances; the conditions (i.e., time to conduct systemwide, meaningful staff development, as well as time to practice and refine the related skills; access to professional journals and literature, the availability of supplementary materials, access to the Internet that facilitate the development of successful partnerships); and the expected outcomes of these partnerships.

CONCLUSION

In the early 1990s, Renzulli and Reis said, "What remains is for us as a field to take seriously the importance of collaboration with content specialists, school administrators, support personnel, and classroom teachers in new configurations that will allow the . . . needs of the gifted to be taken seriously" (J. S. Renzulli & S. M. Reis, personal communication, April 20, 1991). The research contained in this article highlights two facets of the collaborative process that we must understand and practice if we want to tap into the power and benefits of collaboration to provide high level, differentiated educational services for all of our students. First, collaboration is built upon the interaction and resulting relationships between and among people. Second, collaborators who seek to design high level services for young people enter the collaborative alliance with different, yet complementary, sets of expectations. These expectations need to be understood and, if necessary, bridges must be built in order to ensure the success of these potentially powerful alliances between classroom teachers and teachers of the gifted or enrichment specialists.

REFERENCES

Council for Exceptional Children. (1994). *Toward a common agenda: Linking gifted education and school reform.* Reston, VA: Council for Exceptional Children.

Debuse, M., & Shoemaker, B. J. E. (1993). The changing role of the TAG teacher: An Oregon case study. *Roeper Review, 16,* 58–61.

Dettmer, P. (1993). Gifted education: Window of opportunity. *Gifted Child Quarterly, 37,* 92–94.

Donaldson, G. A. (1993). Working smarter together. *Educational Leadership, 51*(2), 12–16.

Fox, R. J., Crask, M. R., & Kim, J. (1988). Mail survey response rate. A meta-analysis of selected techniques for inducing response. *Public Opinion Quarterly, 54*(4), 467–491.

Friend, M., & Cook, L. (1992). *Interactions: Collaborative skills for school professionals.* New York: Longman.

Fullan, M. G. (1992). Visions that blind. *Educational Leadership, 49*(5), 19–20.

Fullan, M. G. (1997). Emotion and hope: Constructive concepts for complex times. In A. Hargreaves (Ed.), *Rethinking educational change with heart and mind* (pp. 216–237). Alexandria, VA: Association for Supervision and Curriculum Development.

Hanninen, G. (1994). Blending gifted education and school reform. ERIC Digest #E525.

Holcomb, E. L. (1993). The rule for role change: Show, don't tell. *Educational Leadership, 51*(2), 17–18.

Lincoln, Y. S., & Guba, E. G. (1985). *Naturalistic inquiry.* London: Sage Publications.

Monson, M. P., & Monson, R. J. (1993). Who creates curriculum? New roles for teachers. *Educational Leadership, 51*(2), 119–121.

Purcell, J. H. (1995). Gifted education at a crossroads: The Program Status Study. *Gifted Child Quarterly, 39,* 57–65.

Renzulli, J. S. (1994). *Schools for talent development: A practical plan for total school improvement.* Mansfield Center, CT: Creative Learning Press.

Salend, S. J. (1994). *Effective mainstreaming: Creating inclusive classrooms.* Englewood Cliffs, NJ: Macmillan Publishing.

Schack, G. D. (1996). All aboard or standing on the shore? Gifted educators and the educational reform movement. *Roeper Review, 18*(3), 190–197.

Strauss, A. & Corbin, J. (1990). *Basics of qualitative research: Grounded theory procedures and techniques.* Newbury Park, CA: Sage Publications.

Tomlinson, C. A., Coleman, M. R., Allan, S., Udall, A., & Landrum, M. (1996). Interface between gifted education and general education: Toward communication, cooperation and collaboration. *Gifted Child Quarterly, 40,* 165–171.

Tomlinson, C. T., Tomchin, E. M., Callahan, C. M., Adams, C. M., Pizzat-Tinnin, P., Cunningham, C. M., Moore, B., Lutz, L., Roberson, C., Eiss, N., Landrum, M., Hunsaker, S., & Imbeau, M. (1994). Practices of preservice teachers related to gifted and other academically diverse learners. *Gifted Child Quarterly, 38,* 106–114.

Treffinger, D. (1991). School reform and gifted education: Opportunities and issues. *Gifted Child Quarterly, 35,* 6–11.

VanTassel-Baska, J. (1991). Gifted education in the balance: Building relationships with general education. *Gifted Child Quarterly, 35,* 20–25.

8

Changing General Education Classroom Practices to Adapt for Gifted Students

Susan K. Johnsen

Baylor University

Patricia A. Haensly

Western Washington University

Gail R. Ryser

Austin, Texas

Randal F. Ford

University of Texas—Arlington

Funded by the Jacob K. Javits Gifted and Talented Education Act, the Mustard Seed Project's major goal was to train teachers to differentiate curricula for gifted students in the general education classroom. This study addressed the changes in classroom practices and the factors that

Editor's Note: From Johnsen, S. K., Haensly, P. A., Ryser, G. R., & Ford, R. F. (2002). Changing general education classroom practices to adapt for gifted students. *Gifted Child Quarterly, 46*(1), 45-63. © 2002 National Association for Gifted Children. Reprinted with permission.

influenced these changes. Changes were measured using the Classroom Instructional Practices Scale (Johnsen, 1992). The sample included 1 urban and 5 rural sites, 8 principals, 74 teachers, 17 mentor teachers, and 18 community representatives. Throughout the two years of implementation, the majority of teachers at each site made changes. Changes in classroom practices and influencing factors were determined from interviews, field notes, formal and informal observations, and a final survey. Participants cited staff-development activities, leadership, mentoring, resources, and project support as extremely beneficial.

Meeting the needs of gifted and talented students in the general education classroom is a crucial concern for professionals and advocates of gifted education. With the growing emphasis on inclusion and the pressure to disband special programs for gifted students, it is imperative that general education teachers be trained to offer differentiated instruction (Reis, Gentry, & Maxfield, 1998; Westberg, Archambault, Dobyns, & Salvin, 1993).

Researchers have proposed ways that the classroom environment can be altered to adapt to gifted learners. Practices that address learner differences include acceleration (Brody & Benbow, 1987; Southern & Jones, 1991), curriculum compacting (Reis, Burns, & Renzulli, 1992), enrichment (Feldhusen & Kolloff, 1986; Renzulli & Reis, 1997), learning centers (Feldhusen, 1986; Lopez & MacKenzie, 1993); creative problem solving (Parnes, 1979; Treffinger, 1980); independent study (Doherty & Evans, 1981; Johnsen & Johnson, 1986; Treffinger, 1980); inter-disciplinary curricula (Kaplan, 1986; VanTassel-Baska, 1985; Ward, 1980); problem-based curricula (Gallagher, Stepien, & Rosenthal, 1992; VanTassel-Baska, 1994), and instructional style preferences (Renzulli & Reis, 1997).

Putting the Research to Use

To learn about the latest innovations, schools are frequently involved in professional development activities—providing workshops, traveling to conferences, attending seminars, and registering for university courses. Administrators and supervisors hope that these opportunities will lead to the implementation of effective practices in the classroom. Unfortunately, because innovative changes involve a complex set of factors that must work together, single professional development events seldom produce the desired effects. This article describes how one project's activities were able to change almost 100% of the 74 teachers' classroom practices over a two-year period.

Given these results, educators will want to consider incorporating these components into their professional development activities. First, it is important to involve all of the stakeholders who will be affected by the change—teachers, counselors, the community, and administrators (particularly the principal). Second, the professional development must simulate the desired practices so that the participants will identify with the innovation and be stimulated to make changes. Third, the practices need to be clearly defined so that the teacher will be able to make a transfer of new practices to the classroom. In this project, the Classroom Instructional Practices Scale (Johnsen, 1992) provided specific information about the desired practice and a developmental hierarchy for noting progress. Fourth, the teachers should have a voice in the type and the degree of change that they will incorporate into their classrooms. This freedom to choose goals empowers teachers and builds a positive attitude toward the change. Fifth, teachers need ongoing and consistent material and human support to make the changes. Types of support include staff-development days, peer and mentor support, leadership support, materials, and time to implement. When these components are present, possibilities for change are enhanced.

However, practical experience tells us that changing the general education classroom is not an easy task. It is a complex, slow process that needs to be supported from many directions and involves many factors (Fullan, 1993). These factors include strong leadership, quality professional development, follow-up support, and collaboration among teachers, administrators, and the community (Connor & Lake, 1994; Sarason, 1995; Sergiovanni, 1995). Because change is highly personal, the majority of the support needs to be directed toward the teacher who is the primary initiator of any change in the classroom (Petrie, 1990; Sarason, 1995).

The relative isolation of classrooms requires careful attention to the development of networks that encompass the immediate setting, as well as extend to other settings of practitioners. Technology and mentoring can serve in that linking process by providing information about curriculum and classroom instruction or modeling strategies that need to be implemented (Sullivan, 1992). To successfully implement any innovation, teachers also need time and material resources. It is well known that most teachers invest considerable personal resources to carry out the ideas they want to implement in their classrooms; at some point, this resource pool becomes depleted. In summary, factors that appear to facilitate change include strong leadership, professional development, follow-up support, collaboration, mentoring, resources, and time to implement.

When changes do occur, they frequently are conservational, requiring just a few classroom modifications. For example, adding a library corner in the classroom does not require the teacher to provide flexible grouping arrangements. Changes that require numerous, significant alterations in the classroom—transformational changes—are particularly difficult to achieve. In these cases, a change in one part of the system often demands changes in other parts. For example, providing above-grade-level materials to advanced learners requires new grouping arrangements, different textbook orders, scope and sequence alterations at all grade levels, and revised assessment procedures. These kinds of transformational changes that are more complex create a new set of demands on the researcher and the participants. "The challenge for researchers is to define implementation variables clearly so that they might be observed and measured [over time]" (Ryser & Johnsen, 1996, p. 489). In this way, the researcher and those involved will know what changes to make, when they are getting more of the desired results, and how long to continue in the same direction. However, few studies actually *observe the degree* of change in the classroom. How does innovation look in its beginning and later stages? Is there a sequence to implementation? Does one change step relate to others, or is there a constellation of factors that must be in place for the differentiation to occur? Since transformational changes take time and may not be implemented in the second or even third or fourth year of the study, the researcher must describe the characteristics of the new practice and the steps that show movement toward the change. Only then can the observer systematically collect data at each step to determine the level of implementation and its relationship to the desired outcome.

Funded by the Jacob K. Javits Gifted and Talented Education Act, the Mustard Seed Project's major goal was to train teachers to differentiate curricula for gifted students in the general education classroom. Using the literature of recommended practices, the principal investigators attempted to define clearly the desired changes, observe and measure the changes over time, and use a model that incorporated the factors that influence change. This study is part of the Mustard Seed Project that describes factors influencing classroom changes. More specifically, two questions are addressed in this study:

1. What changes did teachers make in their classroom practices?
2. What factors influenced these changes?

METHOD

Sample

Site and administrators. A project advisory committee was formed to establish criteria for selecting project sites. This committee included consultants from two regional educational service centers, administrators from urban and rural school districts, and the project staff. Based on the literature and Javits grant requirements, the following criteria were developed:

1. 40–50% of the students were economically disadvantaged, the site was rurally isolated, or both;

2. the project and school objectives were similar;

3. strong instructional leadership was present;

4. a majority of the faculty was interested in the changes proposed by the project;

5. a teacher who might serve as a mentor was available;

6. the site-based team included community representation;

7. no schoolwide behavior management problems were evident; and

8. a nonmobile student population provided opportunities for longitudinal study.

The project director presented a standardized overview to 13 potential sites. The overview included a summary of the project objectives, timelines, available human and technological support systems for project teachers, and benefits to individuals and schools involved in the project. Using the eight criteria above, the project staff and the regional educational service center consultants collaborated on the final selection of the eight campus buildings that were located in six sites—one urban and five rural school districts. In some cases, these school districts were distributed more than 300 miles apart from one another (see Table 1 for site demographics). Only one school, R2, had a pull-out program for gifted and talented students. The rest of the schools served the gifted and talented children within the general education classroom.

Mentors. After the selection was made, each of the eight building principals attended a meeting with the project staff to identify criteria and a process for selecting the first-year mentor and cohort teachers who would receive training. Mentor teachers were to collaborate with the cohort teachers on their campus and provide follow-up support for individual teacher goals developed during the training. After reviewing the literature, the project staff proposed this list of mentor characteristics to the principals: (a) a people orientation; (b) good communication skills; (c) good listening skills; (d) committed to the project ideas; (e) interested in helping cohort teachers; (f) respect for other teachers' ideas; (g) tolerant of ambiguity; (h) confident and flexible; (i) good sense of humor; and (j) a love of learning. The principals then determined the selection process. During the project orientation, all of the schools asked the teachers to respond to this statement: "List three teachers you would go to in this school to ask for help in adapting for differences among students in your classroom." Teacher responses to this statement and the above criteria were used to select the mentor. At four sites, the principal selected the mentor. At R2 and R5, the participating teachers elected the mentor teacher. There were 7 mentor teachers selected for the first

Table 1   Site Demographics

	Number			% Free/ Reduced Lunch	% Minority
Site	Schools	Teachers	Student		
U1	1 (PK–5)	27	516	50	31
R1	2 (PK–2; 3–5)	100	1730	60	51
R2	2 (K–5; 6–8)	80	880	45	51
R3	2 (PK–2; 3–6)	43	682	68	54
R4	1 (K–6)	22	271	46	21
R5	1 (PK–5)	35	411	44	22

Table 2   Mentor Teacher Demographics

	Gender		Current Grade Assignment		Years of Teaching Experience		Years of G/T Experience	
Site	Y1	Y2	Y1	Y2	Y1	Y2	Y1	Y2
U1	F	M	K	K	15	5	0	0
R1	F	F, F	3	K, 5	4	8,12	0	0,0
R2	F	F, F, F	GT	K, 2, 3	15	5, 10, 7	4	0,0,0
R3 (P)	F	F	1	2	7	5	0	0
	M	F	5	3	23	5	0	0
R4	F	F	4	4	22	23	0	0
R5	F	F	1	1	15	8	0	0

Note. Y1 = year 1; Y2 = year 2; P = Primary grades K–2; E = Elementary grades 3–6.

year of implementation and 10 selected for the second year. R3 selected a mentor for each of its two campuses the first year. While the mentors had an average of 11 years of teaching experience, only one reported any experience working with gifted and talented students (see Table 2 for Year 1 and Year 2 mentor teacher demographics).

Cohorts. In selecting the two groups of cohorts, administrators and the project staff focused on teachers who would be willing to adapt to a wider range of student differences and who possessed many of the mentor characteristics. Administrators, mentor teachers, faculty, and the project staff collaborated on the selection of two cohort teams of five to seven teachers at each site for the two years (see Table 3 for cohort teacher demographics). Similar to the mentors, only two of the cohort teachers reported having any experience working with gifted and talented students.

Table 3   Cohort Teacher Demographics

				Experience			
Site	Teachers	M	F	0–5 yrs.	6–15 yrs.	16+ yrs.	G/T Exp. Tchr/yrs.
UI	10	1	9	2	2	6	0
R1 (P)	5	0	5	1	2	2	0
(E)	5	0	5	1	1	3	1/2
R2	14	0	14	4	10	0	1/3
R3 (P)	6	0	6	3	2	1	0
(E)	7	0	7	6	1	0	0
R4	8	0	8	1	2	5	0
R5	12	0	12	4	4	4	0
Total	67*	1	66	22	23	21	. 2/5

Note. P = Primary grades K–2; E = Elementary grades 3–6; M = Males; F = Females; *Year 1 Cohort mentor teachers omitted from these demographics.

The total number of cohort teachers who participated in the training was 71. Ten of these cohort teachers became mentor teachers during the second year of training. Altogether, 78 mentor and cohort teachers participated in the training. Four of these teachers left school before the second observation and were excluded from this study, leaving a sample of 74.

Community representatives. During the first year, the principal at each site selected two community representatives for a total of 12. The following year, four of the sites sent two additional representatives. All of the community representatives were members of the site-based management team and volunteered at the school. There were 17 females and 1 male. All except one from R4 had a child or children in the site schools. These community members were to act as liaisons with the rest of the community and support the teachers in making changes.

Instrumentation

Qualitative and quantitative data were collected throughout the three stages of the project: pretraining, training, and posttraining.

Qualitative. The project director and the six research assistants gathered qualitative data through field notes, systematic and narrative observations, informal and open-ended structured interviews, and the final survey evaluation. Research assistants wrote field notes for each contact, whether by phone or on site, in a narrative form. These notes were transferred to a contact summary form that synthesized the main issues, themes, questions, and future contacts. Project personnel made approximately 400 on-site contacts. During each site visit and observation, the research assistant systematically addressed the following questions:

1. How do teachers make changes during an innovation?

2. How are teachers adapting for learner differences differently since the training and follow-up support?

3. How does the administrative organization support/not support teachers in making changes to adapt for learner differences?

4. How does the mentor teacher support/not support teachers in making changes to adapt for learner differences?

5. How does the community support/not support teachers in making changes to adapt for learner differences?

6. How did the training support/not support the teachers in making changes to adapt for learner differences?

7. How is the follow-up phase of the project supporting/not supporting the teachers in making changes to adapt for learner differences?

8. What evidence is there that teachers are meeting their goals to adapt for learner differences?

9. How are the various personnel within the school responding to the innovation?

10. What evidence is there that peer coaching or mentoring is occurring?

Research assistants conducted open-ended, standardized interviews with administrators, community representatives, mentor teachers, and cohort teachers at each site prior to and after training. Because the project used multiple research assistants, standardized interviews included the same questions in the same sequence for all participants. Pretraining interview questions addressed knowledge and feelings about the grant and its objectives, grant benefits, the school decision-making process, concerns, the degree of adaptation for differences, the degree of collaboration, and the degree of support. Posttraining interview questions addressed training expectations, training effectiveness, and needs for follow-up support. During baseline observations, research assistants also conducted interviews with students in cohort and mentor teacher classrooms to gain insight into their daily classroom practices. The project director also visited each of the sites a minimum of once a month, observing classrooms and making field notes, and the mentor teachers kept logs of contacts with cohort teachers.

Quantitative. The project staff collected systematic observations and rated the teachers' classroom practices using the Classroom Instructional Practices Scale

(CIPS; Johnsen, 1992). This checklist was designed to measure how teachers organize their classrooms in adapting for learner differences in content, rate, preference, and environment. The description of each area is hierarchical, beginning with the least adaptive classroom practice for individual differences and progressing to the most adaptive classroom practice (see Table 4). The descriptors and hierarchy of steps were developed after observing approximately 200 teachers who were involved in changing their classroom practices to adapt for gifted learners.

Content consists of seven descriptors (C1 through C7) that describe the way the teacher organizes and sequences skills, concepts, strategies, and generalizations within and across disciplines. For example, the lowest rating, C1, describes a content that is organized around the book's scope and sequence, while C7 describes content organized around individual student interest. Rate consists of nine descriptors (R1 through R9) that describe how the teacher uses assessment to vary the amount of time needed by students in learning new content. Again, a teacher who receives an R1 rating provides the same amount of time for every student in the classroom, while a teacher receiving an R9 uses a pre-assessment to identify students who may need or may choose in-depth study, enrichment, or acceleration. Environment consists of six descriptors (E1 through E6) that describe the way the teacher arranges the physical environment to facilitate interaction and learning among students. The lowest rating, [E1] describes a classroom in which the teacher limits interaction between students and with learning materials, whereas an E6 rating describes a classroom where students learn from one another and use the community and the school as learning centers. Preference consists of five descriptors that define how the teacher aligns activities with the content and provides for individual student choice. At the lowest rating, the student has no choice of learning materials and uses materials that have a similar format such as paper-pencil; at P5, the student may select or create learning activities. At the highest level these activities also vary the task (i.e., visual, auditory, kinesthetic) and the response (i.e., written, oral, physical). For example, a teacher who would attain the highest rating in each category would be able to organize a classroom so that one gifted student could be learning content of interest to him or her (C7); pursuing that content through an independent study, with time bought from pretesting of core curriculum (R9); and choosing activities that relate to the area of interest (P5), which might include mentors or resources outside of the school (E6).

Teachers and two students in each classroom were probed to gather additional information for verification of the observations. Reliability was established among research assistants through training sessions that produced an interrater reliability of .92 (Ryser & Johnsen, 1996). To accurately assess teachers' classroom practices, each teacher was observed a minimum of three times during baseline. Research assistants observed each teacher who participated during the first year of the project in the classroom three times: the spring before training, the first spring after training, and the second spring

Table 4   Classroom Instructional Practices Scale

Research Assistant _____

Teacher _____   Grade _____

School _____   Date/Time Observed _____

Discipline/Subject _____

Content

__C1 book or curriculum guide organizes content

__C2 includes creative and critical thinking skills

__C3 integration of multiple disciplines; single discipline-based topics; not authentic methods

__C4 interdisciplinary; broad-based themes; authentic methods

__C5 specified attributes of generalizations, concepts

__C6 student performance determines sequence

__C7 student interest guides content

Environment

__E1 arrangement with limited student interaction; no interest or learning centers present

__E2 arrangement with limited student interaction; interest or learning center present

__E3 arrangement with student interaction

__E4 arrangement with student interaction; interest centers present

__E5 arrangement with student interactions; learning centers present

__E6 use of school and/or community as learning centers

Rate

__R1 have same/varied amount of time for tasks; early finishers do no task

__R2 have same/varied amount of time for tasks; early finishers do an unrelated task

__R3 have same/varied time for completion of tasks; early finishers do a related task

Preference

__P1 no variation in tasks and/or response dimensions; not correlated

__P2 variation in tasks and/or response dimensions; not correlated

__P3 no variation in tasks and/or response dimensions; correlated

Rate With Assessment

__R4 postassessment at set times with no recycling

__R5 postassessment at varied times with no recycling

__R6 postassessment at set times with recycling and/or in-depth study/enrichment/acceleration

__R7 postassessment at varied times with recycling and/or in-depth study/enrichment/acceleration

__R8 pre/postassessment at set times with recycling and/or in-depth study/enrichment/acceleration

__R9 pre/postassessment at varied times with recycling and/or in-depth study/enrichment/acceleration

__P4 variation in tasks and/or response dimensions; correlated

__P5 student choice of varied tasks and/or response dimensions

Additional observations in terms of adapting for differences:

after training during the follow-up and support phase of the project. Research assistants also observed cohort and mentor teachers who participated in the second year of the project twice: the fall before training and the first spring after training. In addition, research assistants were in the schools on a weekly basis, observing and recording impressions. The project director also visited each site monthly, verifying the observations that were made by the research assistants.

At the end of the third year, each teacher was sent a final survey to assess the value of a variety of staff development and support activities during the length of the project. The participants rated these 14 project components on a Likert scale from "not at all beneficial" (1) to "extremely beneficial" (5): curriculum units, research assistants, computer, staff-development days, summer training, spring celebration, site visits to your campus, site visits to other campuses, mentor teachers, community representatives, campus administrator, communications, the Keeping in Touch (KIT) packet, and money for materials.

Procedures

Each school was assigned a research assistant from the project who was responsible for collecting data and providing follow-up support. These six research assistants were all graduate students, former teachers, or both. They were selected based upon educational experience in working with gifted and accelerated programs, experience designing curricula, and a willingness to support the project goals. Project information was presented in three stages: pretraining, training, and follow-up.

Pretraining. After the schools and participants were selected, the research assistants interviewed administrators, community representatives, mentor teachers, and students who were in mentor and cohort teachers' classes. They also collected baseline data by observing in each participating teacher's classroom using the CIPS (Johnsen, 1992; see Table 4). From this information and from an extensive review of the literature, the project staff designed a set of training curricula that included 22 units that covered these general topics: learner differences, differentiated curriculum, assessment, managing the learning environment, learning strategies, teacher facilitation, acceleration, mentoring, peer coaching, collaboration, support, and change. Each of the units provided information in different formats: teacher-directed instruction, games, self-paced instruction, showcase, reading, audio-visual, role-play, and problem solving. To learn the selected unit objectives, teachers were able to use the format that best suited their preference or learning style during the training.

Training. Administrators, community representatives, and mentor teachers participated in a three-day training session during the spring of the first and second years of the grant. They focused primarily on the units that examined learner differences, particularly characteristics of gifted and talented students and follow-up methods for assisting teachers. At the end of this training session, all of the participants identified goals that would support teachers during the change process. Mentor teachers also identified changes that they wanted to make in their own classroom practices.

During the summers, the mentor teachers returned to assist and support the cohort teachers in a training session that lasted for 10 days. On the first day, the mentor teachers met with the project staff to identify ways of enhancing the training for each teacher from their schools. The cohort teachers arrived on the second day, and, by the end of the first week, each teacher set short-term goals for the next week. During the second week, the mentor and cohort teachers returned to their classrooms to begin implementing some of their initial goals and then came back to the training site to report on their progress and set long-term goals for the next school year. During the final goal-setting time, the project research assistant and school mentor were present to identify ways that they might support the cohort teacher in making changes. All of the goals related to changes in content, rate, preference, and environment classroom practices (see Table 4). For example, a teacher might decide to organize content in problem-based units (C4), to use assessment to identify and organize activities that match student needs (R6), arrange the needed materials in classroom learning centers (E5), and allow the student to select or develop related activities based on interest (P5).

Both training sessions were individualized so that administrators, teachers, and community representatives could select units that *matched their personal goals for change*. For example, if a teacher were interested in developing performance-based assessment procedures, he or she would use the learning activities that related to Unit 3. On the other hand, if a teacher were interested in developing an accelerated curriculum, he or she would use the learning activities that related to Unit 6.

During the training, six variables were modified to simulate and model lesser to more adaptive classroom practices. These variables included the instructor's use of time and assessments, the organization of groups and materials, and the provision for student and teacher choices (i.e., management systems). As these variables changed, participants made personal reflections regarding their engagement in the class activities and their feelings about each management or classroom organization system. This simulated process enabled them to experience first-hand the effects that various classroom practices have on the learner.

Posttraining. During the fall following the summer training, the research assistants interviewed the participants regarding training expectations, training effectiveness, and needs for follow-up support. Throughout the school year, the research assistants maintained a contact summary form to record information from weekly site visits and to target concerns. During the spring of the next year, research assistants observed teacher classrooms using the CIPS to identify changes in classroom practices. The research assistants followed up each of their observations with interviews of teachers and three of their students to verify their observations and ratings. The project director also visited each of the sites a minimum of once a month throughout the two years, observing in classrooms, and keeping a log of these visits. Mentor teachers also kept logs of contacts with cohort teachers to record progress. All of these data were used in determining the number of changes that were made by each of the cohort and mentor teachers.

Follow-up of teachers was provided in the forms of human and material support. In terms of human support, the majority of research assistants visited the sites weekly. Along with the mentor teachers, they provided in-class support to the teachers, collected materials to assist in the change process, and arranged intersite visits and planning days. In terms of material support, the project purchased a computer with a modem and fax for each of the mentors' classrooms, enabling the sites to be electronically linked. Teachers communicated with teachers at other sites and exchanged successful curriculum ideas. The project also provided a KIT of materials for each mentor that included resources from the training, such as curriculum units, books, and a summary of each of the professional development units. Project teachers received $100 for purchasing classroom materials that might help them in reaching their goals. The project reimbursed substitute pay for six days of staff development for the team of mentor and cohort teachers. The mentor teacher and research assistant provided the leadership for the use of these days. The staff development days were spent visiting other project sites, designing materials at the regional service centers, specialized training sessions, or attending state gifted and talented association meetings.

Meetings were also scheduled for project participants who were in similar roles. Mentor teachers met twice to exchange ideas and collaborate on solving problems. They also presented at the project advisory board meeting and at the state association for the gifted and talented. They developed curricula for the second-year mentor training and provided small-group sessions at that training. The administrators met at a working luncheon to exchange ideas about support for the teachers. They targeted scheduling, staff development, budgeting, selecting instructional materials, and sharing project success stories. Community representatives met twice to construct games and to brainstorm ways for creating a positive support system for the teachers. They discussed methods for establishing a materials workroom. They shared ideas for assisting the teachers and compiled a booklet for site information.

During the second and third years, the project organized a weekend "Spring Celebration" for all project participants at a central location. The agenda included small-group presentations about the positive changes made in the classrooms, ways to facilitate more changes, and the sharing of successful strategies for meeting the needs of individual learners within each of the groups.

Data Analysis

To determine changes in classroom practices, field notes, observations, interviews, and the CIPS were analyzed. Because the CIPS is an ordinal scale, a one-tailed Wilcoxon matched-pairs signed rank test was used to analyze the ratings to determine if teachers made changes in their classroom practices. The Wilcoxon is a nonparametric statistical test for ordinal-scaled variables and is used with matched or correlated samples. In this study, we had a matched sample. We compared ratings from the spring before training to the spring after training for all teachers who participated in the project in the four areas identified on the CIPS: content, rate, preference, and environment (i.e., Year I Cohort and Year 2 Cohort). We also compared CIPS ratings from the first spring after training to the second spring after training for teachers who participated during the first year of the project (i.e., Year 1 Cohort). In our study, we subtracted the first rating (e.g., baseline or pre-training) from the second rating (e.g., post-training). The absolute values of the differences were rank ordered, and the ranks were summed for positive and negative differences. The smaller sum of ranks is the observed Wilcoxon value. This sum is compared with the critical value to determine statistical significance. We hypothesized that teachers who received a higher rating were adapting more for individual differences in content, rate, preference, environment, or some combination. Therefore, we expected to have more positive than negative differences.

To determine factors that influenced changes, field notes, observations, and interviews were analyzed across all six sites. Data obtained from the qualitative instruments were entered in a software package called HyperQual® that assisted in finding trends and patterns among sites. The researcher then used the constant comparative method (Glasser & Strauss, 1967) to begin to think of categories in relation to other categories. This process provided a means for continuous refinement as initial categories were changed, merged, or omitted and new categories were generated (Maykut & Morehouse, 1994). Second, all observations were analyzed and discussed by the project staff and an external project evaluator at monthly project meetings throughout the two years of implementation. Those factors that reached 90% agreement among the project staff and were verified by mentors and administrators were considered influential. The final survey results were also summarized descriptively using percentages and triangulated with the project staff, administrator, and mentor perceptions.

RESULTS

What Changes Did Teachers Make in Their Classroom Practices?

Changes in classroom practices were measured by the CIPS, an observation instrument; interview probes with teachers and students in their classrooms; and field notes. Prior to training, 45% of the teachers in both cohorts used the book to organize their curriculum (C1; see Table 5). In the first cohort, 34% of the teachers used topics such as "dinosaurs" to organize units, but did not use methods that were authentic to the discipline, such as problem solving and the scientific method (C3). Students were given the same amount of time to learn the content in 72% of the teachers' classrooms (R1 and R2); however, 61% allowed the early finishers to do extra work that was not related to the lesson, such as reading their library books (R2). A variety of physical arrangements were found in the two cohort teachers' classrooms, with 27% allowing interaction among students (E2) and 23% having interest centers, independent areas that students could use when they finished their "work" (E4). Surprisingly, 18% of the teachers organized their desks in rows and columns and allowed extremely limited interaction among students. In the preference area, 58% of the teachers in both cohorts used independent tasks that were similar in format (P1 and P3; i.e., primarily paper-pencil), yet only 22% of these related to the lesson objective (P3). Overall, the classrooms could be described as teacher controlled. Students had limited opportunities to move beyond the book, to choose enrichment or independent activities, or to accelerate in the standardized curriculum.

During the two years of implementation, 73 of the 74 teachers made 249 changes and moved a total of 641 steps higher as measured by formal classroom observations on the CIPS, interviews with teachers and students following each of the formal observations, and research assistant and director notes that were gathered on a bimonthly basis (see Table 6). Almost half of the teachers (49%) decided to make changes in the language arts area, 22% in math, 16% in interdisciplinary units, 6% in social studies, and 4% in science. In organizing their curriculum, 16% continued using only the book (C1), but 34% of the teachers began using integrated units (C3), 27% began using more concept-based units with authentic methods (C4 and C5), and 7% allowed students to pursue their interests (C7; see Table 5). By the second year of implementation, 43% of Cohort 1 teachers were using concept-based units (C4 and C5) and 20% of the teachers organized content around student interest (C7). With the exception of one teacher who selected math, all of these teachers had chosen to make their content changes in the language arts or interdisciplinary areas. In rate, 48% of the teachers began using assessments to accelerate, enrich, provide opportunities for in-depth studies (R6–R9). In addition, 27% of the teachers provided related activities for students who finished early (R3). After training, no teachers asked students to simply wait or "put their heads on their desk" while others finished (R1). By the end of the second year, 57% of the teachers in the Year 1 Cohort were using assessments to recycle, compact the curriculum, provide enrichment, or allow students to pursue topics of interest to them. Seventy-seven percent of teachers who chose to change their math classroom practices also chose to accelerate instruction (R6–R8). In preference, 71% of the teachers began offering a variety of learning activities that varied format and responses, as opposed to only 13% before the training (P4 and P5). In 20% of the teachers' classrooms, students were even able to choose what activities they wanted to use (P5). By the end of the second year, 77% of the teachers in the Year 1 Cohort were varying the types of activities that students could use (P5 and P6). These changes in preference, of course, influenced changes in the classroom environment. The majority of teachers (67%) established independent areas or learning centers (E5 and E6), centers that were not viewed as "something to go to when students are finished with their work," but an integral part of the learning environment. By the second year of implementation, 86% of students in the Year 1 Cohort were using learning centers within and/or outside the classroom.

While almost all of the project teachers made some changes, not all made a change that "transformed" the way they adapted for individual differences. Connor and Lake (1994) have described these kinds of transformational changes as those that cause numerous, significant alterations in the classroom. For example, pretesting students and using the results (R8 and R9) is a transformational change for most teachers. In these cases, teachers must be able to organize flexible groups, plan a variety of activities, monitor progress on independent studies, and/or accelerate students into advanced-grade-level books or materials. On the other hand, changes that require few alterations are described as conservational. These changes tend to support what the teacher is already doing. For example, teachers may teach a newly adopted textbook series in the same way that they used the "old" series. Of the 74 teachers who made changes, surprisingly 66 made a transformational change in one or more areas (i.e., content steps 4–7, rate steps 6–9, preference steps 4 and 5, and environment steps 5 and 6; see Tables 5 and 6). The percentage of transformational changes by Year 1 Cohort teachers actually rose from the first to the second year at sites U1, R1, R2, and R3 (see Table 6). This increase may be partly due to the number of steps that need to be changed before a classroom transformation occurred. For example, one of the teachers changed her environment by adding independent learning areas (E5) and a variety of materials (P4) during the first year of implementation before actually using assessment results to plan multiple activities during the second year (R7). The vast majority of the transformational changes at most sites occurred in the preference and environment areas (see Table 7). With a few exceptions, the areas of rate (e.g., varying the time that a student has to learn new concepts or study them in depth) and content (e.g., changing to concept-based units with authentic methods), appeared to be the most difficult to change. In fact, at Rural Site 4, all teachers continued using their textbooks in organizing the curriculum (see Table 7). In some cases, leadership and strong support became an important factor in sustaining and increasing changes. For example, the principal retired and the superintendent was removed at R4, which directly and personally impacted the Year 1 Cohort teachers who made no transformational changes during the second year (see Table 6).

Because the CIPS is hierarchical, a one-tailed Wilcoxon matched-pairs signed rank test was used to determine statistical significance; alpha was set at 0.05. Results of the Wilcoxon T tests revealed that both teacher cohorts made statistically significant changes in their classroom practices in all four areas from before training to after training (see Tables 8 and 9). As these tables illustrate, the number of positive differences, indicating that the teacher was adapting

Table 5 Classroom Practices From Baseline to Postobservation 1 and Postobservation 2 by CIPS Area and Step

| CIPS Area | Cohort 1 (n=41) | | | Cohort 2 (n=33) | | Total %* | | |
	Baseline	Post O1	Post O2	Baseline	Post O1	B (N = 74)	P1 (N = 74)	P2 (n =35)**
Content								
1	13	9	5	20	3	33 (45%)	12 (16%)	5 (14%)
2	7	4	4	5	6	12 (16%)	10 (14%)	4 (11%)
3	14	10	3	6	15	20 (27%)	25 (34%)	3 (9%)
4	5	5	5	1	4	6 (8%)	9 (12%)	5 (14%)
5	2	6	10	0	5	2 (3%)	11 (15%)	10 (29%)
6	0	2	1	1	0	1 (1%)	2 (3%)	1 (3%)
7	0	5	7	0	0	0	5 (7%)	7 (20%)
Rate								
1	2	0	0	6	0	8 (11%)	0	0
2	32	12	5	13	2	45 (61%)	14 (19%)	5 (14%)
3	4	10	6	1	10	5 (7%)	20 (27%)	6 (17%)
4	3	1	4	7	3	10 (14%)	4 (5%)	4 (11%)
5	0	1	0	1	0	1 (1%)	1 (1%)	0
6	0	6	4	3	9	3 (4%)	15 (21%)	4 (11%)
7	0	6	9	0	3	0	9 (12%)	9 (26%)
8	0	1	5	1	5	1 (1%)	6 (8%)	5 (14%)
9	0	4	2	1	1	1 (1%)	5 (7%)	2 (6%)
Preference								
1	12	3	2	15	3	27 (36%)	6 (8%)	2 (6%)
2	6	1	1	8	3	14 (19%)	4 (5%)	1 (3%)
3	12	7	5	4	4	16 (22%)	11 (15%)	5 (14%)
4	10	20	14	6	18	16 (22%)	38 (51%)	14 (40%)
5	1	10	13	0	5	1 (1%)	15 (20%)	13 (37%)
Environment								
1	3	1	0	10	0	13 (18%)	1 (1%)	0
2	13	1	1	7	2	20 (27%)	3 (4%)	1 (3%)
3	5	3	1	6	4	11 (15%)	7 (9%)	1 (3%)
4	10	6	3	7	8	17 (23%)	14 (19%)	3 (9%)
5	8	20	16	1	12	9 (12%)	32 (44%)	16 (46%)
6	2	10	14	2	7	4 (5%)	17 (23%)	14 (40%)

Note. O1 = Observation 1; O2 = Observation 2; May not equal 100% because of rounding to the nearest whole percent; **Includes Year 1 Cohort only; 6 teachers left (see Table 6).

more for individual differences after training, was greater than the negative differences or ties. In addition, the results of the Wilcoxon T for ratings obtained one year after training and two years after training are found in Table 10. This

Table 6   Positive Changes Recorded on the CIPS by School Site

	U1	R1	R2	R3	R4	R5
Year 1 Cohort (n = 41)						
First Year						
Teachers Who Changed	6	6	7	8	4	6
No. of Changes (Steps)	16 (37)*	17 (39)	19 (45)	25 (75)	7 (26)	15 (41)
% Transformational	11 (69%)	12 (71%)	8 (42%)	21 (84%)	6 (85%)	14 (93%)
Second Year						
Teachers Who Changed	5**	6	3***	9	3	4****
No. of Changes (Steps)	10 (22)	11 (24)	5 (9)	19 (60)	4 (5)	8 (13)
% Transformational	10 (100%)	10 (91%)	4 (80%)	19 (100%)	0	7 (88%)
Year 2 Cohort (n = 33)						
First Year						
Teachers Who Changed	5	4	8	6	4	6
No. of Changes (Steps)	14 (34)	13 (38)	20 (50)	21 (73)	12 (27)	13 (23)
% Transformational	10 (71%)	11 (85%)	10 (50%)	19 (90%)	5 (42%)	7 (54%)
Total						
Number of Teachers	11	11	15	15	9	13
Teachers Who Changed	11 (100%)	11 (100%)	15 (100%)	15 (100%)	8 (89%)	13 (100%)
Teachers With Transformational Change	10 (91%)	11 (100%)	13 (87%)	15 (100%)	6 (67%)	11 (85%)
Teachers With No Change	0	0	0	0	1	0
No. of Changes (Steps)	40 (93)	41 (101)	44 (104)	65 (208)	23 (58)	36 (77)

Note. *Number of change made on the CIPS. For example, movement from R1 to R4 is one change, but three steps; **One teacher left for a bonus incentive to teach in another school in the district; ***Four teachers left: One left for maternity leave; one moved to a smaller district; one returned to graduate school; one became a research assistant For the Mustard Seed Project; ****One teacher moved with her husband.

table illustrates that teachers continued to make statistically significant changes in the area of rate during the third year of the project. None of the other three areas—content, preference, and environment—were statistically significant. As mentioned before, teachers tended to alter preference and environment first, leaving less room for change in these areas. In addition, it may be that a teacher needs to gather materials and organize them for independent use before assessing students' needs and forming multiple groups.

What Factors Influenced These Changes?

Field notes, interviews, observations, and the final survey were analyzed to determine the factors that influenced changes in classroom practices. The patterns that emerged were categorized, providing insight into the complexity of the change process.

Positive attitudes. Because the schools, including principals and teachers, were able to choose whether or not to become a part of the project, the participants

Table 7   Conservational (C) and Transformational (T) Classroom Practices From Baseline to Postobservation 1 and Postobservation 2 by CIPS Area and School Site

Site Area	Cohort 1				Cohort 2		Total %*	
	Post 1		Post 2		Post 1			
	C	T	C	T	C	T	C	T
Urban 1 (n = 11)**								
Content	2	4	1	4	4	1	7 (44%)	9 (56%)
Rate	3	2	1	4	3	3	7 (44%)	9 (56%)
Preference	2	4	0	5	1	4	3 (19%)	13 (81%)
Environment	1	5	0	5	3	2	4 (25%)	12 (75%)
Rural 1 (n = 11)								
Content	5	2	1	6	1	3	7 (39%)	11 (61%)
Rate	6	1	7	0	0	4	13 (72%)	5 (28%)
Preference	2	5	1	6	2	2	5 (28%)	13 (72%)
Environment	2	5	0	7	2	2	4 (22%)	14 (78%)
Rural 2 (n = 15)***								
Content	6	1	2	1	8	0	16 (89%)	2 (11%)
Rate	4	3	2	1	6	2	12 (67%)	6 (33%)
Preference	3	4	1	2	3	5	7 (39%)	11 (61%)
Environment	3	4	0	3	4	4	7 (39%)	11 (61%)
Rural 3 (n = 15)								
Content	3	6	1	8	1	5	5 (21%)	19 (79%)
Rate	8	1	0	9	1	5	9 (38%)	15 (63%)
Preference	1	8	1	8	1	5	3 (13%)	21 (88%)
Environment	1	8	0	9	1	5	2 (8%)	22 (92%)
Rural 4 (n = 9)								
Content	5	0	5	0	4	0	14 (100%)	0
Rate	2	3	5	0	3	1	10 (71%)	4 (29%)
Preference	3	2	5	0	2	2	10 (71%)	4 (29%)
Environment	3	2	4	1	2	2	9 (64%)	5 (36%)
Rural 5 (n = 13) ****								
Content	2	5	2	4	6	9	10 (53%)	9 (47%)
Rate	0	7	0	6	3	3	3 (16%)	16 (84%)
Preference	0	7	0	6	1	5	1 (5%)	18 (95%)
Environment	1	6	1	5	2	4	4 (22%)	15 (79%)

Note. *May not equal 100% because of rounding to the nearest whole percent; **One teacher left after first year. ***Four teachers left after first year; ****One teacher left after first year.

were, for the most part, positive and willing to give up two weeks of summer vacation time for training. The principals at U1, R2, R3, R4, and R5 all expressed "excitement" about being involved. For example, one principal said that she

Table 8   Changes for Year 1 Cohort From Baseline to First Posttraining Observation

| | Changes | | | | |
Area	Pos.	Neg.	None	Wilcoxon T	p
Content	18	6	14	43.0	.002
Rate	27	3	6	9.3	.000
Preference	26	3	9	42.0	.000
Environment	27	1	10	14.5	.000

Table 9   Changes for Year 2 Cohort From Baseline to First Posttraining Observation

| | Changes | | | | |
Area	Pos.	Neg.	None	Wilcoxon T	p
Content	20	4	8	32.0	.001
Rate	24	4	4	51.0	.000
Preference	22	0	10	0.0	.000
Environment	25	2	5	23.0	.000

Table 10   Changes for Year 1 Cohort From First to Second Posttraining Observation

| | Changes | | | | |
Area	Pos.	Neg.	None	Wilcoxon T	p
Content	15	8	11	86.5	.113
Rate	17	5	10	57.0	.023
Preference	11	7	16	65.0	.350
Environment	12	4	18	35.5	.073

was happy that "it would give the teachers help in adapting for learner differences" because she knew that "[the] gifted program was not what it needed to be." At R1, one of the principals was very positive, while the other was "negative," resulting in follow-up support from only one campus administrator. Unfortunately, this site was added after the mentor/principal spring training because one of the original schools dropped out due to superintendent changes. For this reason, these principals were not trained with their mentors, which appeared to be important in building a positive team at the school and establishing goals. For example, after training, one principal said, "[I gained] better insight into the classroom teachers and their mindset."

The vast majority of the teachers paralleled the principals' excitement. Before the training, the mentors said, "[I'm] excited—can't wait to find out more"; "I'm not certain about my role. But, I have confidence that whatever we gain will be of a positive nature." After the training, the teachers' attitudes were still positive, yet more focused: "I changed my attitude. I was very structured. I decided that regimentation may not be best for students"; "I realized that there are differences; I dropped the letter of the week [with my students]." For the most part, mentor and cohort teachers maintained their positive attitudes throughout the two years of the grant, although they acknowledged that some changes were difficult: "We've had some conflict, but things were settled in a professional manner and everyone is positive now."

The principal, mentor, and project's support tended to play an important role in sustaining positive attitudes toward the project. For example, one cohort teacher at R3 commented, "Our principal has been real supportive. He gets our class covered if we need to meet and tries to get materials we need." On the other hand, a mentor at another site where changes were more conservational remarked, "I strongly would like our school in this. I want you to sell the principals because I'm not sure they really are totally into it. I don't think they've seen the big picture. All the teachers are excited." At the same school, one research assistant observed, "The principal insists on everyone in the same grade being on the same spelling word, the same page in the phonics program." In such situations, sustaining positive attitudes toward change was indeed difficult.

A clear vision. The project provided a clear vision for all participants that was modeled in the training simulation and appeared to motivate teachers in setting and working toward their goals. One mentor summarized the effects of the summer training: "I think during the summer the teachers were motivated to make some changes because of the training they received. They felt very positive and upbeat, which was a new feeling for us. Also, I think during the summer the teachers received some real tools to help them make some changes. . . . It made them feel that they were capable of making changes." A cohort teacher described the effect of the vision provided by the training on her classroom organization: "The project has really allowed me to teach to individual needs, particularly gifted students, rather than teaching 'second grade.' It could not have come at a better time because the group I have had this year has cried out for differentiation. They have learned to become more independent of me and think for themselves more. I have learned different ways to group children with different abilities. . . . The units allowed flexibility and some structure at the same time." Another teacher talked about how the training affected her personally: "Well, it really reminded me of the choices that children need to make. I do that, but it really reminded me. After being in the classroom 11 years, we start being a dictator, rather than a facilitator." Finally, the training appeared to provide a framework for principals who began to have a picture of individual differences. One principal commented, "It gave [me] some insight on how different ways children learn and different ways children approach learning. It helped with [adapting] for differences in rate and speed with gifted kids."

Freedom to choose goals. All of the participants were allowed to identify and establish goals for the next year. This goal setting involved the project staff, the mentor, the cohort teachers, and, when possible, the principal and community representatives. Cohort and mentor teachers could decide the degree or amount (i.e., conservational or transformational), the quality and type (i.e., area on the CIPS), and the subject area of change (i.e., math, science, social studies, language arts). Participants focused on a variety of goals: organizing the room and materials, designing assessments for flexible pacing, compacting the curriculum and using contracts, developing concept-based units, incorporating problem solving, providing for extensions and independent studies. Some of the mentor teacher's goals were personal and included such statements as "I need to model good listening, to make sure I am not judgmental, and to remember to praise the smallest improvement." Other goals were collaborative: "We need to work together as a team to show the others this can work." Overall, the teachers felt that they had a choice in deciding how they wanted to change. As one mentor commented about one of the training effects, "An assurance that the teachers I will be working with have the freedom to choose how they want to conduct their classroom and the project will support and help make whatever kind of classroom they want." Because of this freedom, teachers who set their own goals made progress. At one site, the cohort teacher commented, "To be perfectly honest, I'm not only meeting them, I'm exceeding them!"

Staff-development activities. Teachers were asked to rate various project activities on a final survey with 1 indicating "not at all beneficial" and 5 indicating "extremely beneficial." The project director distributed this survey to all teachers. It was completed confidentially and returned through the mail. Eighty-one percent of the teachers completed the survey. Three of the highest rated activities (i.e., = 4.0) related to staff development—summer training, staff-development days, and site visits to other campuses (see Table 11).

The results from these surveys were corroborated by participant comments during interviews. Regarding the summer training, teachers said, "Training answered quite a few unanswered questions—with the different types of learning"; "Actually having to take a pretest and apply it to what I've learned was great!"; "It gave me an insight into how the gifted child thinks differently." While all principals also commented positively about the training during their interviews, it affected them differently. One stated empathetically, "I've got a better appreciation of my teachers and how hard they work and the different levels they must teach to and the different problems or unique approaches that they have." Another commented about the nature of needed support, "My primary responsibility is to make sure my teachers have time off together to try new things without being afraid of failing," while another principal reflected about a student-centered classroom by saying, "I'm a concrete sequential guy,

Table 11   Composite of Total Mean Scores on Final Survey

	Mean Scores							
Factors	U1 $n=8$	R1 $n=12$	R2 $n=7$	R3 $n=15$	R4 $n=9$	R5 $n=9$	Total $n=60$	Range
1. Units	3.8	2.8	2.9	3.3	3.6	3.0	3.3	.9
2. Research assistants	3.5	3.8	3.7	3.0	3.2	3.3	3.4	.7
3. Computer	2.5	1.3	2.1	2.3	3.3	2.1	2.3	2.0
4. Staff development days	4.6	4.4	4.7	4.3	4.1	4.7	4.5	.6
5. Summer training	4.5	4.7	4.9	3.7	4.0	4.2	4.3	1.2
6. Spring celebration	3.4	4.5	3.7	3.3	3.0	3.0	3.5	1.5
7. Site visits to your campus	4.6	4.1	2.5	0*	2.8	4.0	3.6	2.1
8. Site visits to other campuses	4.8	4.8	4.1	2.7	4.0	4.2	4.1	2.1
9. Mentor teachers	4.8	3.3	4.3	4.1	4.0	3.4	4.0	2.5
10. Community representatives	2.5	2.3	3.4	1.5	2.9	2.2	2.5	1.9
11. Campus administrator	4.0	3.4	4.4	4.2	3.8	3.0	3.8	1.4
12. PMS communications	3.4	3.4	3.7	3.5	3.7	3.4	3.5	.3
13. The KIT	3.6	2.8	2.5	2.8	3.4	3.0	3.0	1.1
14. Money for materials	4.5	4.8	5.0	4.5	4.1	4.2	4.5	.9

Note. *Site R3 was located approximately 250 miles away from any of the other sites.

and it really bothered me." These reactions eventually were manifested in the types and quality of support provided by the leadership at each school.

For staff-development days each month, the project paid for substitutes. These days provided time for mentors and cohort teachers to collaborate in working toward individual or school goals. Teachers commented, "It allowed for several of us to work together. Sometimes, it's hard for some of us to see each other at school on a regular basis, so I appreciated those days where we could sit together and brainstorm"; "We loved the days together. We are a team!"

With the exception of R3 and R4, which were located farther away from the other school districts, cross-site visits were rated as extremely beneficial. At these meetings, mentors and cohort teachers were able to meet in other teachers' classrooms. A teacher remarked, "I enjoyed getting together with the other schools and sharing ideas. It was the first time we were with the other teachers in a real training opportunity."

Mentoring. All first-year mentor teachers reported feeling initially "excited" to be the mentor teacher, except the primary mentor teacher at R3, who commented that she was "doing this because the principal asked me to." The mentor teacher at R2 left at the end of the year to work for the project; all other mentors remained at their sites for the second year of implementation. First-year mentors formed a Trailblazer group, met twice to brainstorm positive mentor techniques and solve problems, and presented at two state conventions and for the grant advisory board. After presenting at a state convention for the gifted and talented, one mentor commented, "This project has made me feel like a professional and has given me the opportunity to work with other teachers from other towns. Thank you [research assistant] for encouraging me to grow. Your visits and seeing you and talking with you keeps it [the project] on my mind. I see myself differently now!" Second-year mentor teachers uniformly reported enthusiasm for the job. Along with the first-year mentors, each school had an additional mentor teacher during the second year. Observational data corroborated the "enthusiasm and support" of the second-year mentors. The project director commented that, "Being experienced in the project seems to give the second-year mentors the maturity and assurance to positively support the cohort teachers" (Ford, 1996, p. 195).

All of the teachers rated the mentors as beneficial to extremely beneficial, although the mentors varied in their expertise and their communication skills (see Table 11). About a second-year mentor, one teacher reported, "He is a collaborator, and the group became a team because of his insight and his involvement in the training program. The teachers mention often about how [the mentor] is so organized, encouraging, and positive." However, at the same school one research assistant observed that the first-year mentor was able to incorporate many of the strategies in her classroom, but was impatient with others who were struggling to incorporate those strategies. "Her efforts at mentoring became authoritative, rather than peer assistance; she directed, rather than collaborated. The cohort teachers hesitated to seek her advice or assistance, and they had difficulty forming a team." The research assistants noted that these differences indicate that the choice of mentor is personal and cannot be imposed by schools or administrators (Griffin, 1997).

Support among teachers. While mentors provided support, peer support among cohort teachers was also present to varying degrees at different schools. In some cases, cohort teachers actually became models for others: "Since she taught third grade, the intermediate teachers have observed her innovations and have begun to question her about the changes and the time it took to implement these changes." Cohort teachers also preferred working with others in the same or similar grade levels. For example, one of the teachers said, "When I want to develop a thematic unit, I go to Melissa [another cohort teacher] because she teaches on the same grade level and she knows the basic skill requirements for our students . . . and the materials available."

In other cases, however, divisions occurred among project and nonproject teachers. After the first summer training, one research assistant observed after a faculty meeting that a division developed between the upper and lower grade teachers. She noted that the upper grade teachers were hesitant to try the new practices and resisted their implementation. While some of the upper grade teachers appeared to resent those who did make changes, the primary teachers were strongly committed to change, and their numbers strengthened that resolve. The principal's reaction to the negative group of teachers was to ignore them, eventually replacing retirements and transfers with teachers more interested in the innovations. At smaller sites, all or most of the teachers eventually became involved in the training, although those resisting more transformational changes were still a vocal group in some project schools where poor leadership was present.

Leadership support. Most participants rated the administrator as providing moderate to extremely beneficial support. Comments regarding strong principal support for the project were evident at U1, R1 (elementary), R2, and R3. Teachers' positive comments about the principals focused on building recruitment, teamwork, supplying extra materials, and encouraging professional development. Prior to mentor training, one teacher said, "Our principal approached me about this, and, from our discussion, she convinced me to give it a try. Her support and confidence in me was a deciding factor." One R2 teacher described her principal by saying, "He is very cooperative about making sure we get to have our work days. He tries to make sure that the things that we need here at the school in a physical way are taken care of. He really stuck his neck out to help us get the tables and chairs we need so we can rearrange our rooms." When the U1 principal was interviewed after training, she said, "Oh, I think it's great! I'm excited! I'm enthusiastic. When I believe in something, there is no stopping me!" This principal eventually integrated the project's summer training into the school's staff development and used project teachers to train all beginning teachers at her school.

During the second year, however, leadership inconsistency was particularly evident in the quality of the changes (i.e., transformational vs. conservational). At R5, a new superintendent redirected the principal's energy away from the project's goals to new grants. While teachers continued to make small changes in their practices, only 54% were transformational (see Table 6). At R4, the dearth of leadership was even more dramatic. The principal retired; the new principal didn't attend training; the superintendent was fired; and the superintendent's wife, who was a second-year mentor, lost enthusiasm. As can be seen in Table 6, the Year 1 Cohort made no transformational changes during the second year.

Central office support tended to be mixed. Most sites had initial support that dwindled through the project's implementation. In some cases, the central administration had a negative impact on the site, particularly in the loss of teachers. As one research assistant at R2 commented, "Central administration has not been supportive of the teachers in general, and therefore there is a feeling of distrust among the staff. Tight control seems to be the style of the superintendent. We lost one teacher because of lack of support for the teacher from the central office and may lose the mentor teacher by the end of the year. That would leave only one of the original cohort group at the site." Disgusted with the central administration, a mentor suggested, "I would like for [the project] to be more important to our administrative people. I would like for them to understand so much of what we're trying to achieve that it would become as important to them as it is to us." The exception was at U1, which had both central office and later superintendent support when it was named a magnet school for gifted students and offered the project training to teachers in the district.

Community support. During the first year, two community representatives from each site, with the exception of R3 and R4, attended support training; the community representatives from R1 attended a training session after the teachers were trained. All sites except R3 had community representatives involved in the second support training. However, with the exception of R2, most of the participants did not view the community representatives as beneficial. Some of the mentors described the community's limited or lack of involvement: "The VIP's are helping make materials, but the rest of the community doesn't know too much about it"; "Right now, this is the weakest area of our situation here. We are receiving no community support that I'm aware of. . . . We have learned from this, and hopefully in the future we will arrange to select some good, strong community people and help them understand how they can help."

Teachers sometimes did not want the community's help. For example, at U1, they did not "trust" the community representatives to make "professional looking" materials for them. At R5, the two community representatives had opposite views of the community's involvement in the schools. One felt the community was excluded from school activities, while the other reported that the school was the "hub" of the community. Some community representatives became less involved when their children were not placed in a project room. One remarked, "I was excited about working with the project until my kid wasn't put in a project room. Then, I just got uninterested."

Research assistants support. Most of the project's research assistants visited the sites weekly. They provided support to the mentor teachers, identified needs, and collected data. In fact, they became second-level mentors to both the mentor teachers and the cohort teachers. While two research assistants changed during the second year of implementation, all sites rated research assistants as beneficial on the final survey. One of the mentors described her relationship with the research assistant: "I think the thing that's helping me the most is knowing that I have someone I can call on if I hit a snag. And I have sat down many times with Mary to bounce ideas off her or say I'm having a little bit of a problem here. What would you suggest? Just having someone I can talk to and get suggestions from has helped a great deal." In addressing the effect of changes on her students, one mentor reflected, "They [research assistants] have been very supportive in the way they have encouraged and supported me. This helps especially when I received little encouragement from my school staff. It felt good! I found I really missed that. It also helped me stop and think that maybe my students missed the encouragement they needed to take risks."

Material resources. With the exception of the urban site, the participants from rural schools viewed their resources as limited prior to training: "We are a poor school. When you don't have money, you have difficulty in recruiting quality in-service, computers, materials." For this reason, the participants consistently rated the $100 project stipend as extremely beneficial on the final survey. While not a large stipend, the teachers viewed this money as a trust from the project in their development of classroom practices that related to their goals.

The project also gave each mentor one computer and a modem so that the project schools might share materials and establish a network. In all but one school, it was the first time that a computer had ever been in a teacher's classroom. For this reason, it was not rated highly by many of the teachers. The project hired a consultant at the beginning of the second year of implementation to help each site learn how to use the computer and interact with other sites. As the teachers became more computer literate, they began to use it with their students and in e-mailing one another. However, for the majority of teachers, the computer was only mentioned as an incentive for becoming a mentor teacher, but not in relationship to changing practices.

Effects on students. Teachers were also affected by changes that they observed in their students. In reflecting about her changes, one teacher commented, "I looked back and one of my goals . . . was having my homeroom kids work on contracts. . . . I feel that these kids were so successful and enjoyed it so much that I am now ready to branch out and have three or two of the other classes [use contracts] with my ultimate goal [being] all five math classes." Case studies with six gifted students also revealed a high degree of satisfaction when learning adapted for rate and provided for student choice (Davalos, 1996). One gifted child wrote an essay entitled "Visualizing Schools in the 21st Century" that described transformational classroom practices implemented in her classroom: "They are doing different projects for different subjects at different times so they can have fun while they learn. . . . Lessons learned will be connected in some way. . . . They are allowed to go on to any grade they are comfortable with so they can be in a class that will not bore them so they can learn at their own rate of learning" (p. 81). Other positive effects on gifted students in classrooms that transformed their practices included more satisfaction with school, increases in confidence, feelings of acceptance, and self-esteem (Davalos & Griffin, 1999). However, when change was conservational and limited to adding activities that were not particularly challenging, the gifted students expressed little or no satisfaction with the classroom modifications (Davalos & Griffin, 1999).

Current practices. Baseline observations revealed that 7 teachers were at a transformational level in content, 1 in rate, 11 in preference, and 8 in environment. With the exception of one teacher, all of these made a transformational change in one or more areas. Since the majority of teachers tended to make changes in preference and environment before making changes in content and rate, their current practices influenced the degree to which they were able to implement the more difficult steps. Changes in one practice did appear to influence other practices. For example, teachers who began providing more varied activities tended to change their environment, as well.

Inhibiting factors. Teachers and research assistants cited these factors as inhibiting change: departmentalization or organization of the school, finances, lack of time, coworkers, and administrative support. For example, one teacher said, "I'm meeting my goals okay. I'm working on some new activities to do. . . . It's just real hard to work with departmentalization . . . they can't work in depth." Others said, "I'm not sure there will be enough time to start something new"; "The only frustration that I've had is I feel that some other staff members have not been very supportive as far as I'm trying something new." At one school, the research assistant observed, "There is constant talking about TAAS [state assessment] to the exclusion of everything else. Every time I go to the primary school, the principal complains about the project. He says that his teachers need to concentrate on TAAS."

In summary, a constellation of factors appears to influence change in schools. The vast majority of participants viewed staff-development activities, leadership, the mentor teachers, and project support as being beneficial to extremely beneficial. The project training was effective in changing attitudes, establishing a common vision, and developing change goals for each participant. Effects on students also influenced teacher change. The only support team member who was not rated highly was the community representative. The low rating might have been the result of not only the participants' lack of understanding of how to use the community representative effectively, but also the attitude of the parent toward the school and the lack of consistent follow-up by the project staff. The project staff focused their efforts primarily on the culture within the school: the principal, the mentor teachers, and the cohort teachers. In some cases, teachers had to overcome their peers' resistance, administrative changes, limited resources, and school structures to implement their goals. Without the simulated training, strong follow-up, leadership, material resources, and eventual collaboration among teachers, change most likely would not have occurred.

DISCUSSION

Systems theory describes settings in which organizational and transformational changes take place, with schools consisting of several systems (Lunenburg & Ornstein, 1991; Ouchi, 1982). The process of educational change is therefore complex, with each school presenting a unique culture that must be addressed. Indeed, when humans attempt new innovations, a multiplicity of factors must work in concert for change to occur. Before the Mustard Seed Project, classrooms were primarily teacher directed, with little adaptation for gifted students. In its brief duration, the project was able to support 99% of the participants in changing their classroom practices to adapt for gifted students. Given the difficulty with educational reform, those who have been change agents may be surprised by these results. A number of factors appear to have contributed to the success of the project.

First, the sensitivity of the observation instrument and its alignment with the desired changes in classroom practices provided opportunities for the researchers to identify the teachers' smallest changes. The instrument clearly established the attributes of the practices and included ways to measure their degree of implementation. In addition, the research assistants and mentors could identify relationships among areas of change and use this knowledge to support the teacher in establishing new goals. Transformational changes in environment and preference occurred first for the majority of the teachers, perhaps because they were more visible or easier to accomplish. It did appear that changes in environment or preference were precursors to more substantial changes in rate and content, whether these changes are sequential or cyclical is unknown without further study. While the small steps may not have had much effect on the gifted students' satisfaction, they appeared to lead to future changes that did have positive effects, particularly in the second year of implementation (Davalos & Griffin, 1999). For example, when teachers changed practices in rate, allowing students opportunities for independent and/or in-depth studies, and in content, providing more challenging concepts and authentic methods, the gifted students responded positively. One child described her teachers as being very supportive of her and interesting, saying, "They're both wonderful." Later, she elaborated on their characteristics: "[They] let us do things like projects that other classes don't get to do, because those teachers think you have to do all these worksheets. You don't get anything out of that. In our class, we try to make it realistic, like when I pretended my career was a geologist in the cave project" (Davalos, 1996, pp. 61–62). While these case studies suggest that transformational practices in rate and content appear to relate to increases in confidence, feelings of acceptance, and self-esteem (Davalos & Griffin, 1999), it is still unknown if changes in these areas relate to other student performances or outcomes, such as achievement and general problem-solving strategies.

Second, the simulated training experience acted as a catalyst, modeled concrete examples, and clearly defined the vision for the teachers. This initial impetus was critical in breaking established frameworks. Before new practices are adopted, individuals must free themselves from previously held attitudes—in this case, an attitude toward organizing instruction around the book, rather than children's abilities, styles, or interests (Lewin, 1951). In addition, the common language developed during the training facilitated collaboration among the teams of teachers and other project sites, developing an internal and external support structure.

Third, the teachers established their own change goals at the end of the training. The mentor and research assistant supported all of these goals and developed new ones in collaboration with each classroom teacher.

Fourth, within each school, strong, consistent follow-up from the principal, mentor teacher, and/or research assistant contributed to the teachers' changes in classroom practices and was evident in those schools with the greatest percentage of teachers who made changes. Equally important was the development of a cohort team that included the principal. This team learned to trust one another and formed positive, supportive, and professional working relationships. In sites where leadership and central office support was lacking or transitory, fewer teachers made changes. In one case, the district was trying to implement multiple innovations at the same time. The leadership never grasped the "big picture," viewing each as separate entities, which dissipated the teachers' energies toward the Javits project. Leadership is therefore a critical component.

As in any study that involves qualitative assessments, previous experiences may create bias and alter perceptions. While every attempt was made to collect data from multiple sources and standardize the process, subjectivity was still present in observations, interpretations, and in the categorization of data.

Many questions still remain. Is experiential staff development more effective than other forms? What are the critical characteristics of mentors and cohort teams in supporting change? What constellation of system factors is most important in influencing short- and long-term changes? What changes are sustained over time? What are the long-term effects on gifted students? A two-year implementation timeline is too brief to institutionalize changes within the school and the community. Longitudinal studies have recently been conducted at the sites to determine which factors are indeed critical in sustaining classroom changes (Hay, 2000).

One conclusion is consistently supported in the literature: The nature of change is not only complex, but highly personal. If the teacher is not involved in the process, no change will be effective or long lasting. As Goodlad and Klein (1994) suggested, "For the schools to change, the people in them must change. Changing people, especially full-grown people, is the most difficult of all human enterprises" (p. 117). Change agents must therefore identify the innovation clearly and responsibly research the effects of their endeavors, particularly on students and teachers, to make sure that they assume roles of improving, rather than using the system.

REFERENCES

Brody, L. E., & Benbow, C. P. (1987). Accelerative strategies: How effective are they for the gifted? *Gifted Child Quarterly, 31*, 105–109.

Connor, P. E., & Lake, L. K. (1994). *Managing organizational change* (Rev. ed.). Westport, CT: Praeger.

Davalos, L. R. A. (1996). *The impact of teacher training for individualization on highly gifted students in heterogeneous classrooms.* Unpublished doctoral dissertation, Texas A&M University, College Station, TX.

Davalos, P., & Griffin, G. (1999). The impact of teachers' individualized practices on gifted students in rural, heterogeneous classrooms. *Roeper Review, 21*, 308–314.

Doherty, E., & Evans, L. (1981). Independent study process: They can think, can't they? *Journal for the Education of the Gifted, 4*, 106–111.

Feldhusen, H. J. (1986*). Individualized teaching of gifted children in regular classrooms.* East Aurora, NY: D.O.K.

Feldhusen, J. F., & Kolloff, M. (1986). The Purdue three-stage model for gifted education at the elementary level. In J. Renzulli (Ed.), *Systems and models for developing programs for the gifted and talented* (pp. 126–152). Mansfield Center, CT: Creative Learning Press.

Ford, R. F. (1996). *A study of the effects of training on teacher attitudes and classroom instructional practices.* Unpublished doctoral dissertation, Baylor University, Waco, TX.

Fullan, M. G. (1993). *Change forces: Probing the depths of educational reform.* New York: Farmer Press.

Gallagher, S. A., Stepien, W. J., & Rosenthal, H. (1992). The effects of problem-based learning on problem solving. *Gifted Child Quarterly, 36,* 195–200.

Glasser, B. G., & Strauss, A. L. (1967). *The discovery of grounded theory.* Chicago: Aldine.

Goodlad, J. L., & Klein, M. F. (1994). *Looking behind the classroom door.* Worthington, OH: Charles A. Jones.

Griffin, G. L. (1997). *The phenomenon of teachers mentoring teachers in the midst of change.* Unpublished doctoral dissertation, Texas A&M University, College Station, TX.

Hay, B. J. (2000). *A longitudinal study of factors sustaining changes in instructional practices.* Unpublished doctoral dissertation, Baylor University, Waco, TX.

Johnsen, S. K. (1992). *Classroom instructional practices scale.* Unpublished manuscript, Baylor University, Waco, TX.

Johnsen, S. K., & Johnson, K. (1986). *Independent study program.* Waco, TX: Prufrock Press.

Kaplan, S. (1986). The grid: A model to construct differentiated curriculum for the gifted. In J. Renzulli (Ed.), *Systems and models for developing programs for the gifted and talented* (pp. 182–193). Mansfield, CT: Creative Learning Press.

Lewin, K. (1951). *Field theory in social science.* New York: Harper and Row.

Lopez, R., & MacKenzie, J. (1993). A learning center approach to individualized instruction for gifted students. In C. J. Maker (Ed.), *Critical issues in gifted education: Programs for the gifted in regular classrooms* (pp. 282–295). Austin, TX: PRO-ED.

Lunenburg, F. C., & Ornstein, A. C. (1991). *Educational administration: Concepts and practices.* Belmont, CA: Wadsworth.

Maykut P., & Morehouse, R. (1994). *Beginning qualitative research: A philosophic and practical guide.* Washington, DC: The Falmer Press.

Ouchi, W. G. (1982). Theory Z and the schools. *School Administrator, 39*(2), 12–19.

Parnes, S. J. (1979). Creativity: The process of discovery. In J. J. Gallagher (Ed.), *Gifted children: Reaching their potential* (pp. 44–54). New York: Trillium.

Petrie, H. G. (1990). Reflections on the second wave of reform: Restructuring the teaching profession. In S. L. Jacobson & J. A. Conway (Eds.), *Educational leadership in an age of reform* (pp. 14–29). New York: Longman.

Reis, S. M., Burns, D. E., & Renzulli, J. S. (1992). *Curriculum compacting: The complete guide to modifying the curriculum for high-ability students.* Mansfield Center, CT: Creative Learning Press.

Reis, S. M., Gentry, M., Maxfield, L. R. (1998). The application of enrichment clusters to teachers' classroom practices. *Journal for the Education of the Gifted, 21,* 310–334.

Renzulli, J. S., & Reis, S. M. (1997). *The schoolwide enrichment model: A how-to guide for educational excellence* (2nd ed.). Mansfield Center, CT: Creative Learning Press.

Ryser, G. R., & Johnsen, S. K. (1996). Toward more research on effective practices with gifted students in general-education settings. *Journal for the Education of the Gifted, 19,* 481–496.

Sarason, S. (1995). *School change: The personal development of a point of view.* New York: Teachers College Press.

Sergiovanni, T. J. (1995). *The principalship: A reflective practice perspective* (3rd ed.). Boston: Allyn and Bacon.

Southern, W. T., & Jones, E. D. (Eds.). (1991). *Academic acceleration of gifted children.* New York: Teachers College Press.

Sullivan, C. G. (1992). *How to mentor in the midst of change.* Alexandria, VA: Association for Supervision and Curriculum Development.

Treffinger, D. J. (1980). *Encouraging creative learning for the gifted and talented: A handbook of methods and techniques.* Ventura, CA: Office of the Ventura County Superintendent of Education for the National/State Leadership Training Institute on the Gifted and the Talented.

Van Tassel-Baska, J. (1985). Appropriate curriculum for the gifted. In J. F. Feldhusen (Ed.), *Toward excellence in gifted education* (pp. 45–67). Denver, CO: Love.

Van Tassel-Baska, J. (1994). *Comprehensive curriculum for gifted learners* (2nd ed.). Boston: Allyn and Bacon.

Ward, V. S. (1980). *Differential education for the gifted.* Ventura, CA: Office of the Ventura County Superintendent of Education for the National/State Leadership Training Institute on the Gifted and the Talented.

Westberg, K. L., Archambault, F. X., Jr., Dobyns, S. M., & Salvin, T. J. (1993). The classroom practices observation study. *Journal for the Education of the Gifted, 16,* 120–146.

9

A Curriculum Study of Gifted-Student Learning in the Language Arts

Joyce VanTassel-Baska

Li Zuo

Linda D. Avery

Catherine A. Little

College of William and Mary

This curriculum study of gifted-student learning in the language arts explores questions of curriculum efficacy related to the nature of the learner, the type of grouping model employed, and the strength of a curriculum treatment emphasizing literary analysis and interpretation and persuasive writing. The study further explores the use of curriculum effectiveness

Editor's Note: From VanTassel-Baska, J., Zuo, L., Avery, L. D., & Little, C. A. (2002). A curriculum study of gifted student learning in the language arts. *Gifted Child Quarterly*, 46(1), 30-44. © 2002 National Association for Gifted Children. Reprinted with permission.

data to improve instruction the next time a unit of study is taught. Findings suggest that the curriculum treatment produces both significant and important learning outcomes for gifted students across 18 school district entities. Implications for further research and practice are highlighted.

INTRODUCTION

The call for high-quality curricula for the gifted matches a similar call in the general educational community for higher standards for all students. Attempts to bring standards-based reform to U.S. classrooms have been met with skepticism, resistance, and concern by many (Cohen & Hill, 1998). In gifted education, concerns that the standards may be driving out appropriate curricula for the gifted have also been voiced (Reis, 1999). The challenge for gifted education remains to demonstrate that the standards—and the professional disciplines whose voices lie behind them—may be used as a filter through which high-quality curricula for the gifted might emanate.

The connection of the standards to gifted-education intentions, pedagogy, and assessment practices has already been demonstrated in other work (VanTassel-Baska, 1995; VanTassel-Baska, Bass, Ries, Poland, & Avery, 1998; VanTassel-Baska, Johnson, Hughes, & Boyce, 1996). This work has noted the importance of key emphases that are present in both sound curricula for the gifted and in the standards, emphases such as learner outcomes of significance, authentic assessment, use of inquiry and hands-on approaches, substantive content, higher level thinking, intra- and interdisciplinary connections, and the use of metacognition. These connections provide the basis for building more differentiated curricula for the target audience of gifted learners.

Although the standards connections are important curriculum design requirements, they are insufficient to create curricula designed for a special population of learners; one must also assess the curriculum's efficacy with those learners to ensure that appropriate learning gains are forthcoming. The purpose of the study reported here was to assess gifted student learning outcomes as a result of using a specially designed language arts curriculum that wedded the standards work to differentiation features of a gifted curriculum. Specifically, the study asked the following questions:

- To what extent do gifted learners using the special curriculum outperform equally able learners not using it in the dimensions of literary analysis and interpretation and persuasive writing?
- To what extent are there gender and socioeconomic effects from using the curriculum?
- To what extent does grouping impact student performance?
- To what extent do these performance-based assessment tasks yield valuable data for continued instructional planning?

Putting the Research to Use

The findings from this curriculum study serve several purposes for practitioners. First, the study solidifies our understanding of the capacity for differentiated curricula that are faithfully implemented to enhance learning for gifted students. Consequently, it provides a credible case for the defensibility of gifted programs. Secondly, the study suggests that quality differentiated curricula must address advanced content, sophisticated processes, and higher level interdisciplinary concepts in an integrated way to be effective. Thus, accelerated and enriched curricula appear to provide the strongest base for effective learning of the gifted. Thirdly, the study provides a strong case for the use of the William and Mary curriculum in school regardless of ability grouping patterns. Results suggest that students register significant and important learning regardless of the grouping model employed. Fourth, the study illustrates that the curriculum treatment is highly effective with economically disadvantaged minority students, a special population that is of particular interest to our field. Finally, the study contributes to our understanding of effective and consistent strategy use over time to enhance learning. The continuous employment of the literature web and prepared higher order questioning used in an inquiry discussion model throughout the unit contributed to student learning in literary analysis and interpretation. Moreover, the repeated use of the hamburger model for persuasive writing facilitated student growth demonstrated in that area.

REVIEW OF RELEVANT LITERATURE

In order to understand what interventions would be most successful with gifted learners in the language arts area, we must first understand several strands of existing research. These strands may be characterized as (1) what we know about teaching literature and writing to all students; (2) what we know about teaching to the new standards, which call for higher level student responses; and (3) what we know about effective approaches to teaching the language arts as subject matter to gifted learners. These areas of research were briefly reviewed as a prelude to presenting the current study. Although a similar literature review was conducted at the beginning of the curriculum development work in 1990, newer studies have further informed our understanding of teaching and learning the language arts.

Teaching Literature and Writing to All Students

Response-based approaches to teaching literature have been advocated strongly in the work of English educators over the past two decades (e.g., Langer, 1994; Rosenblatt, 1982), and action research in classrooms, even at the primary level, has substantiated student growth in thinking as a result when the approach is balanced between teacher-initiated activities and student response (Baumann & Ivey, 1997; Jewell & Pratt, 1999). Research on enhancing thinking through the teaching of English has been carried out on older students, as well. Kral (1997) found that high school students improved their scientific reasoning significantly on the American College Test (ACT) after being taught a model for hypothetical-deductive thinking in English class and applying it to a study of literature and writing. Similar reasoning gains have been seen for the model when used in science classes, as well (Lawson, 1995).

The importance of instructional moves in teaching reading comprehension and interpretation has been highlighted in the work of Beck and McKeown (1999). These researchers have emphasized research-based teacher strategies such as refraining, synthesizing, connecting, and modeling for students in the act of holding discussions in literature. Such techniques appear to provide an important basis for effective literary discussion and resultant student learning.

Recent research has also suggested the benefits of integrating reading and writing tasks (Bottomley, Truscott, Marinak, Henk, & Melnick, 1999; Henry & Roseberry, 1996; Newell, 1996). Reviews and meta-analyses on the teaching of writing over the past 15 years (Hillocks, 1986; Levy & Ransdell, 1996; Sadoski, Willson, & Norton, 1997) have demonstrated the significance of key instructional variables in the process. It has been found that a combination of (1) inquiry activities, (2) analyzing or responding to literature, (3) pre-writing preparation, and (4) the use of scales reflecting specific criteria enhanced student gains in writing. Making writing about literature central to the instructional approach was also found to be predictive of higher scores for writing quality (Applebee, Langer, Mullis, Latham, & Gentile, 1994). More eclectic combinations of instructional approaches did not improve quality. Feedback on writing produced moderate to high effect sizes if it was positive feedback (.43) and, more importantly, if it was linked to operationally clear instructional objectives (.74). While these same studies have demonstrated a decrease in writing gains as students move from elementary to secondary schools and on into college, Hillocks (1986) maintained that these decrements may be best explained by lack of instruction, rather than developmental limitations of learners.

Thus, the employment of integrated literature and writing models that incorporate the research-based key features suggested by English educators should prove to be successful when employed with specific populations of gifted learners. Moreover, when the emphasis within the relevant teaching models is on teaching thinking, the results should also be positive.

Teaching to the New Standards

Researchers also have found, based on the expectations of standards-based reform, essential ingredients for helping students learn at higher cognitive levels (Donovan, Bransford, & Pellegrino, 1999). One of these elements is teaching for understanding and knowledge utilization (Gardner, 1991; Greeno, 1991; McLaughlin & Talbert, 1993), suggesting the need for a strong knowledge base from which learners are encouraged to work. A second element involves assessment practices that provide ongoing learning experiences in higher level thinking (Vye, Goldman, Hmelo, Voss, & Williams, 1998; Wiggins, 1993). A third ingredient discussed extensively in the literature is the role of context as studied from various perspectives, including establishing learning communities (Brown & Campione, 1994), orchestrating cooperation in problem solving (Newstead & Wason, 1995), providing group structures for argumentation (Goldman, 1994; Salmon & Zeitz, 1995), and linking classroom work to how students spend leisure time (Csikszentmihalyi, Rathunde, & Whalen, 1993) and how parents facilitate learning at home (Moll, Tapia, & Whitmore, 1993). These understandings about how students learn are important underpinnings to enhancing the learning standards in any subject area, but they also contribute to the orchestration of viable instructional approaches to aid the cognitive development of high-ability learners.

Teaching Gifted Learners in the Language Arts

A recent analysis of curriculum models employed in gifted education revealed a paucity of evidence for approaches that are nonaccelerative in orientation (VanTassel-Baska & Brown, 2000), yet school districts rarely employ acceleration strategies with gifted learners in the language arts. The more common approach is to use advanced reading materials that are complex in form and meaning (Baskin & Harris, 1980; Hauser & Nelson, 1988). Thus, many language arts programs for the gifted use supplementary materials such as Junior Great Books to satisfy advanced readers in their classrooms. Junior Great Books constitutes one of the most effective literature programs available for gifted learners. It is the only program that was highly rated by Aldrich and McKim (1992) in their review of programs and materials purported to be effective with the gifted. Moreover, it offers a strong inquiry-based training program for teachers, and the program has been found to be most effective at improving students' quality of discourse and enhancing their interest in literature (Nichols, 1992, 1993).

Research evidence is limited in respect to what works with gifted students in a language arts program. Typically, studies have examined reading practices separate from writing approaches. A few research studies have focused on effective reading practices with the gifted, with mixed findings. One study on precocious readers (Henderson, Jackson, & Mukamal, 1993) found that such readers need to be assessed carefully concerning specific areas of strength within the language arts area, lest assumptions be made about skills in which they may not be advanced or about connections between skill areas that may not be present, such as between reading and writing or oral language and reading. Yet, in another study, fifth and sixth graders who participated in a literary analysis class once a week showed significant gains over a control group on both reading comprehension and vocabulary when they were assessed with an off-grade-level standardized achievement measure (Aldrich & Mills, 1989).

Reasonable consensus exists that a reading program for the gifted should be specialized and focus on critical and creative reading behaviors (Collins & Alex, 1995), implying the need for various forms of instructional grouping. Yet, whole-language advocates have sought to dismantle all forms of reading groups by instructional level, albeit for reasons related more to the use of narrow skill instruction than to thwart advanced learning of the gifted (e.g., Rosenblatt, 1982). In a descriptive study of gifted students in general education classrooms, Matthews (1992) found that teachers who were most effective at whole language were also most effective at differentiating for the gifted and that both sets of strategies were positive experiences for the gifted.

Literature programs at middle and high school levels should involve gifted students in reading high-quality adult literature and should help them develop skill and enthusiasm in the intellectual and aesthetic experience of literature (Mallea, 1992). Some sentiment exists for the use of good young-adult literature, as well (Rakow, 1991). The use of the seminar approach to teach literature to secondary gifted students has been strongly advocated because of its context for stimulating discussion and interaction (Dixon, 1993; Taylor, 1996).

Just as reading programs enhance critical thinking behaviors, well-conceptualized writing programs can provide similar support. Journal writing offers an important avenue for self-expression in the gifted, giving students the opportunity to better understand themselves and others (Bailey, Boyce, & VanTassel-Baska, 1990; Hall, 1990). Schunk and Swartz (1992) found that the teaching of a writing model through a deliberate strategy coupled with feedback on progress enhanced both the achievement of gifted learners and their sense of self-efficacy. Even teaching the strategy without providing feedback was found to be beneficial. The strategy goal approach exposed students to the following task demands: (1) write down ideas, (2) pick a main idea, (3) plan a paragraph, (4) write a topic sentence, and (5) write other sentences. Thus, the study provided evidence that strategy instruction facilitates gifted students' achievement and transfer of learning (Scruggs, Mastropieri, Jorgensen, & Monson, 1986) and that self-efficacy is positively related to performance (Schack, 1989). Moreover, it substantiated earlier research on the superior metacognitive performance of gifted students over other types of learners, specifically in monitoring their learning progress and generating their own strategies (Rogers, 1986; Scruggs & Mastropieri, 1985).

In a more recent study, gifted learners in grades 4–6 showed significant improvement in persuasive writing when provided with a visual model, specific strategies for replicating it in written form that included an analysis of exemplary writing, explicit teaching of the rubric for assessment, and peer and teacher feedback (VanTassel-Baska et al., 1996). Another recent study found that teachers who participated with their students in writing enhanced the overall fluency of writing in the classroom (Armstrong, 1994), suggesting that the role of the teacher, as well as strategy employment, enhances the writing behavior of gifted learners.

Recent studies of effective differentiation practices for gifted learners have focused on strategies such as compacting (Reis & Purcell, 1993), problem-based learning (Gallagher & Stepien, 1996), inquiry approaches (Hertzog, Klein, & Katz, 1999), and independent investigation (Delcourt, 1994; Renzulli, 1999). While these studies demonstrate in many different ways the effectiveness of a single approach, little evidence exists for how the approaches work together within a core curriculum framework or how they are sustained over time, multiple teachers, and curriculum sequence.

Existing studies in teaching and learning the language arts demonstrate important considerations for curriculum development and implementation in this subject area. Clearly, we need effective models or strategies for teaching core skills in the language arts, especially writing. The current research also suggests the need to use these models consistently and purposefully over time, rather than employing an eclectic approach to the process. Yet, research studies on effective strategies with gifted students continue to suggest that multiple strategies such as compacting, inquiry, and independent study have positive effects on gifted learners, even though each has been studied separately without the benefit of alternative strategy comparison. Gaps in our understanding of working effectively with gifted learners in the language arts persist in several key areas. Few studies have investigated effective approaches to teaching literature, language, or oral communication to high-ability learners, nor have studies demonstrated how critical thinking enhances performance in the language arts. Although concept or theme-based curricula are popular for teaching the language arts, no studies currently illuminate their effectiveness in enhancing learning. The William and Mary curriculum work in language arts offers a rich set of applied research questions for exploration since it incorporates many of the differentiated features of curricula about which we know little.

The study reported on in this paper, however, focuses on the effectiveness of a curriculum for teaching literary analysis and interpretation and persuasive writing as language arts manifestations of higher level thinking. Thus, it contributes to our understanding of the importance of embedding higher order skills into context and builds on prior understanding of effective research-based strategies for teaching writing.

DESIGN AND PURPOSE OF THE STUDY

By using a quasi-experimental design mode (Campbell & Stanley, 1969), the researchers sought to demonstrate the effects of particular units of study on gifted learners at primary, intermediate, and middle school levels. Each unit was organized around the Integrated Curriculum Model (ICM; VanTassel-Baska, 1986, 1995) and thus sought to enhance learning through an integrated approach of using advanced literature, embedding a reasoning model into the teaching of the language arts, requiring a high-quality student product, and organizing and teaching to the major concept of change as it applies to literature, writing, language study, and oral communication.

Sample

Seventeen public school districts and one private school furnished student data for this study. The districts and schools were quite diverse and drawn from 10 states. Three of the districts were rural, three were urban, and the remainder would be classified as suburban or exurban. The private school was located in an urban area. In all, 46 schools across these districts participated in the study.

Students participating in the study (N = 2,189) were all preidentified gifted learners in grades 2–8 in their local school district. Given the relative standard of giftedness applied to identification procedures at the local level coupled with the variety of state definitions of giftedness (Stephens & Karnes, 2000), the range of general ability and verbal aptitude varied in the sample to some extent. Identification criteria employed in the 10 participating states included ability and aptitude measures coupled with teacher recommendations. Threshold scores for identification on group ability measures ranged from 94–99% and on group on-grade verbal aptitude measures from 94–99%.

Curriculum Treatment

The curriculum materials used in the study were four of a series of six units developed under a federal Javits grant in the mid-1990s. The curriculum framework for all of the units, based on the ICM, includes goals addressing advanced content, higher level processes, and abstract concepts. The six goals for the units are as follows:

- to develop analytical and interpretive skills in literature;
- to develop persuasive writing skills;
- to develop linguistic competency;
- to develop listening/oral communication skills;
- to develop reasoning skills in the language arts; and
- to understand the concept of change in the language arts.

Each unit employs advanced literature as the driving force to encourage students to develop the skills listed above, with integration of a specific model of reasoning (Paul, 1992) and discussion and activities around the concept of change. Specific models for teaching literary analysis and interpretation and persuasive writing are also employed throughout the units, based on theories of discourse and argument (e.g., Beck & McKeown, 1999; Toulmin, 1958). In addition, each unit emphasizes interdisciplinary connections and involves students in issue-based research.

Differentiation of the units for gifted students occurs at multiple levels of unit analysis. The goals are differentiated through the focus on higher level thinking and concept development. The use of literature that meets criteria for intellectually gifted learners further contributes to the differentiation of the materials and matches it to their intended users. The consistent use of strategies like research, inquiry, and various forms of independent learning exemplify differentiated teaching of gifted learners.

The units include pre- and postassessments for literary analysis and interpretation and for persuasive writing. Other assessments, including both formative and summative measures, are also included.

The four units included in this study were *Journeys and Destinations, Literary Reflections, Autobiographies,* and *The 1940s: A Decade of Change.* The first of these was written for grades 2–3, the second two for grades 4–6, and the last for grades 7–9. This study focused on the pre-post results of the literature and writing tests.

Each of the teachers involved in the study received one to four days of training on the curriculum materials. These workshops were conducted by project staff and/or by local teachers or administrators who had themselves been trained for workshop leadership. Training workshops introduced teachers to the curriculum framework and to the specific teaching models used in the units, with discussion of how those models promoted accomplishment of the goals. The workshops also explored the specific units and the activities and literature pieces involved. In addition, the workshops included discussion of implementation issues, including suggestions for utilizing the units in various organizational settings.

Instrumentation

The two assessments used in the study measured literary analysis and persuasive writing skills. The same task demands were consistent across the units, although different stimuli were used to evoke student responses in each unit. At the beginning and at the end of each unit, students were asked to read a selection and to complete the two assessments based on that selection. Both assessments were piloted with relevant populations and formed the basis of an earlier curriculum effectiveness study (VanTassel-Baska et al., 1996). The first assessment was a performance-based test of literary analysis and interpretation. This test, modeled on the NAEP assessment in reading (National Assessment Governing Board, 1992), included four questions, addressing the following topics: (1) main idea, (2) analysis of a quote, (3) relationship of the concept of change to the selection, and (4) creating a title with a rationale to support it. The second assessment was a performance-based persuasive writing assessment that asked students to develop an argument to support whether or not they would require all the students in their grade to read the given selection. In each unit, students read and responded to a different selection in the pretest than in the posttest, although the two selections in each unit represented the same genre. Both assessments were reviewed for content validity by experts in gifted education and in English education. These experts offered favorable reviews regarding the content validity of both instruments. Recent interrater reliability estimates for scoring each instrument exceeded .90 for each scorer team.

Scoring

Pairs of trained scorers on the project staff scored the assessment measures. The rubric used for the literature test was developed by project staff, piloted, and utilized in the earlier study (VanTassel-Baska et al., 1996). This rubric gave a range of 0–3 points for each of the four questions, for a total score range of 0–12. For each item, a response could receive a score of 0, meaning no response; 1, indicating a vague or inaccurate response; 2, for an accurate but literal response; or 3, indicating an insightful response. Interrater reliability on this rubric has been reported as .81 (VanTassel-Baska et al., 1996).

The rubric for the writing test was based on Toulmin's (1958) criteria for judging quality of claim, data, and warrant as adapted by Burkhalter (1995). This rubric gave a range of 0–20 total points, with a 0–6 range for each of the elements of claim, data, and warrant, and a 0–2 range for conclusion. In the areas of claim, data, and warrant, a score of 0 indicated no response; a 2 indicated a limited attempt at a response; a 4 indicated a clear and accurate response meeting the task demand as stated; and a 6 indicated a response exceeding expectations. In the case of the conclusion, a 0 indicated the absence of a conclusion, while a 2 indicated its presence. Interrater reliability on the writing rubric has been reported as .77 for claim, .56 for data, and .66 for warrant (Connor, 1990).

The scoring protocol for the assessments involved practice scoring based on training and using a consensus model to ensure inter-rater reliability. Scorers were trained in workshops that involved an overview of the units, reading and discussion of the selections used as stimuli for the assessments, examination of the rubric and sample responses for each score, and then a supervised scoring of at least 10 tests where scorers were able to agree at least at a .90 level. Pairs of trained scorers then separately scored sets of tests. A third scorer reviewed those responses on which there was not agreement and met with the initial scorers to arrive at a consensus.

Methods

Analysis of covariance (ANCOVA) was used in the comparisons across groups to answer the questions of whether the treatment and comparison groups were significantly different in their posttest performance after controlling for pretest differences, whether males and females were significantly different in their posttest performance after controlling for pretest differences, whether grouping models for gifted students made any difference in student posttest difference after controlling for pretest differences, and whether students from high or low socioeconomic status (SES) were significantly different in their posttest performance after controlling for pretest differences. Paired samples *t*-test was used for comparison within each group formed by the gifted-student grouping model or repeated exposure to units to investigate within-group improvement in performance after curriculum intervention. Descriptive statistics were used for item-level analysis to diagnose students' strengths and weaknesses after the treatment.

Limitations of the Study

One limitation of the study, a common difficulty in social scientific research, was the lack of random selection or assignment. Intact classes had to be used, taught by teachers who volunteered to implement the units. For this study, the project staff took care at the beginning to instruct the participating teachers about how to set up appropriate comparison groups. In the actual statistical analysis, only the data from the schools that had both experimental and comparison groups were used for the examination of the treatment effect and the assumptions for ANCOVA were dutifully tested, as well.

Data collection constituted the second difficulty, as the project staff had to depend on participating teachers' cooperation and commitment and, to some extent, students' participation through the entire treatment period. The study involved over 2,000 students and spanned five years of data collection; thus, missing records and variables were unavoidable consequences. As a result, unbalanced group sizes complicated the analysis process.

Finally, though the performance-based assessment instruments used in the units were technically adequate based on the procedures described and highly relevant to the curriculum taught, additional more standardized assessment measures might have strengthened the case made for student growth.

RESULTS

Findings from this study were drawn from six major analyses: (1) comparisons between treatment and comparison groups, (2) gender comparisons within the treatment group, (3) pre- and posttest item analysis, (4) comparisons among and within grouping models, (5) comparisons based on single- and multi-year exposure, and (6) high and low SES comparisons. All of these analyses involved both performance-based measures, the first dealing with literary analysis and interpretation and the second with persuasive writing. Students were used as the unit of analysis in all cases. Table 1 shows the summary of study demographics employed in the various analyses undertaken.

The results from the comparisons between treatment and comparison students are presented in Table 2. This sub-sample was drawn from the larger sample based on comparability of comparison-group composition. Thus, only sites with identified comparison students were selected for the analysis. These results showed that there was a statistically significant difference ($p < .001$)

Table 1 Summary of the Study Demographics

Table	Content	Analysis	Group	N*	Data Source
2	Treatment effect	ANCOVA	Experimental & Comparison	366	9 schools with both experimental & comparison groups
3	Gender effect	ANCOVA	Experimental	1,449	Cases with gender specification
4	Subanalysis	Descriptive	Experimental	486	2 districts with available item scores
5	Grouping model	t-test	Experimental	534	2-5 graders with grouping model specification
6	Grouping model	ANCOVA	Experimental	534	2-5 graders with grouping model specification
7	Exposure effect	t-test	Experimental	52	8 schools from 1 district that used units in sequence
8	SES effect	ANCOVA	Experimental	171	5th graders from 5 schools with extreme high or low SES

Note. *Before listwise deletion in analysis.

between the experimental and comparison groups on the posttest after adjusting for pretest differences between the groups by using the ANCOVA. Furthermore, the effect size using the Eta squared statistic was medium for literature (.070) and large for persuasive writing (.242; Cohen, 1988), suggesting that the curriculum treatment is both statistically and educationally significant.

The results of separate analyses, conducted at the unit level, are consistent with the results combined across units. In other words, virtually any language arts unit within the William and Mary curriculum, when implemented, can be expected to produce a significant treatment effect.

The results from the comparisons based on gender are reported in Table 3. These results showed that there were no differences by gender for literature, but a statistically significant difference was found for persuasive writing ($p < .01$). However, that difference was found to be of little practical importance when effect size was computed. This suggests that boys and girls benefited relatively equally from their exposure to the curriculum.

An item analysis for each instrument was undertaken to identify how the instructional process could be informed by analyzing student performance at the item level on each instrument. This analysis was restricted to two units (*Literary Reflections* and *Autobiographies*) and drawn from the data from two implementation sites. The results provide the basis for suggesting areas in

Table 2

A: Analysis of Covariance for Literature Assessment in Comparison and Experimental Groups

Group	n	Pretest Mean (SD)	Posttest Mean (SD)	Adjusted Mean (SD)	F	Effect Size (η^2)
Comparison	85	5.88 (1.96)	5.88 (1.72)	5.88 (.19)	17.75*	.070
Experimental	155	5.88 (1.81)	6.86 (1.88)	6.86 (.14)		

B: Analysis of Covariance for Writing Assessment in Comparison and Experimental Groups

Group	n	Pretest Mean (SD)	Posttest Mean (SD)	Adjusted Mean (SD)	F	Effect Size (η^2)
Comparison	76	7.24 (3.56)	7.21 (3.44)	7.59 (.36)	70.00*	.242
Experimental	146	8.40 (3.27)	11.53 (3.59)	11.34 (.26)		

Note: *$p < .001$

Table 3

A: Analysis of Covariance for Literature Assessment in Experimental Males and Females

Group	n	Pretest Mean (SD)	Posttest Mean (SD)	Adjusted Mean (SD)	F	Effect Size (η^2)
Male	606	6.10 (0.77)	7.33 (1.99)	7.41 (0.07)	1.056	.001
Female	537	6.49 (1.59)	7.61 (1.86)	7.52 (0.08)		

B: Analysis of Covariance for Writing Assessment in Experimental Males and Females

Group	n	Pretest Mean (SD)	Posttest Mean (SD)	Adjusted Mean (SD)	F	Effect Size (η^2)
Male	561	8.87 (3.30)	11.07 (3.83)	11.22 (0.15)	6.758*	.006
Female	497	9.61 (3.41)	11.94 (3.63)	11.78 (0.16)		

Note: *$p < .001$

which instruction needed reinforcement in order to strengthen learning outcomes, as well as areas in which instruction appeared to make a sizable difference. The results from this analysis are presented in Table 4.

The results of the analysis showed that student performance varied from item to item. In *Literary Reflections*, students' gain scores in interpreting a line of literary text (.46) and in illustrating the concept of change in the textual material (.38) showed the most improvement. Students' abilities to state an important idea showed much less growth (.19), and their skills in supplying a new title for

Table 4   Descriptive Statistics of Individual Item in Literature and Writing Assessment

Test Item	Maximum Score	Literary Reflections				Autobiographies			
		n	Mean	SD	Gain	n	Mean	SD	Gain
Important Idea (pretest)	3	250	1.51	.64		212	1.65	.59	
Important Idea (posttest)	3	251	1.70	.68	.19	209	2.03	.73	.38
Interpret a Line (pretest)	3	250	1.63	.61		212	1.60	.55	
Interpret a Line (posttest)	3	251	2.09	.70	.46	209	2.01	.73	.42
Idea of Change (pretest)	3	250	1.56	.67		212	1.63	.54	
Idea of Change (posttest)	3	252	1.94	.71	.38	209	1.92	.69	.29
Supply a Title (pretest)	3	250	1.85	.59		212	175	.54	
Supply a Title (posttest)	3	251	1.91	.55	.06	209	2.16	.61	.41
Opinion/Claim (pretest)	6	236	4.14	1.95		208	3.71	1.70	
Opinion/Claim (posttest)	6	235	4.64	1.70	.50	204	4.34	1.68	.63
Data/Support (pretest)	6	236	3.03	1.11		208	2.77	1.05	
Data/Support (posttest)	6	235	3.14	1.21	.11	204	3.18	1.20	.41
Elaboration (pretest)	6	236	.70	1.04		208	.93	1.16	
Elaboration (posttest)	6	235	1.17	1.45	.47	204	1.61	1.69	.68
Conclusion (pretest)	2	236	1.17	.99		208	.95	1.00	
Conclusion (posttest)	2	235	1.40	.92	.23	204	1.23	.98	.28

the stimulus showed virtually no change. However, the pretest scores for this last item were higher than for the other items, a factor that may have affected the growth rate.

Student performance in relation to items on the persuasive writing instrument for the *Literary Reflections* unit showed larger gains per item, consistent with the larger point spread on the rubric, but still well below the ceiling on the instrument. The item showing the greatest gain dealt with stating an opinion (.50), but the item showing the most evidence of increasing sophistication in writing based on the rubric, use of elaboration, also showed strong gains. However, this item also had the lowest pre- and posttest means, suggesting that there is still much room for growth. The students' abilities to articulate reasons, another hallmark of sophistication, showed very little change, suggesting more instructional time needs to be devoted to this area.

In the *Autobiographies* unit, students' gain scores across the items dealing with literature showed less variability, ranging from .38 to .42 for three of the items. However, for the item assessing students' abilities to illustrate the concept of change in the textual material, growth was more constrained (.29). Although this group of students started with a slightly higher pretest score on this item than their counterparts in *Literary Reflections*, their posttest performance was actually lower, again suggesting room for improvement in helping students grapple with an abstract concept.

Student gains on items from the persuasive writing instrument for *Autobiographies* showed a more consistent pattern of growth across all items, ranging from .28 to .68. Again, despite a relatively large gain in the area of elaboration, both pre- and posttest scores were still relatively constrained, suggesting continued room for growth.

The item showing the least amount of gain dealt with stating a conclusion (.28). The gain score was fairly consistent with the gain score of the corresponding item from the *Literary Reflections unit* (.23). Unlike the other items on the instrument, this item is scored dichotomously; a student who provides a conclusion receives two points and a student who does not receives zero. The pattern for student performance across both units suggests that, at the pretest stage, about half of the students are able to do this without teaching. By the posttest, an additional 20% or more of the students demonstrate this skill. Because the model used to teach persuasive writing incorporates this component, it is interesting that even more students do not demonstrate this skill on the posttest.

The results from the comparisons based on grouping arrangement are reported in Table 5. The variable of grouping model was coded based on four alternative ways of grouping students for language arts instruction using the William and Mary curriculum: (1) self-contained, (2) pullout, (3) cluster grouped in the heterogeneous classroom, and (4) language arts block. Schools participating in the study selected the designation that best fit their situation. Information on the type of grouping models of the gifted students in the classrooms where the units were implemented was provided by teachers or district coordinators. Unknown cases were excluded from the analysis. To ensure comparability, only elementary grades were involved in the comparison. Results indicated that students showed significant and important gains in both literary analysis and persuasive writing, regardless of the grouping model employed.

The researchers further analyzed the grouping data to determine whether the grouping models employed varied significantly from one another and which

Table 5

A: Comparison of Student Performance in Literature Assessment
Within Each Grouping Model

Grouping Model	n	Pretest Mean (SD)	Posttest Mean (SD)	t
Self-contained	171	5.77 (1.58)	6.91 (1.77)	7.15*
Pull-out	54	5.11 (1.56)	6.44 (1.33)	7.21*
Cluster of gifted	160	6.92	8.08 (1.82)	6.75*
Language arts block	113	6.19 (1.52)	6.89 (1.37)	4.21*

B: Comparison of Student Performance in Writing Assessment
Within Each Grouping Model

Grouping Model	n	Pretest Mean (SD)	Posttest Mean (SD)	t
Self-contained	168	7.92 (3.20)	11.30 (4.14)	9.89*
Pull-out	54	6.04 (2.71)	10.80 (4.33)	7.87*
Cluster of gifted	152	9.34	11.03 (3.08)	6.53*
Language arts block	100	7.30 (2.85)	8.82 (3.19)	4.01*

Note: *p < .001

grouping models appeared to be effective in facilitating student gains. Table 6 presents these results. Because of the different group sizes, the assumption of homogeneity of variance was not met ($F = 7.46$, $p < .001$ in literature assessment, and $F = 10.64$, $p < .001$ in writing assessment). As larger variances were associated with larger group sizes in literature assessment where a significant grouping effect was found, the statistical test employed was conservative in respect to Type I error (Stevens, 1990). In writing, the small group had large variance, which signified the danger of using a liberal statistical test, so a more stringent α level was used to avoid Type I error. Bryant-Paulson post hoc procedure was used to follow up the significant result in the omnibus test in literature and writing ($F = 12.06$, $p < .001$ in literature, and $F = 10.18$, $p < .001$ in writing). Results from a pairwise comparison using a formula for nonrandomized design and harmonic means showed the grouping models of self-contained, pull-out, and language arts block as each significantly different from that of heterogeneous cluster grouping, which showed the highest posttest adjusted mean. The self-contained, pull-out, and language arts block were not significantly different from each other (BP = −6.65 for the comparison between self-contained and heterogeneous cluster, BP = −6.15 for the comparison between pull-out and heterogeneous cluster, and BP = 7.04 for the comparison between language arts block and heterogeneous cluster). In all of these cases, $p < .01$.

In the writing pairwise comparisons, language arts block was found to be significantly different, with a lower posttest adjusted mean from the other three grouping models in terms of students' writing performance (BP = 8.30 for the

Table 6

A: Comparison of Student Performance in Literature Assessment
Among G/T Grouping Models

Grouping Model	n	Pretest Mean (SD)	Posttest Mean (SD)	Adjusted Mean (SD)	F	Effect Size (η^2)
Self-contained	171	5.77 (1.58)	6.91 (1.77)	7.01 (.13)		
Pull-out	54	5.11 (1.56)	6.44 (1.33)	6.72 (.23)	12.06*	.068
Cluster of gifted	160	6.92 (1.55)	8.08 (1.82)	7.88 (.13)		
Language arts block	113	6.19 (1.52)	6.89 (1.37)	6.88 (.15)		

B: Comparison of Student Performance in Writing Assessment
Among G/T Grouping Models

Grouping Model	n	Pretest Mean (SD)	Posttest Mean (SD)	Adjusted Mean (SD)	F	Effect Size (η^2)
Self-contained	168	7.92 (3.20)	11.30 (4.14)	11.34 (.27)		
Pull-out	54	6.04 (2.71)	10.80 (4.33)	11.57 (.48)	10.18*	.061
Cluster of gifted	152	9.34 (3.09)	11.03 (3.08)	10.52 (.29)		
Language arts block	100	7.30 (2.85)	8.82 (3.19)	9.10 (.34)		

Note: *$p < .001$

comparison between self-contained and language arts block, BP = 6.82 for the comparison between pull-out and language arts block, and BP = 5.05 for the comparison between heterogeneous class with cluster of the gifted and language arts block). The p values in these comparisons were also less than .01.

The results from analyzing repeated exposure to the units are reported in Table 7. Results indicated that students registered increasing and mostly significant ($p < .05$) progress each time they were exposed to the units. Subanalysis was done by grade level to control the effect of developmental maturation, and the results showed that the observed improvement from repeated use of the units could not be solely attributed to natural growth in cognition.

Table 8 reports the results of treatment by socioeconomic level of schools. Seventy-two percent of the low-SES group were students on free or reduced lunch status, and 67% of that group represented a minority. The high-SES group was comprised of students who came from schools with fewer than 20% minority students or students on free or reduced lunch. The comparison was based on the same unit, *Autobiographies*, used with fifth graders. Students having been taught two William and Mary units in these schools were excluded from the

Table 7   Student Outcome From Repeated Exposure to Units

Assessment	Usage	N	Pretest Mean (SD)	Posttest Mean (SD)	t
Literature	1st time	52	5.21 (1.09)	6.48 (1.60)	4.60**
	2nd time	52	7.31 (1.54)	8.38 (2.20)	3.60**
Writing	1st time	49	10.12 (3.01)	11.37 (3.61)	1.92
	2nd time	49	12.24 (3.78)	13.67 (3.17)	2.55*

Note: *$p < .05$; **$p < .001$

Table 8

A: Comparison of Student Outcome in Literature Assessment Between Experimental Students Low and High in SES

Group	n	Pretest Mean (SD)	Posttest Mean (SD)	Adjusted Mean (SE)	F	p
Low SES	57	5.89 (1.47)	7.21 (1.59)	7.28 (.26)	2.50	.12
High SES	49	6.94 (1.38)	7.98 (2.19)	7.90 (.28)		

B: Comparison of Student Outcome in Writing Assessment Between Experimental Student Low and High in SES

Group	n	Pretest Mean (SD)	Posttest Mean (SD)	Adjusted Mean (SE)	F	p
Low SES	53	7.70 (3.20)	13.06 (4.85)	13.47 (.56)	2.38	.13
High SES	52	10.15 (3.43)	15.15 (3.15)	14.74 (.57)		

comparison. Although test scores in literature assessment favored high-SES groups, the difference was not statistically significant ($p = .12$).

In writing assessment, the equal variance assumption was not tenable, but the SES effect was not significant either ($p = .13$). Interestingly, although the low-SES group started much lower than the high-SES group as shown by their pretest scores, they gained much after the curriculum treatment, indicating their effective mastery of the hamburger model for persuasive writing. An important point is that both low-SES and high-SES students can improve significantly from the curriculum intervention. In literature, score differentials for low-SES students were 1.32 ($t = -4.836$, $p < .001$) while for high-SES students, the gain score differential was 1.04 ($t = -2.98$, $p < .001$). In persuasive writing, gain score differentials for low-SES students were 5.36 ($t = -7.969$, $p < .001$), while they were 5.00 for high-SES students ($t = -8.82$, $p .001$).

DISCUSSION

The data suggested that the use of the William and Mary language arts units produces significant and important gains for gifted learners in key aspects of the language arts as assessed by demonstration of high-level thinking on performance-based measures. Such findings contribute to our understanding of teaching literature and writing in an integrated way, teaching for deeper understanding, and teaching for thinking within a subject area, all aspects found to be important in enhancing learning in teaching to the new standards and research on teaching both literature and writing (e.g., Hillocks, 1986; McLaughlin & Talbert, 1993). The deliberate use of instructional models, such as the literature web, hamburger model, and the Paul model of reasoning within the curriculum, used to promote student automaticity in thinking and writing about ideas, appears to have had a positive effect on student learning. It may be important to adjust training cycles for teachers in order to highlight these findings and to demonstrate how the integrated model of instruction itself may contribute to higher level learning.

The subanalyses conducted to understand the pattern of student responses on individual items provided an important basis for using test results to diagnose student areas of weakness and key emphases to be stressed in future teaching. These data clearly suggest the need to work more with students on their abstract thinking skills and elaboration skills. It also may be important to track students' performance over time. Do they grow more when teachers have more experience in teaching the units? Do students exposed to multiple units show differential gains? These questions are important considerations in continuing to use the units with the same or different learners. The data might also be interpreted to suggest that broader use of the units among teachers and deeper training would enhance student learning to a greater extent. Thus, there is a need to consider training more teachers in using the curriculum and to consider advanced training for teachers using the curriculum currently.

Small gender differences found in this study demonstrated a direction of female superiority in the verbal areas not typically reported in the literature (Callahan & Reis, 1996). Perhaps the more frequent use of performance-based measures to assess authentic learning will uncover subtle differences in performance between groups not found by use of more standardized measures. Performance-based assessment and protocols require the demonstration of higher level thinking in a domain (Wiggins, 1993) and an open-ended response that encourages fluency, providing the opportunity for students to reveal depth of understanding, rather than speed. Yet, the effect sizes suggest that the findings are not educationally important. Thus, opportunities to learn abound for both genders in using the curriculum.

The findings on grouping echo the Kulik and Kulik study (1992) that noted the importance of curriculum intervention in the understanding of benefits of grouping models. The fact that students showed important gains across grouping models attests to the importance of the curriculum as opposed to the particular grouping approach employed. It was particularly heartening to find strong gains for students in cluster-grouped heterogeneous classes, since many gifted students are served under that model of instruction, as well as strong gains in pull-out programs.

The findings also support the use of the curriculum with special populations, in particular minority students from low-SES backgrounds. Recommendations for serving such students include the call for the use of multicultural literature, activities that are open-ended, and alternatives in assignments that promote learning among minority and disadvantaged groups (Ford, 1996). The William and Mary curriculum contains all of those features, and teachers are provided training in the application of models that promote student engagement. It may be that the incorporation of these features attracted and motivated students from low-SES backgrounds. Moreover, the findings suggest the need to balance teacher-initiated use of direct instruction with student-initiated work. The direct teaching of scaffolds to support learning appeared to benefit these learners greatly, especially in the area of persuasive writing, where they outperformed more advantaged students even though they were less competent when they began the unit.

The findings related to the use of two units in comparison to one also reinforce the need for facilitating depth of student understanding of higher level skills and concepts. The assumption that gifted learners develop to higher levels on their own without purposeful instructional guidance and powerful learning stimuli is clearly challenged by these results. Strong curricula, coupled with the use of effective research-based content and focused teaching strategies, provide the best chance for sustaining growth in gifted learners. Such approaches have already been found as central to students' learning in mathematics and science reform projects (Kennedy, 1999).

CONCLUSIONS

The use of the William and Mary language arts curriculum made a difference in student learning in regard to both literary analysis and interpretation skills and persuasive writing skills based on an accumulated database drawn from multiple unit use across multiple school districts over a five-year period. Importantly, the treatment was effective with both economically disadvantaged and economically advantaged students. It was also equally effective with males and females when educational importance was used as the criterion to examine small differences. The grouping model used showed minimal evidence of impact on student performance, with all grouping models showing strong evidence of learning gains. An item analysis of group performance on each instrument illustrates internal variations of student performance and may be used to highlight strengths and weaknesses of student profiles in relation to the skills assessed. Clearly, students benefited from their exposure to the William and Mary curriculum in language arts, and these benefits were documented in terms of learning outcomes of statistical and educational significance on performance-based assessment measures. Furthermore, this study showed how curricula derived from standards-based reform can be assessed using instruments that require demonstration of higher order reasoning in the language arts domain.

Implications of the Study

Several implications emerge from these study findings that have meaning for both researchers and practitioners. A set of questions still remains to be answered at a deeper level about curriculum implementation of the William and Mary units. For example, how do the variables of length of treatment time, intensity of treatment, and transfer use of the core teaching models to other material in and out of the language arts context impact student learning results? Moreover, what are the longer term advantages of using the curriculum across years and beginning it early at the primary level, rather than later at the intermediate? Another area of special interest in the field of gifted education would be how the curriculum works with various special populations beyond the economically disadvantaged, especially the learning disabled. Moreover, there remains to be answered a set of questions related to how effective this curriculum might be with less gifted students. This study has demonstrated that it works, based on nationally normed tests, with the upper 6% of school-aged populations and with low-SES students scoring within the top 10% of the population, but it has not demonstrated effective learning for a broader range of ability. Research also needs to investigate more fully the teacher variable in respect to the effects of background, training in gifted education and language arts, and specific training on unit implementation, as this variable may influence student learning levels. Grouping effects also need to be studied under more controlled conditions than were possible in this study. Finally, this study's results suggest a need for more comparative intervention studies that would tease out what curricular and instructional approaches work best in each subject area with gifted learners at different stages of development.

Implications for practitioners are also evident from these findings. The use of a defined differentiated curriculum for gifted learners that also addresses national and state standards is supported by this study and suggests the need for clarity in deciding the focus of gifted programs. This study also clarifies the value of using advanced literature integrated with writing as an effective approach with gifted populations. This study further substantiates other research on the effects of teaching higher order thinking embedded in content, rather than separate from it. Both performance-based assessment tools used in the study set out tasks that required higher level thinking to accomplish them. Another implication of this study for practitioners is the importance of teaching models of learning in a systematic way to enhance overall cognitive development in literary analysis and interpretation and persuasive writing. The use of strong combinational models that have demonstrated learning effects in other studies (e.g. Hillocks, 1986) lends support to the premise that broad eclecticism in teaching the language arts is not supported by research. Finally, this study suggests that high-powered curricula can produce growth gains for gifted learners regardless of the nature of the learner or the grouping model employed. Such understanding should aid school-based programs in shifting their focus of attention from the administrative aspect of program delivery to the classroom-based arena of appropriate curriculum and instruction.

REFERENCES

Aldrich, P., & McKim, G. (1992). *The consumer's guide to English-language arts curriculum.* New York: Saratoga-Warren Board of Cooperative Educational Services.

Aldrich, P., & Mills, C. J. (1989). A special program for highly able rural youth in grades five and six. *Gifted Child Quarterly, 33,* 11–14.

Applebee, A. N., Langer, J. A., Mullis, I. V. S., Latham, A. S., & Gentile, C. A. (1994). *NAEP 1992 writing report card.* Washington, DC: Office of Educational Research and Improvement.

Armstrong, D. C. (1994), A gifted child's education requires real dialogue: The use of interactive writing for collaborative education. *Gifted Child Quarterly, 38,* 136–145.

Bailey, J. M., Boyce, L. N., & VanTassel-Baska, J. (1990). Writing, reading, and counseling connection: A framework for serving the gifted. In J. VanTassel-Baska (Ed.), *A practical guide to counseling the gifted in a school setting* (pp. 172–189). Reston, VA: Council for Exceptional Children.

Baskin, B. H., & Harris, K. H. (1980). *Books for the gifted child.* New York: Bowker.

Baumann, J. F., & Ivey, G. (1997). Delicate balances: Striving for curricular and instructional equilibrium in a second-grade, literature/strategy-based classroom. *Reading Research Quarterly, 32,* 244–275.

Beck, I. L., & McKeown, M. G. (1999). Comprehension: The sine qua non of reading. *Teaching and Change, 6,* 197–211.

Bottomley, D. M., Truscott, D. M., Marinak, B. A., Henk, W. A., & Melnick, S. A. (1999). An affective comparison of whole language, literature-based, and basal reader literacy instruction. *Reading Research and Instruction, 29,* 115–129.

Brown, A. L., & Campione, J. C. (1994). Guided discovery in a community of learners. In K. McGilly (Ed.), *Classroom lessons: Integrating cognitive theory and classroom practices* (pp. 229–270). Cambridge, MA: MIT Press.

Burkhalter, N. (1995). A Vygotsky-based curriculum for teaching persuasive writing in the elementary grades. *Language Arts, 72,* 192–196.

Callahan, C., & Reis, S. (1996). Gifted girls, remarkable women. In K. Arnold & R. Subotnik (Eds.), *Remarkable women* (pp. 171–192). Cresskill, NJ: Hampton Press.

Campbell, D. T., & Stanley, J. C. (1969). *Experimental and quasi-experimental designs for research.* Chicago: Rand McNally.

Cohen, D., & Hill, H. (1998). *Instructional policy and classroom performance: The mathematics reform in California* (Research Report NO. RR-39). Philadelphia: University of Pennsylvania, Consortium for Policy Research in Education.

Cohen, J. (1988). *Statistical power analysis for the behavioral sciences* (2nd ed.). Hillsdale, NJ: Erlbaum.

Collins, N. D., & Alex, N. K. (1995). *Gifted readers and reading instruction.* Bloomington, IN: ERIC Clearinghouse on Reading, English, and Communication. (ERIC Document Reproduction Service No. ED 379 637)

Connor, U. (1990). Linguistic/rhetorical measures for international student writing. *Research in the Teaching of English, 24,* 67–87.

Csikszentmihalyi, M., Rathunde, K. & Whalen, S. (1993). *Talented teenagers: The roots of success and failure.* New York: Cambridge University Press.

Delcourt, M. (1994). Characteristics of high-level creative productivity: A longitudinal study of students identified by Renzulli's three-ring conception of giftedness. In R. F. Subotnik & K. D. Arnold (Eds.), *Beyond Terman: Contemporary longitudinal studies of giftedness and talent* (pp. 401–426). Norwood, NJ: Ablex.

Dixon, F. A. (1993). Literature seminars for gifted and talented students. *Gifted Child Today, 16*(4), 15–19.

Donovan, M. S., Bransford, J. D., & Pellegrino, J. W. (1999). *How people learn: Bridging research and practice.* Washington, DC: National Academy Press.

Ford, D. Y. (1996). *Reversing underachievement among gifted black students: Promising practices and programs.* New York: Teachers College Press.

Gallagher, S. A., & Stepien, W. J. (1996). Content acquisition in problem-based learning: Depth versus breadth in American studies. *Journal for the Education of the Gifted, 19,* 257–275.

Gardner, H. (1991). *The unschooled mind: How children think and how schools should teach.* New York: Basic Books.

Goldman, A. I. (1994). Argument and social epistemology. *Journal of Philosophy, 91,* 27–49.

Greeno, J. (1991). Number sense as situated knowing in a conceptual domain. *Journal for Research in Mathematics Education, 22,* 170–218.

Hall, E. G. (1990). Strategies for using journal writing in counseling gifted students. *Gifted Child Today, 13*(4), 2–6.

Hauser, P., & Nelson, G. A. (1988). *Books for the gifted child* (Vol. 2). New York: Bowker.

Henderson, S. J., Jackson, N. E., & Mukamal, R. A. (1993). Early development of language and literacy skills of an extremely precocious reader. *Gifted Child Quarterly, 37,* 78–83.

Henry, A., & Roseberry, R. L. (1996). A corpus-based investigation of the language and linguistic patterns of one genre and the implications for language teaching. *Research in the Teaching of English, 30,* 472–489.

Hertzog, N. B., Klein, M. M., & Katz, L. G. (1999). Hypothesizing and theorizing: Challenge in an early childhood curriculum. *Gifted and Talented International, 14,* 38–49.

Hillocks, G., Jr. (1986). *Research on written composition: New directions for teaching.* Urbana, IL: ERIC Clearinghouse on Reading and Communication Skills and National Conference on Research in English.

Jewell, T. A., & Pratt, D. (1999). Literature discussions in the primary grades: Children's thoughtful discourse about books and what teachers can do to make it happen. *The Reading Teacher, 52,* 842–850.

Kennedy, M. (1999). Form and substance in mathematics and science professional development. *NISE Brief, 3*(2), 1–7.

Kral, E. A. (1997). Scientific reasoning and achievement in a high school English course. *Skeptical Inquirer, 21*(3), 34–39.

Kulik, J. A., & Kulik, C. L. (1992). Meta-analytic findings on grouping programs. Gifted *Child Quarterly, 36,* 73–77.

Langer, J. A. (1994). *A response-based approach to reading literature* (Report Series 6.7). Albany, NY: National Research Center on Literature Teaching and Language.

Lawson, A. E. (1995). *Science teaching and the development of thinking.* Belmont, CA: Wadsworth.

Levy, C. M., & Ransdell, S. (Eds.). (1996). *The science of writing: Theories, methods, individual differences, and applications.* Mahwah, NJ: Erlbaum.

Mallea, K. (1992). A novel approach for the gifted reader. *Middle School Journal, 24,* 37–38.

Matthews, M. K. (1992, April). *Gifted students and whole language: A descriptive study of four classrooms.* Paper presented at the annual meeting of the American Educational Research Association, San Francisco.

McLaughlin, M. W., & Talbert, J. E. (1993). *Teaching for understanding: Challenges for policy and practice.* San Francisco: Jossey-Bass.

Moll, L. C., Tapia, J., & Whitmore, K. F. (1993). Living knowledge: The social distribution of cultural sources for thinking. In G. Salomon (Ed.), *Distributed cognitions* (pp. 139–163). Cambridge, England: Cambridge University Press.

National Assessment Governing Board. (1992). *Reading framework for the 1992 national assessment of education progress.* Washington, DC: U.S. Department of Education.

Newell, G. E. (1996). Reader-based and teacher-centered instructional tasks: Writing and learning about a short story in middle-task classrooms. *Journal of Literacy Research, 28,* 147–172.

Newstead, S. E., & Wason, P. C. (Eds.). (1995). *Perspectives on thinking and reasoning: Essays in honor of Peter Wason.* Hillsdale, NJ: Erlbaum.

Nichols, T. M. (1992). A program for teachers and students: The Junior Great Books program. *Gifted Child Today, 15*(5), 50–51.

Nichols, T. M. (1993, November). *A study to determine the effects of the Junior Great Books program on the interpretive reading skills development of gifted/able learner children.* Paper presented at the annual meeting of the Mid-South Educational Research Association, Knoxville, TN.

Paul, R. (1992). *Critical thinking: What every person needs to survive in a rapidly changing world.* Sonoma, CA: Foundation for Critical Thinking.

Rakow, S. R. (1991). Young adult literature for honors students? *English Journal, 80,* 48–51.

Reis, S. M., (1999, Winter). Message from the president. *National Association for the Gifted Communique,* 1.

Reis, S. M., & Purcell, J. H. (1993). An analysis of content elimination and strategies used by elementary classroom teachers in the curriculum compacting process. *Journal for the Education of the Gifted, 16,* 147–171.

Renzulli, J. S. (1999). What is this thing called giftedness and how do we develop it? A twenty-five year perspective. *Journal for the Education of the Gifted, 23,* 3–54.

Rogers, K. B. (1986). Do the gifted think and learn differently? A review of recent research and its implications for instruction. *Journal for the Education of the Gifted, 10,* 17–39.

Rosenblatt, L. M. (1982). The literary transaction: Evocation and response. *Theory Into Practice, 21,* 268–277.

Sadoski, M., Willson, V. L., & Norton, D. E. (1997). The relative contributions of research-based composition activities to writing improvement in the lower and middle grades. *Research in the Teaching of English, 31,* 120–147.

Salmon, M. H., & Zeitz, C. M. (1995). Analyzing conventional reasoning. *Informal Logic, 17,* 1–23.

Schack, G. D. (1989). Self-efficacy as a mediator in the creative productivity of gifted children. *Journal for the Education of the Gifted, 12,* 231–249.

Schunk, D., & Swartz, C. (1992, April). *Goal and feedback during writing strategy instruction with gifted students*. Presentation at the annual meeting of the American Educational Research Association, San Francisco.

Scruggs, T. E., & Mastropieri, M. A. (1985). Spontaneous verbal elaboration in gifted and nongifted youths. *Journal for the Education of the Gifted, 9*, 1–10.

Scruggs, T. E., Mastropieri, M. A., Jorgensen, C., & Monson, J. (1986). Effective mnemonic strategies for gifted learners. *Journal for the Education of the Gifted, 9*, 105–121.

Stephens, K. R., & Karnes, F. A. (2000). State definitions for the gifted and talented revisited. *Exceptional Children, 66*, 219–238.

Stevens, J. P. (1990). *Intermediate statistics: A modern approach*. Hillsdale, NJ: Erlbaum.

Taylor, B. (1996). The study of literature: Insights into human understanding. In J. VanTassel-Baska, D. T. Johnson, & L. N. Boyce (Eds.), *Developing verbal talent* (pp. 75–94). Boston: Allyn and Bacon.

Toulmin, S. E. (1958). *The uses of argument*. Cambridge, England: Cambridge University Press.

VanTassel-Baska, J. (1986). Effective curriculum and instructional models for talented students. *Gifted Child Quarterly, 30*, 164–169.

VanTassel-Baska, J. (1995). The development of talent through curriculum. *Roeper Review, 18*, 98–102.

VanTassel-Baska, J., Bass, G. M., Ries, R. R., Poland, D., & Avery, L. (1998). A national pilot study of science curriculum effectiveness for high-ability students. *Gifted Child Quarterly, 42*, 200–211.

VanTassel-Baska, J., & Brown, E. F. (2000). An analysis of gifted education curriculum models. In F. A. Karnes & S. M. Bean (Eds.), *Methods and materials for teaching the gifted* (pp. 93–131). Waco, TX: Prufrock Press.

VanTassel-Baska, J., Johnson, D. T., Hughes, C., & Boyce, L. N. (1996). A study of language arts curriculum effectiveness with gifted learners. *Journal for the Education of the Gifted, 19*, 461–480.

Vye, N. J., Goldman, S. R., Hmelo, C., Voss, J. F., & Williams, S. (1998). Complex mathematical problem solving by individuals and dyads. *Cognition and Instruction, 15*, 435–484.

Wiggins, G. (1993). Assessment: Authenticity, context, and validity. *Phi Delta Kappan, 75*, 200–208, 210–214.

10

Practices of Preservice Teachers Related to Gifted and Other Academically Diverse Learners

Carol A. Tomlinson, Ellen M. Tomchin, Carolyn M. Callahan, Cheryll M. Adams, Paula Pizzat-Tinnin, Caroline M. Cunningham, Barbara Moore, Lori Lutz, Chris Roberson

The University of Virginia

Nancy Eiss

Radford University

Mary Landrum

The College of William and Mary

Scott Hunsaker

The University of Georgia

Marcia Imbeau

University of Arkansas

Preservice teachers face formidable tasks of planning and management as they enter the classroom for the first time as professionals. They also bring with them mental imprints of what teaching and learning are like, images

Editor's Note: From Tomlinson, C. A., Tomchin, E. M., Callahan, C. M., Adams, C. M., Pizzat-Tinnin, P., Cunningham, C. M., Moore, B., Lutz, L., Roberson, C., Eiss, N., Landrum, M., Hunsaker, S., & Imbeau, M. (1994). Practices of preservice teachers related to gifted and other academically diverse learners. *Gifted Child Quarterly, 38*(3), 106-114. © 1994 National Association for Gifted Children. Reprinted with permission.

gained not from their professional preparation programs, but from their years as students. Once in the role of teacher, those views may be reinforced by the circumstances of their apprenticeship. This qualitative study reports five themes in the preservice teaching experience of 10 preservice teachers which may reinforce traditional views of schooling and discourage understanding and addressing unique learning needs of academically diverse learners such as gifted, remedial and special education learners.

INTRODUCTION

Identifying student differences and providing instruction to accommodate those differences are problems frequently mentioned by beginning teachers, yet the complexity of teaching for the novice is so consuming that preservice teachers are often frustrated in their attempts to understand and address the needs of academically diverse students. As there are more and more calls for heterogeneity in classrooms, it is essential that we understand how novice teachers come to understand and address the needs of academically diverse learners, among whom are gifted learners, in their classrooms. Furthermore, it is useful to examine novice teacher attitudes toward a variety of academically diverse learners, rather than a single population of outliers only, because understanding commonalities and differences of beginning teachers' attitudes toward varied groups of outliers may be useful to those charged with facilitating development of the novices both at preservice and inservice levels.

Research on attitudes and practices of novice teachers directly related to student diversity is not abundant. Nonetheless, there is evidence of ways in which novice teachers develop as professionals and ways in which they regard students with diverse learning needs.

REVIEW OF THE LITERATURE

Impact of Teacher Training on Preservice Teachers

There is much evidence that preservice teachers enter and leave teacher preparation programs with a relatively unchanged set of beliefs (Book, Byers, & Freeman, 1983; Copeland, 1980; Finlayson & Cohen, 1967; Kagan, 1992; Lasley, 1980; Ross, 1988; Tabachnick & Zeichner, 1984). There are varied hypotheses for the lack of modification of beliefs as a result of professional training. One suggestion is that the preservice teachers have spent so many hours as students during their own schooling developing models and images of school, that the resulting beliefs are simply too strong to be drastically reshaped (Bullough, 1989; Jordell, 1987; Lortie, 1975; Zeichner & Gore, 1990). This may be further confounded by the fact that most young people who enter teaching as a profession were comfortable and successful with the prevailing models of schooling (Pajares, 1992) which they encountered during their "apprenticeship of observation" (Lortie, 1975). A second hypothesis is that teacher education programs do, in fact, change attitudes of preservice teachers, but that everyday experience in schools washes out whatever changes came about (Veenman, 1984). Koehler (1985) suggests, however, that the key problem is that teacher education programs promote teaching skills and attitudes which the novices do not yet see as relevant or necessary. Others believe that teacher preparation programs transmit beliefs and practices which are largely conservative and in harmony with those held by entering novices and which validate existing school practices (Giroux, 1980; Zeichner & Tabachnick, 1981). Whether one hypothesis or a combination is correct, it appears that novice teachers' attitudes about schooling are not radically shaped by experiences in their teacher training programs. Among beliefs which novices may continue to hold about teaching in spite of, or with reinforcement of, teacher preparation are delineated by McDiarmid (1990):

1. Teaching subject matter involves telling or showing.

2. Every child is special and deserves an education tailored to his/her particular needs.

3. Different objectives and standards should be applied to different students.

4. Some children are not capable of learning basic skills in reading and mathematics.

5. Pupils are responsible for their school failures because they lack either the right home environment, right attitude, or right ability.

6. The more learners practice, the more they will learn.

7. Subject matter at the elementary school level is "simple" and they already know enough to start teaching before they begin their professional studies. (p. 13)

Attitudes of Preservice Teachers About Gifted and Other Academically Diverse Learners

One set of attitudes which preservice teachers may bring with them to classroom teaching relates to learners such as gifted, remedial, learning disabled, emotionally disturbed, and other students who are academic outliers in that their learning differs in some significant ways from the learning of their more typical agemates. The attitudes will shape ways in which novices interpret their experiences in the classroom (Wood & Floden, 1990).

Veteran educators without training in teaching exceptional students appear to be less tolerant of such students than are educators who have special training

Putting the Research to Use

The novice teachers in this study indicate beliefs that students differ in academic readiness and need. Furthermore, the novices believe that they should adjust instruction in ways which challenge varied learners. Transforming those beliefs into action, however, proves very difficult.

Educational leaders interested in assisting novice teachers to develop skill in understanding and responding to varied student traits and needs should consider intervention at three levels. First, teacher education programs should focus on teacher as assessor and problem solver, learning as construction of meaning, and teaching as facilitating. These views of school offer promise as an antidote to prevailing views of teachers as dispensers of a single body of knowledge and all students as reproducers of that single body of knowledge. Second, teacher preparation programs should assist cooperating teachers or master teachers in refining their skills of differentiating classrooms for academically diverse learners. Cooperating teachers who make responsiveness to student diversity central to the conversation of the apprenticeship could help novice teachers develop skill in identifying and responding to students' learning needs, associate appropriateness of academic fit with classroom management, and develop early habits of classroom practice which invite success in varying students. Third, staff developers and other educational leaders at the public school level should focus resources of experts in gifted education, special education, and compensatory education on beginning teachers. Mentorships established among educators experienced in adapting classroom instruction for diverse needs and novice teachers in the early months or years of their practice could become catalysts for differentiating instruction while teaching habits are more malleable than may be the case in later years.

in exceptionalities (Bryan, 1974; Copenhaver & McIntyre, 1992; Hanninen, 1988; Leyser & Abrams, 1982; Sachs, 1990; Starko & Schack, 1989), although Panda and Bartel (1972) found that training after a certain level of awareness does not appear helpful in changing veteran teachers' perceptions about exceptional students. Preservice teacher attitudes may also correlate positively with their knowledge of gifted students (Morris, 1987; Nicely, Small, & Furman, 1980) or their sense of self-efficacy in meeting the needs of these students (Jordan, Kircaali-Iftar, & Diamond, 1993).

In general, it appears that experienced teachers prefer working with students of average or above-average ability to working with remedial students

(Khan & Weiss, 1972; Leyser & Abrams, 1982; Panda & Bartel, 1972). Nonetheless, many educators tend to view gifted learners in less favorable and more stereotypical ways (Crammond & Martin, 1987; House, 1979; Jacobs, 1975) or to devalue educational programs or provisions for them (Colangelo & Kelly, 1983). Some studies indicate that preservice teachers' attitudes toward the gifted are more positive than those of veteran teachers (Buttery, 1979), some suggest that experience as a teacher may predict positive attitudes toward the gifted (Hanninen, 1988; Rubenzer & Twaite, 1979), and others indicate little significant difference in the attitudes of preservice and experienced teachers toward gifted students (Crammond & Martin, 1987; Guskin, Majd-Jabbari, & Peng, 1988).

Of more interest may be indications that preservice teachers believe students do differ in learning profile and need, and desire to address those needs in meaningful ways (McDiarmid, 1990; Veenman, 1984), but that inexperience frustrates their attempts to do so (Fuller & Brown, 1975; Paine, 1990).

Complexities of Classroom Life for the Preservice Teacher

Even though preservice teachers may enter and leave teacher preparation programs with a similar set of beliefs about schooling, the novices are not able to practice education as would an experienced or expert teacher. It is important to be aware of the process of acclimation to classroom teaching which impacts the ability of the novice to translate beliefs into practice and which may ultimately shape or reinforce beliefs about teaching and learning.

Preservice teachers typically focus on "survival" concerns about personal adequacy, class control, being liked by students, and opinions and evaluations of supervisors. Being praised and failing dominate their thoughts in the early stages of teaching. As a result of the early pressure of teaching, and perhaps in response to the "prevailing ethos of the public school" (Fuller & Brown, 1975, p. 41), preservice teachers become more negative, rigid, and authoritarian— shifting from a more idealistic or humanistic vantage point to a more controlling and custodial one.

Concerns about teaching conditions (e.g., numbers of students, noninstructional duties, inflexible situations, teaching materials) and concerns about pupils (e.g., recognizing the social and emotional needs of students, inappropriateness of curricular materials for certain students, tailoring content for individual students) tend to come later and with much more experience than is available to the novice (Fuller & Brown, 1975).

Novices are more likely to alter lessons in response to student requests or interests than in response to performance cues (Clark & Peterson, 1986), less likely to note and accommodate to student characteristics than to environmental/ physical characteristics (e.g., time of day, importance of the lesson) as they teach (Calderhead, 1991), and more likely to focus on information related to classroom management than on information related to instruction (Clark & Peterson, 1986). Because they perceive fewer cues and interpret them in more limited ways, they are less able to make inferences than veteran teachers (Berliner, 1987). Furthermore, novices have fewer teaching repertoires and modes of assessing student understanding than do experts and are more bound to lesson plans (less able to improvise) than are experts, encountering problems when student questions require explanations not planned in advance (Livingston & Borko, 1989). Shulman (1987) points out that teachers must be able to define and assess key aspects of student ability, culture, motivation, and prior knowledge and skill in order to be able to adjust or tailor a lesson to student needs. Thus the skill level of the novice, which makes instructional leadership in the classroom difficult in general, is likely to impact in significant ways the novice's ability to deal effectively with students who differ from the norm. This study examines factors in the student teaching experience of 10 preservice teachers which relate to their instruction of academically diverse learners, among whom are gifted learners.

BACKGROUND

The National Research Center on the Gifted and Talented at the University of Virginia is currently engaged in a three-phase study (baseline, intervention, and first-year teaching follow-up) designed to facilitate understanding of ways in which preservice teachers develop awareness of needs of exceptional learners, including gifted learners, and how the novices begin meeting the needs of exceptional learners. Five college and university teacher education programs, selected on the basis of willingness to collaborate, access to classrooms in which student teachers instruct a range of academically diverse learners, and qualifications of staff to serve as site directors for the study, are participating in the project. The five university sites represent three states in the South, Southeast, and Middle Atlantic regions of the country, as well as small, medium, and large colleges/universities. During the three phase study, approximately 70 novices and their cooperating teachers will be surveyed, observed, and interviewed. The study looks at attitudes and practices of novice teachers and their cooperating teachers related to academically diverse learners (a) with no research intervention, (b) with a workshop intervention in which the preservice teachers are helped to develop both awareness of and strategies for meeting needs of academically diverse learners, (c) with both the workshop intervention and a mentorship intervention focusing on needs of academically diverse learners, and (d) as the preservice teachers move from student teaching and into their first year of full-time teaching. Data gathering for the larger study utilizes two quantitative instruments (a survey of attitudes and practices and a structured classroom observation format) and two qualitative instruments (a semistructured classroom observation protocol and a semistructured interview protocol). The larger study seeks to answer five questions: (a) Will intensive orientation to the nature and needs of academically diverse learners, including the gifted, and strategies for meeting those needs via instruction and/or mentoring result in changes of attitudes and practices of preservice teachers during student teaching or first-year teaching; (b) will the interventions affect attitudes or practices of cooperating teachers; (c) how will preservice teachers seek out students in their classes for whom differentiation may be appropriate; (d) how do preservice teachers assess the effectiveness of various instructional strategies for differentiating curriculum and instruction; and (e) how do preservice teachers develop in their awareness of themselves as problem solvers capable of assessing and meeting the instructional needs of academically diverse learners?

Reported here are qualitative findings from four sites in phase one (the baseline phase) of the larger study. The four sites are located in two states and represent small, medium, and large colleges/universities. Data were the first available from the larger study and provided an opportunity to refine data collection procedures, develop data analysis procedures, and define and test emergent themes for the larger study.

PROCEDURES

Selection of Participants

Preservice teachers at each participating university site were chosen by a random selection procedure, stratified to ensure presence of academically diverse learners in the preservice teacher's classroom (therefore, for example, preservice teachers with full-time special education placements were removed from lists of potential candidates because of the likelihood that gifted learners and typical learners would be unrepresented or underrepresented in their classrooms) and to ensure participation by elementary, middle, and secondary preservice teachers proportional to the numbers in the institution's teacher education program. Potential participants were then contacted by researchers with an explanation of the study, a description of what participating in it would require, and the option to agree to or decline participation. In the few instances when selected preservice teachers declined participation (typically because of concern about observers in the classroom), replacements were chosen by the same stratified random procedures and subsequent researcher contact. Researchers secured permission to conduct the study, from school district superintendents and principals. Cooperating teachers also had the option of accepting or rejecting participation in the study. In two instances, cooperating teachers declined participation, again because of concern about additional observers in the classroom. In these instances, replacement preservice teachers, were selected by previously described procedures.

Observer/interviewers who gathered data in the study were selected for training and experience as teachers of academically diverse learners and training in qualitative research or classroom observation. All observers had advanced education and teaching experience with gifted and/or special education learners, most had advanced preparation in qualitative research and observation as well. Researchers provided a minimum of 1/2 day of training for all observer/interviewers on basic principles of qualitative observation and interviewing to ensure observer familiarity with principles and practices important in the study. A training manual with extensive information about the project, its procedures, and use of qualitative methods was also provided for all observer/interviewers.

Method

Qualitative research is well-suited to inquiry when researchers need to retain the characteristics of real-life events (Yin, 1989), when they deal with problems of educational practice and extending the knowledge base about various facets of educational practice (Merriam, 1988), when the boundaries between the phenomenon investigated and the context in which it is investigated are not clear, when multiple sources of evidence are used (Yin, 1989), and when the desired end product is a description. Each of these traits is descriptive" of the current study.

Observer/interviewers utilized several modes of data gathering: (a) a modified version of the Classroom Practices Record (CPR) (Westberg. Dobyns, & Archambault, 1990) to document the degree to which gifted learners and remedial/special education learners received differentiated content, process, or products during an observation; (b) observational field notes taken throughout the classroom visit to comment on any aspect of instruction and teacher student interaction which might be relevant to the novice's understanding of or attempt to meet instructional needs of academically diverse learners; and (c) a semistructured interview protocol based on the study's questions and content of the CPR which also encouraged interviewers to pursue topics based on facets of the observation not recorded oil the CPR.

Preservice, teachers were, observed at least three times by the same observer/interview for approximately 1 1/2 hours per observation. One observation occurred early in the student teaching experience, one in the middle, and one near the end. The interview followed each observation with a tape-recorded interview of the novice. Interviews were approximately 30 minutes long.

Following an observation-interview session, data gatherers expanded their field notes to reflect thoughts about the observation and interviews separately, as well as relationships between them and between earlier observations and interviews with the same novice. When available, relevant documents were also obtained (e.g., novice teacher logs, lesson plans, sample assignments).

Interviews were transcribed and case folders established for each novice containing interview transcripts, CPR forms, field notes, demographic data on the class(es) observed, and pre- and post-administrations of a quantitative data gathering instrument (Survey of Practices with Students of Varying Needs) not used in the current findings.

Data Analysis

Using qualitative data analysis computer programs, researchers coded interview transcripts with preordinate codes reflecting the study's questions and with codes which emerged throughout the data analysis period. Redundancy of codes led to development of themes which recur in the cases. Codes and themes were tested, expanded, and modified though use of CPR forms, interviewer/observer field notes, and teacher documents. Ultimately, researchers wrote case summaries for each novice teacher, retaining coded transcripts for additional data analysis across cases.

The research team of seven met at least weekly to discuss coding and met in peer debriefing pairs weekly or biweekly to review one another's codes, themes, and case reports. An audit trail (Lincoln & Guba, 1985) of raw data, coded data, themes, and case reports is available as an aid in establishing confirmability of data analysis procedures.

Findings presented here reflect themes recurrent across several cases and sites. While no finding is applicable to every novice studied, themes presented are the most common among the cases.

RESULTS

The five most common patterns or themes across the cases of the preservice teachers studied are: (a) stated beliefs in the existence and importance of student differences and needs, (b) ambiguity in identifying student differences and needs, (c) incomplete view of differentiating instruction in response to student differences and needs, (d) shallow wells of strategies for enacting differentiation, and (e) the presence of factors which complicate and discourage understanding and addressing student differences and needs. In presenting the themes, every effort has been made to retain the voices of the preservice teachers as they talk about their induction into teaching academically diverse learners. To this end, each presentation of a theme begins with a quotation from one preservice teacher which typifies the comments and practices of others as well.

Stated Belief in Student Differences

"You should do everything that you can to see that all students can be successful, and a lot of times, that involves a lot of different things for a lot of different students."

Like reciting familiar tenets of democracy, the preservice teachers proclaim the existence and rightness of student differences. "They [the students] are going to be different, and that's okay, and I'm going to have to know what to do about it." But as is often the case, when the abstraction becomes real, the reality is less clear-cut than was the belief. "One of my fears now in planning is that I'm afraid I'm going to try to target the center and I won't think about the variation in the class and adapt for each student. It's so hard when you have 23 students in one class period." "Within the classroom, there's only so much I can do, you know, trying to keep up with everyone." "I'm ambivalent because I have trouble making my lessons appropriate for every kid. It's hard having a sign that the bright kids might finish in 5 minutes; the other kids might need the whole class. Do I make it simpler so that every kid can under-stand it, or do I make it harder as to challenge the brighter one, or do I do it somewhere in between?" "There are five or six kids in here who fly through the work. Then what do I do? Then I have these four who can't read. Then what do I do?"

The pull of students exceeds the resources of the young teachers to meet the needs. Because there is not enough skill, time, insight, or even energy to plan or improvise to meet the needs of everyone, various outlier students can become a serious problem. The preservice teachers sense that they must let someone down, and consciously or by default, they choose. Occasionally, the novice says she focuses her energy on higher achieving students. "My expectations in my classroom are usually medium to high, in fact, mostly high, but low enough. I think, for medium ability kids to do pretty well. Kids who are low tend to do not as well in my class, and the only thing that I can do for them is give them time to catch up, you know. More time to do the assignments and constantly remind them." More often among these preservice teachers, however, there was a clear empathy and preference for attending to low-achieving learners. 'Students who are at the lower level, I pay a lot more attention to them . . . I try to make sure there are things they're going to get, or they can at least enjoy while they are trying to do it." "[I find myself] caring more for the kids who need my help . . . I think when I'm between a rock and a hard place, I tend toward giving instruction to the lower kids and maybe let the brighter kids do something on their own." "I think a lot of times teachers don't give [gifted kids] attention because they know they're going to get it done, do a good job, that sort of thing." "I give most attention to the lower group because they need the most help in achieving and because they demand the most time." "If you direct your lessons to the special education students, you know you'll have the other ones covered." "I know gifted learners get the short end as far as being chal-lenged, but they aren't hurt as a result of it."

Throughout their preservice placement, the preservice teachers held on to the belief that students differ in their needs, but from the earliest interviews, there is a clear sense among virtually all of the young teachers that addressing those needs is a near impossibility. Observations indicate that the preservice teachers hold single-mindedly to the idea that one lesson must be crafted to suit the largest number of students possible. Tailoring may then be accomplished in some limited way for a few students, most often academic outliers who struggle with the lesson.

Ambiguity in Identifying Students' Academic Differences

"In defining and serving exceptionalities, I'm flying by the seat of my pants. I hate to admit that, but it's true."

While the preservice teachers talk freely about students who are gifted, highly able, or "way ahead of the others" and those who are remedial, special education students, or "struggling," their inexperience in reading and responding to student traits is apparent in the rubrics they use to identify outliers. Struggling or remedial students are those who "can't do the work," "turn in work late," "can't sit still," "are not responsible," "have bland ideas," "look at me with a blank stare . . . you can tell by their eyes," "don't know how to get it together," "you have to keep an eye on them," and "are apathetic." On the other hand, gifted or advanced students "do the work," "sit still," "listen," "remember more," "get the work in," "do more quantity in the same time," "have high quality sentence structure," "answer questions," "grasp the material," "are not impulsive," "back up their thinking with a reason," "are right on when I need them to answer my questions," and "understand the directions and purpose for activities right away."

As the preservice teachers interpret traits of academically diverse learners, several interesting things commonly occur. First, the teachers often equate compliant behavior with academic readiness. This becomes especially puzzling for the preservice teachers when a given child appears bright and still "misbehaves." Representative are the cases of Jack, who was both "hyperactive" and "very intelligent," and Sam, who "answers questions really well" but "just can't write." These students demonstrate traits of double-labeled learners (e.g., gifted learning-disabled) and are a puzzle to their young teachers, who encounter what to them is the oxymoron of noncompliant intelligence or compliant disability. The teacher is baffled by the contradictions. "I find this child intriguing. He's got a lot of potential. I tend to think he's gifted, you know . . . I lean on him a lot for intellectual discussions in class . . . but like I said, he's behind in his writing . . . his skills are not good . . . every now and then he has some trouble . . . He picks up on theoretical things . . . It's like he has the thought processes, but he can't get it on paper . . . When he gets to the writing, he kind of gives up . . . The writing kills him, and this class is all writing . . . He has to have [writing] to succeed, so I can't give him alternatives."

Second, for gifted learners, the preservice teachers nearly always equate completing school tasks happily, or at least successfully, with high ability. Thus a very creative, independent gifted learner is likely to be overlooked as highly able because work is missing, sloppy, or fails to follow directions. "He doesn't get his work in, you know, so he's not considered a top student. He's not successful."

Third, remedial or struggling learners are assumed to be incapable of understanding because they do not "'cover the material" successfully and do not complete assignments according to specifications. "It's like if you don't have someone standing over them saying, 'You need to do this,' they will sit there and talk and goof off the whole time." Although some of the preservice teachers see a connection between behavior and academic frustration ("I have this student who gets up and walks around and does everything but the assignment, mainly. I think, because he finds it difficult"), more often the novice equates frustration during a given task with inability to learn ("He's not capable of staying on task. He can't recognize basic concepts") or intransigence ("The remedial students who don't know will hopefully sit there and pay attention so they can start learning." "The best thing I can do for a special ed. student is keep an eye on them").

Narrow Views of Differentiating Instruction

"Students are always required to do the same kind of work essentially. How they choose to do it is pretty much up to them. They're all required to do the same, basically, the same amount."

Imprecise in their reading of student ability and need, many of the preservice teachers are also imprecise as they discuss what it means to differentiate in their classrooms. Shulman (1987) suggests that there may be two elements in differentiating instruction to adapt to variations in ability and background among students. Using the analogy of a manufacturer of clothing, he first speaks of creating clothing (curricula/instruction) of an appropriate fit for a given child or group of children. This implies having more than one suit of clothing ready in anticipation of the varied sizes of children in the class. Then, he suggests, a teacher would still tailor a given suit to fit a particular learner perfectly. Differentiation of curriculum might, then, be the equivalent of creating a clothes rack with various sizes of suits (e.g., proactively planning different approaches to content, process, and/or product), and individualization of instruction might be the equivalent of tailoring a suit which is a close fit for a child in order to make it fit as perfectly as possible (e.g., different pacing, expression through preferred learning mode).

For the great majority of the preservice teachers, the notion of proactively differentiating curriculum was absent in both their conversation and practice. There were a few exceptions. One teacher used some advanced assignments for a gifted learner. In one classroom, a novice continued her cooperating teacher's practice of using first-grade reading bins with books of different levels of difficulty in different bins, matching bins to student readiness. In a kindergarten setting, a novice working with the senses taught all of her students about four categories of taste and expanded the lesson for highly able learners by giving them a model of the tongue and having them identify where the four tastes would be detected. In most instances, however, differentiation of curriculum was, at best, synonymous with individualization of instruction. There was a pervasive one-size-fits-all approach to planning lessons, with individualization happening reactively on those occasions when a method of doing so presented itself. ("How do I differentiate? By trial and error.")

For academic outliers, the result is "clothing" which is so much "too big" or "too small" that tailoring it to fit is an impossibility. "In math, everyone does pretty much the same. If someone finishes early, I give them an enrichment sheet. With remedial students, they may not understand, but at least they are being exposed to it. "The quiz is the same for everyone, but I look at them differently for children that have different ability levels." "It's not so much that the assignment was different, but the expectations were different. What was considered to be excellent performance for some students would not have been considered to be [excellent] for others." "They all write the same thing, but it can be typed or written in pen. It all depends on which is more comfortable for them." "I never really individualize. I never set them apart and require something different of them." "I suppose I could ask the gifted child to do something more with the same information." "If gifted students finish early, I'll probably just think, probably unfortunately give them busy work like reading another chapter." "I think she spends a lot of her time bored in the sense that she wants to be moving along and could be moving along. . .she would benefit from moving along. . .But it's kind of like, what do you do, give them more work because they've done such a great job?"

Shallow Well of Strategies for Responding to Academic Diversity

"Since I can't be everywhere at once, I have brighter kids who can tutor or teach the lower ones."

Given the goal of ensuring that everyone learn ("cover") the same thing and complete the same tasks, the overwhelmingly preferred instructional strategy for differentiation becomes use of cooperative learning groups. One preservice teacher even noted, "differentiation means putting kids of different abilities in a single cooperative group." In the context of cooperative learning as practiced by the preservice teachers, there are consistent role expectations for the academic outliers. High-ability children are teachers; remedial children are learners. "I think when they are in a group, [the gifted student] will take on the position of kind of like a teacher. She is the extra help they need in a group, you know." There is only an occasional sense that the 'tutors" may lack original and challenging learning opportunities or that the "learners" may be dependent on very inexperienced guides. "We grouped them, you know. This one is a very high ability, this is a very low one: let's put them together and kind of mix in the middle." "The use of groups is good because some of the lower kids couldn't have done it by themselves." "If they see they are accountable for helping each other, then it's good because 'you have a bunch of little tutors or teachers as opposed to just one." "It's good for the kids who are tutoring, and they don't even realize they are learning because when they explain something, by explaining, you learn something better." "The gifted student was starting to get bored because he knows his letters forwards, backwards probably, but its good to have him here because he can help the others." "It's better having a child who knows strategies to figure out a problem and a child who is less able to think because they could learn from one another." "Right now we try getting a group together so there is a lower ability child and a high ability child in the group so they can help each other. But sometimes I think the higher ability child overshadows and [the low ability children] are still not getting all the help they need." The words of these teachers indicate that cooperative learning, may create rather than diminish lines of demarcation between academic "haves" and "have nots" in the minds of the preservice teachers.

Factors Which Discourage Addressing Academic Diversity

"I'm thinking about so many things right now that I feel like I'm not targeting on any one problem. I'm just trying to deal with it for now. And I don't know that I'll ever reach a time when I can target on any one problem."

Becoming a teacher is a complex task, requiring simultaneous development and application of multiple skills. The preservice teachers we studied were energetic, hard working, and evidenced a desire to grow as effective educators. It is the complexity of teaching rather than a lack of effort which stymies them. At least four factors recurred in their interviews and observations as complicating their ability to understand and address needs of academically diverse learners: (a) issues of management, (b) views of teaching and learning, (c) weak role of assessment and (d) lack of emphasis from superordinates on differentiation.

Not surprisingly, managing student behavior was a priority for these preservice teachers. Having students learn from different materials, at different rates, or in different ways appeared too risky to the preservice teachers. "The class works pretty much as a whole. I lecture a lot to avoid confusion." "[The remedial students] definitely need some one-on-one instruction, but we haven't been able to do that because there's too many kids." "I guess the whole time we just move steadily through in trying to keep everybody together and everyone moving together so that it's obvious that the class is ready to move on to the next step." "You can't put one kid ahead of everyone else. It'd throw you off for the whole year." Meeting diverse needs of students interjects more variables into management, and the preservice teachers often rejected the risk: "I tried giving two different articles to various groups in one class to read and discuss, It's a big mistake because when you try to discuss it as a class, then the groups that didn't have the particular article aren't paying attention because they don't get it, you know, and I don't blame them."

A second complicating factor in addressing academic diversity is the clear presence of traditional images of teacher as dispenser of knowledge ("When a gifted kid asks me a question beyond and I can satisfy them, then I think I'm doing something good"), student as consumer of knowledge ("They have to learn to take what I say and put it on paper"), and content as a discrete body of prescribed information to be covered in a specific period of time ("It's hard to be spontaneous when you have to cram so much in one class"). This view makes it difficult for preservice teachers to picture and construct a classroom in which diversity can be accommodated.

Further confounding the task of assessing and addressing needs of academic outliers is a lack of understanding and application of assessment strategies. In the absence of a clear picture of what a student knows or understands, it is easy to assume that the single lesson of the day is appropriate for everyone. "How can I assess them? I don't see them that much." "I don't know what appropriate responses *are*." "Essentially, evaluation comes down to 'did you do it' as opposed to 'how well did you do it.' That way, more students succeed." "To me, assessment is checking to see if the work is in." "What do you mean by 'readiness'? Like, do they have their work?"

A fourth obstacle to addressing academic diversity is the perceived near absence of advice and encouragement from cooperating teachers, university supervisors, and even teacher preparation programs toward that end. "I don't feel like I've been taught in college how to deal with different levels. You are taught there is the gifted program, and there's the LD and BD program, and you're taught little things about each group. You're told you have to keep the lower level students on task, and it's got to be a task they can perform. You've got to teach the upper level students and keep them from getting bored, and you have to keep the average students going along at a good pace. They don't really tell you how to do that." "There've never been any comments about that from my university supervisor that I can think of. I don't know if there have been any comments like that at all. It seems most advice is along the lines of advice about behavior." "The only advice I've gotten about addressing student differences is that it wasn't a good idea when I assigned a learning disabled student to be the reporter in a group." "No one has said anything to me about differentiating for student differences." "I asked my cooperating teacher if we could do something a little more advanced, a little extra with third period, because they're ahead, you know. But she said we had to keep them all together because they have to take the same test at the end of the year." "We had a course about exceptional children, and it was a good class except that it packed a lot into 2 hours a week, so it was hard to sift through." "I don't know what kinds of things we should do, and no one has given me any advice."

DISCUSSION

The role of a preservice teacher is a confounding one at best. Attempts to understand and meet the needs of academically diverse learners complicate issues of planning and management and require subtle understandings and applications of both content and pedagogy. On one level, it is easy to suggest that preservice teachers may not yet be ready for the task of creating classrooms appropriate for the needs of academic outliers such as gifted, special education, or remedial learners. Rather, one might argue that preservice teaching experiences are the equivalent of a medical internship or residency when the young practitioners can learn to specialize from their previous general knowledge.

There are at least two dangers in that assumption, however. First, these preservice teachers appear to enter teaching with images of classrooms that perpetuate teacher-centered, coverage-driven practices. Thus the "generalist" skills which the preservice teachers hone in the classroom maintain a status quo of schooling which is dubious in its value even for the typical learner for whom schools are designed. The liability for academic outliers is that despite proclamations of the existence of individual differences and the responsibility of the teacher to meet them, basic practices may close off avenues of "specialization" necessary for addressing the needs of gifted, remedial, and special education students. The second danger lies in the apparent reality that there is little support for the preservice teachers in changing either their images of schooling or their single size practice of it. These preservice teachers sense that differentiating instruction for academically diverse learners is a low priority for their teacher education institutions, cooperating teachers, and university supervisors. If that is the case, rather than being a time of internship or residency during which special diagnostic and prescriptive skills will be developed for addressing needs of academically, diverse learners, preservice teachers will gain tacit permission to dispense learning as though all students need the same prescription or treatment.

Because qualitative research does not claim generalizability, it is important to conduct similar research with other preservice teachers to determine the presence or absence of similar themes in their experience. There is also a need to follow preservice teachers into their first year of teaching to see whether patterns noted in this study persist or are modified during the first year of full-time teaching. Finally, it is important to examine the influence of interventions designed specifically to impact practices of preservice teachers with academically diverse learners in order to develop strategies for facilitating teacher efficacy with gifted, special education, and remedial learners.

REFERENCES

Berliner, D. (Ed.). (1987). Ways of thinking about students and classrooms by more or less experienced teachers. In J. Calderhead (Ed.), *Exploring teachers' thinking* (pp. 60–83). London: Cassell.

Book, C., Byers, J., & Freeman, D. (1983). Student expectations and teacher education traditions with which we can and cannot live. *Journal of Teacher Education, 34*(1), 9–13.

Bryan, T. (1974). An observational analysis of classroom behaviors of children with learning disabilities. *Journal of Learning Disabilities, 7,* 26–34.

Bullough, R. (1989). *First-year teacher: A case study.* New York: Teachers College Press.

Buttery, T. (1979). Pre-service teachers' attitude regarding gifted children. *College Student Journal, 12,* 288–289.

Calderhead, J. (1991). The, nature and growth of knowledge in student teaching. *Teaching and Teacher Education, 7*, 531–535.

Clark, C., & Peterson, P. (1986). Teachers' thought processes. In M. Wittrock (Ed.), *Handbook of research on teaching* (3rd ed., pp. 255–296). New York: Macmillan.

Colangelo, N., & Kelly, K. (1983). A study of student, parent, and teacher attitudes toward gifted programs and gifted students. *Gifted Child Quarterly, 27*, 107–110.

Copeland, W. (1980). Student teachers and cooperating teachers: An ecological relationship. *Theory into Practice, 18*, 194–199.

Copenhaver, R., & Mclntyre, D. (1992). Teachers' perception of gifted students. *Roeper Review, 14*, 151–153.

Crammond, B., & Martin, C. (1987). Inservice and preservice teachers' attitudes toward the academically brilliant. *Gifted Child Quarterly, 31*, 15–19.

Finlayson, D., & Cohen, L. (1967). The teacher's role: A comparative study of the conceptions of college of education students and head teachers. *British Journal of Educational Psychology, 37*, 22–31.

Fuller, F., & Brown, O. (1975). Becoming a teacher. In K. Ryan (Ed.), *Teacher education* (74th Yearbook of the National Society for the Study of Education. Part 2, pp. 25–52). Chicago: University of Chicago Press.

Giroux, H. (1980). Teacher education and the ideology of social control. *Journal of Education, 162*, 5–27.

Guskin, S., Majd-Jabbari, M., & Peng, C. (1988). Teachers' perceptions of giftedness. *Gifted Child Quarterly, 32*, 216–221.

Hanninen, G. (1988). A study of teacher training in gifted education. *Roeper Review, 10*, 139–144.

House, P. (1979). Through the eyes of their teachers: Stereotypes of gifted pupils. *Journal for the Education of the Gifted, 2*, 220–224.

Jacobs, J. (1975). Teacher attitude toward gifted children. *Gifted Child Quarterly, 17*, 23–26.

Jordan, A., Kircaali-lftar, G., & Diamond, C. (1993). Who has a problem, the student or the teacher? Differences in teachers' beliefs about their work with at risk and integrated exceptional students. *International Journal of Disability, Development, and Education, 40*(1), 45–62.

Jordell, K. (1987). Structural and personal influences in the socialization of beginning teachers. *Teaching and Teacher Education, 3*(3), 165–177.

Kagan, D. (1992). Professional growth among preservice and beginning teachers. *Review of Educational Research, 62*, 129–169.

Khan, S., & Weiss, J. (1972). Teaching of affective responses In R.Travers (Ed.). *Second handbook of research on teaching* (pp. 759–804). Chicago: Rand McNally.

Koehler, V. (1985) Research on preservice teacher education. *Journal of Teacher Education, 36*, 23–30.

Lasley, T. (1980). Preservice teacher beliefs about teaching. *Journal of Teacher Education, 31*(4), 38–41.

Leyser, Y., & Abrams, P. (1982). Teacher attitudes toward normal and exceptional groups. *The Journal of Psychology, 110*, 227–238.

Lincoln, Y. & Guba, E. (1985). *Naturalistic inquiry.* Beverly Hills, CA: Sage.

Livingston, C., & Borko, H. (1989). Expert-novice differences in teaching: A cognitive analysis and implications for teacher education. *Journal of Teacher Education, 40*(4), 36–42.

Lortie, D. (1975). *School teacher.* Chicago. IL: University of Chicago Press.

McDiarmid, G. (1990). Challenging prospective teachers' beliefs during early field experience: A Quixotic undertaking? *Journal of Teacher Education, 41*(3), 12–20.

Merriam, S. (1988*). Case study research in education: A qualitative approach.* San Francisco: Jossey-Bass.

Morris, S (1987). Student teachers' attitudes toward gifted students. *Creative Child and Adult Quarterly, 12*, 112–114.

Nicely, R., Jr., Small, J., & Furman, R. (1980). Teachers' attitudes toward gifted children and program: Implications for instructional leadership. *Education, 101*, 12–15.

Paine, L. (1990). *Orientation towards diversity: What do prospective teachers bring?* East Lansing. MI: National Center for Research on Teacher Education. (ERIC Document Reproduction Service No. ED320 903)

Pajares, M. (1992) Teachers' beliefs and educational research: Cleaning up a messy construct. *Review of Educational Research, 62*, 307–322.

Panda, K., & Bartel, N. (1972). Teacher perception of exceptional children. *The Journal of Special Education, 6*, 261–266.

Ross, E. (1988). Becoming a teacher: The development of preservice teacher perspective. *Action in Teacher Education, 10*, 101–109.

Rubenzer, R., & Twaite, J. (1979). Attitudes of 1,200 educators toward the education of the gifted and talented: Implications for teacher preparation. *Journal for the Education of the Gifted, 2*, 202–213.

Sachs, J. (1990). The self-efficacy interaction between regular educators and special education students: A model for understanding the mainstream dilemma. *Teacher Education and Special Education, 13*, 235–230.

Shulman, L. (1987). Knowledge and teaching: Foundations of the new reform. *Harvard Educational Review, 57*(1), 1–22

Starko, A., & Schack, G. (1989). Perceived need, teacher efficacy, and teaching strategies for the gifted and talented. *Gifted Child Quarterly, 33*, 118–122.

Tabachnick, B., & Zeichner, K. (1984). The impact of the student teaching experience on the development of teacher perspectives. *Journal of Teacher Education, 35*(6), 28–36.

Veenman, S. (1984). Perceived problems of beginning teachers. *Review of Educational Research, 54*, 143–78.

Westberg, K., Dobyns, S., & Archambault. F. (1990). *The training manual for The Classroom Practices Record.* Storrs. CT: The National Research Center on the Gifted and Talented.

Wood, E., & Floden, R. (1990). *Where teacher education students agree: Beliefs widely shared before teacher education.* (ERIC Document Reproduction Service No. ED 331–781).

Yin, R. (1989). *Case study research: Design and methods.* Newbury Park, CA: Sage.

Zeichner, K., & Gore, J. (1990). Teacher socialization. In W. R. Houston (Ed.), *Handbook of research on teacher education* (pp. 329–348) New York: Macmillan.

Zeichner, K., & Tabachnick, B. (1981). Are the effects of university teacher education 'washed out' by school experience? *Journal of Teacher Education, 32*(3), 7–11.

11

Deciding to Differentiate Instruction in Middle School: One School's Journey

Carol Ann Tomlinson

The University of Virginia

As many schools move toward serving a broad range of students in heterogeneous settings, it is important to assist teachers in developing classrooms responsive to the needs of academically diverse learners. Understanding what impedes and what facilitates appropriately differentiated instruction is essential for educational leaders if schools are to move away from one-size-fits-all teaching and if heterogeneous classrooms are to become viable for "academic outliers" such as gifted, struggling, and special education learners. This case study examines the experience of one middle school confronted with a district mandate for differentiated instruction and presents the factors which impeded or facilitated their movement toward appropriately differentiated classrooms.

Editor's Note: From Tomlinson, C. A. (1995). Deciding to differentiate instruction in middle school: One school's journey. *Gifted Child Quarterly, 39*(2), 77-87. © 1995 National Association for Gifted Children. Reprinted with permission.

"That students differ may be inconvenient, but it is incapable. Adapting to that diversity is the inevitable price of productivity, high standards, and fairness to students" (Sizer, 1984, p. 194). Over time, American schools have sought various solutions to dealing with student diversity, including academic diversity.

In recent years, many voices in education have called for reduction or abandonment of homogeneous grouping of students by ability. Advocates for more inclusive classrooms make their case based largely on equity of learning opportunity (e.g., Kozol, 1991; Oakes, 1985; Page, 1991; Slavin, 1987; Wheelock, 1992). Use of heterogeneous grouping is especially commended by proponents of a middle school philosophy (Carnegie Task Force on the Education of Young Adolescents, 1989; National Middle School Association, 1992). Simultaneously, a philosophy of inclusion has become prevalent in the field of special education (Hallahan & Kauffman, 1994). As a result, many advanced and struggling learners who once had special learning needs addressed through special classes and/or resource room programs are now served almost entirely through the regular heterogeneous classroom.

Well-documented in the literature of schooling is a tendency to "teach to the middle." or to develop and deliver a standard, one-size-fits-all curriculum in American schools (Darling-Hammond & Goodwin, 1993; Goodlad, 1984; Welsh, 1986). Research indicates that regular classroom teachers make very few modifications in their instruction for gifted learners (Archambault et al., 1993; Westberg, Archambault, Dobyns, & Salvin, 1993) or for low performers (Bateman, 1993; International Institute for Advocacy for School Children, 1993; McIntosh, Vaughn, Schumm, Haager, & Lee, 1993).

Thus an issue with the broad movement toward heterogeneous grouping is whether teachers can and will appropriately address academic diversity in the regular classroom or whether the teach-to-the-middle practice will continue to prevail. It is important to understand what occurs when a school attempts to ensure appropriate differentiation of instruction based on students' learning needs. Insight into what facilitates teacher adaptation for academic diversity may well be a first step in determining whether heterogeneity can succeed in the long term for gifted learners, as well as for other students with diverse needs.

METHOD

Qualitative case study research is appropriate for exploring and interpreting educational phenomena in a real-life setting when "how" and "why" questions are the focus of the study, when multiple sources of evidence will be used, when multiple views of reality are likely to exist, and when the boundaries between the phenomenon to be studied and the setting in which it occurs are blurred (Glesne & Peshkin, 1992; Merriam, 1988; Yin, 1989).

This exploratory qualitative case study sought to understand how middle school teachers responded to a school district initiative to differentiate instruction for academically diverse students through a heterogeneous classroom. It also probed why various teachers responded to the initiative as they did.

Putting the Research to Use

If a school or district goal is to establish classrooms in which regular class-room teachers effectively address needs of academically diverse learners, intensive and sustained staff development will be required. Teachers need assistance in developing a rationale for differentiated instruction, help and support in unlearning entrenched patterns of whole-class instruction which assume that all students need to learn the same information in the same way at the same time and over the same duration, and ongoing support as they develop new ways to think about their students and instruction. Staff development has an opportunity to model differentiation for teachers, building on their readiness, interests, needs; engaging in individual goal setting; establishing individual timelines; and assessing individual progress, just as differentiated teaching would ask them to respond to the differing profiles of their students.

The case studied was Midland Middle School (pseudonym). Data were gathered by the author through prolonged engagement (Lincoln & Guba, 1985) with Midland staff, parents, and students over an 18-month period which included three school semesters and a summer staff development institute. Data sources and methods included interviews with teachers, administrators, students, and parents (totaling 28 hours); classroom observations (totaling 30 hours); attendance at and participation in teacher team meetings (totaling 11 hours), faculty meetings (totaling 4 1/2 hours), and staff development sessions (totaling 34 hours); and documents (e.g., district memos, teacher lesson plans, assignment handouts for students, and letters and notes from teachers and parents to the researcher). All data collection and analysis were conducted by the author. Triangulation via multiple sources and methods allows flexible study of emerging themes and increases the credibility or trustworthiness of findings (Lincoln & Guba, 1985). An audit trail of data and data analysis has been preserved and includes tape recorded interviews, transcripts of the interviews, original notes from observations, field notes, field documents, the researcher's reflective journal, records of evolving themes, and drafts of all figures.

Interviews were tape recorded, except in one case when a teacher requested that the recorder not be used. Transcribed recordings, field notes, and researcher memos generated throughout the research period were hand coded and ultimately analyzed for recurring coding categories (Bogdan & Biklen, 1982) leading to themes (Strauss, 1989). At several points in the research process, member checks (Lincoln & Guba, 1985) were used with some Midland teachers and students to verify or extend researcher understanding. In addition, preliminary findings were repeatedly shared and discussed with individual teachers and administrators as well as small and large groups of district administrators and Midland staff.

As researcher, I was a participant observer (Bogdan & Biklen, 1982). During the first 6 months of the study period, my role was more toward the observer end of a continuum as I interacted with informants only to conduct interviews and observe classrooms and meetings. In the later months of the study, teachers and administrators began actively seeking dialogue and information regarding differentiation of instruction from me, and my role shifted toward that of participant in the process. In the context of "workshop dialogues" and staff development sessions conducted both by me and by Midland administrators, I had the opportunity to hear, record, and ultimately understand questions and thinking of teachers about developing differentiated classrooms at a much more specific and detailed level than would likely have been the case had I persisted only with formal interviews and classroom observations.

BACKGROUND OF MIDLAND AS A RESEARCH SITE

Midland Middle School is in a relatively affluent community in the upper midwestern United States. Teacher salaries are high compared with those of many districts, resulting in a stable and experienced teaching staff. The student population contains a large number of high-ability or advanced learners, as well as students with learning problems. In this instance, the terms *high-ability* or *advanced* will be used to designate students (a) identified by the district by virtue of multiple criteria including scores at least 2 years above grade level on local norms for standardized achievement tests (local norms in Midland are well above national norms), teacher recommendation, and grades or (b) identified by teachers through classroom performance as being ahead of classmates in skills and knowledge for the subject studied. The terms *students with learning problems* or *struggling* will refer to students (a) identified by a professionally qualified child study team based on observations of the child, individually administered diagnostic instruments, and parent input as having special learning needs such as learning disabilities or mental retardation or (b) identified by teachers through classroom performance as being behind classmates in skills and knowledge for the subject studied. Although the school and district conducted formal assessment of student achievement and aptitude for special services, teachers in heterogeneous differentiated classrooms also became diagnosticians for student readiness for specific tasks—thus the two pronged definitions.

In the past in the Midland district, homogeneous grouping was employed as a means of addressing academic diversity. As is the case with many school districts, leaders in the Midland schools have more recently embraced movement toward heterogeneity, believing that it is possible to serve a wide range of academic needs in such settings while simultaneously avoiding the social stratification of students which may result from homogeneous groupings. Midland has not relinquished all homogeneity or special services for advanced or struggling learners but has moved markedly in the direction of heterogeneous classes in which teachers will serve academically diverse populations.

Following recommendations from a community study committee regarding services to academically diverse learners, the Midland Superintendent of Schools took the stance that if heterogeneous classrooms were to be effective, they would have to do more than pay lip service to addressing the needs of students with broadly differing academic profiles. Thus the Superintendent and the School Board mandated that the Midland district focus efforts and resources on ensuring that appropriately differentiated instruction would take place in its classrooms and that teachers in those classrooms develop and use skills of differentiation of instruction.

Midland Middle School had a staff of approximately 50 and a student body of approximately 550 in Grades 6 through 8. Among schools in the Midland district, Midland Middle School seemed to move most directly toward working with teachers to differentiate instruction in heterogeneous classrooms. Heterogeneity is a hallmark of middle school philosophy, and Midland Middle School administrators expressed a clear belief that such an initiative was appropriate for middle schools in general and their school in particular.

Midland was an attractive research site, then, because there was broad leadership support for ensuring that heterogeneity did not become an opportunity for one-size-fits-all instruction. Furthermore, its teachers were skilled; its staff was stable: it provided ample resources for teachers and students; and its students were relatively unassaulted by poverty, violence, poor discipline, drugs, and similar circumstances which can make both teaching and learning more difficult. It seemed to be, in many ways, a best case scenario for addressing academic diversity in a heterogeneous setting. As a Midland administrator noted. "If we can't pull this off here where we have excellent staff, strong student bodies, cooperative parents, and experts to help, then there's probably not a lot of reason to be optimistic it'll happen anywhere."

The Midland study yields generous information. Following are key insights which should be helpful to educational leaders whose role it is to assist teachers in moving toward differentiation of instruction in academically diverse classrooms. Teachers' voices are used to provide dimensionality and reality to researcher insights. Sections in the report begin with comments from Midland Middle School staff which in some way represent a prevailing view about the topic of the section.

NEED FOR DIFFERENTIATED INSTRUCTION

"We're producing good test scores, so isn't that enough?"

In the early days of the differentiation focus at Midland Middle School, many teachers expressed a clear conviction that single-size schooling as it was largely practiced at Midland was "working" and that there was little need for significant adjustment in instruction for academically diverse learners. Some educators were direct in their opposition to the idea of differentiation. Sometimes the objections were based on satisfaction with the status quo. "We're doing a good job here. We have high test scores. Parents are satisfied. I don't see any students complaining." Sometimes objections arose from an inability to grasp how differentiation would work in practice. "My job is to make sure every kid gets the material. How do I do that if they don't all do the same thing?" "How am I fair if I jiggle my expectations for different students?" "It makes no sense. Theoretically, a kid could spend a whole class on one problem. But we have this text to cover."

Other Midland educators (fewer at first) expressed support for the concept of adapting instruction in response to learner needs. "If we don't have homogeneous classes any more, then we have to figure out a way to meet kids where they are in the heterogeneous class." "We are trying to look beyond a class and see individual kids, and beyond a textbook to see individual needs." "Differentiation belongs in middle school because the middle school wants to focus on the child." "In our mission statement, we say we have the interest of students at heart and that we are going to move kids along at the best level of challenge for them. We've said that. I'm not sure we really mean it." Another teacher explained: "Kids start at different points and we are supposed to help them stretch and be successful from those various points. That's so easy to say—and so hard to do." A third teacher reflected a similar sentiment: "We spend a year on our textbook. I know some of my kids could finish it in half a year. Others need 2 years. I don't know how to do that without making somebody look bad."

If educators differed widely in their acceptance of the idea of differentiated instruction early on, there was unanimous support for the idea among students interviewed who were advanced or struggling in a given subject, and among the parents of such students. One student who was well beyond grade level expectations in several subjects explained: "Our book in social studies is really easy. It just doesn't tell us much stuff about anything." Another said, "All you have to do in science is skim the chapter and the test is so easy you get 100." A third reflected: "Our project is pretending to be Zeus, and you don't really have to know anything to do it. The project has no substance." Another student who seemed to have a grasp of differentiation misdefined explained: "Sometimes when our teachers try to do different things, they just give me *more* stuff. I wish they'd give me *harder* stuff [emphasis in voice]. I'd really like a challenge."

A student who struggled because of a learning disability said: "Sometimes I get really frustrated. I want to ask the teacher to stop talking and let me work a little longer on something. I think I could get it then." Another student who found academics difficult felt a better academic fit in a special services resource room than in her regular classes: "I'd feel lost without the Learning Center. Somebody there can always help me figure out a different way to do things. They have different books and all. They let me take my time, too. My classes aren't like that, though."

A parent mused: "Sometimes I feel like he's considered a burden, a threat. It's sad if a child feels he has no control in a classroom. What adult would want to stay in that situation?" Another parent reflection also pointed to the need for instruction modified to meet the unique profiles of academically diverse learners. "I want my child to be appreciated for his best efforts, to learn to face and overcome a true challenge, to handle frustration and disappointment. These are important skills he's not learning in a classroom. He has learned to do the bare minimum and to be praised for his lack of effort."

Midland began a journey toward modifying instruction for academically diverse learners with varied degrees of staff resistance and openness to the idea, and with a general lack of understanding of how to make differentiation a reality, even when the idea itself made sense to them.

A NEED FOR CLARITY OF DEFINITION

"Does this mean putting the smart kid in the next book?"

One contributor to the ambiguity regarding differentiating instruction in the early phases of the initiative was that there was no widely disseminated definition of differentiation from which all parties could operate. Thus a continual refrain from teachers was, "Nobody knows what differentiation means." The lack of a common definition was clear. "Does differentiation mean enrichment or acceleration for the high-end learner? Does it mean slowing down the same material or using different material for the learner who finds the work too difficult?" "Do we let kids make choices or do we choose for them?" Along with ambiguity, there was misconception. "If we differentiate instruction, we'll just lower standards because we won't let anybody fail."

In the absence of an operational definition, the most often repeated assumption among Midland teachers was, "We already do that." One teacher explanation typified many: "Good teachers have always differentiated instruction. It's really nothing new for us, except somebody downtown gave it a new name."

An interesting early finding of the research at Midland stemmed from the we-already-do-that stance. Because so many teachers asserted in interviews the pervasiveness of differentiated instruction in the middle school, I began observations with the expectation that I would see many examples of differentiated instructional practice. In fact, I found almost none. Knowing that the teachers were not being untruthful in their assertions, I concluded that our definitions of differentiation must differ. I then began asking each teacher prior to an observation, "When I see you differentiate instruction in your class today, what will I see?" The majority of teachers could readily tell me. What they called differentiation is what Shulman (1987) called individualization or tailoring. Using the analogy of a clothes rack, Shulman suggested that differentiation of instruction involves a teacher's understanding that different learners will require different sizes of garments (different input or content, different process or sense making, and/or different products or output) based on their readiness to learn. Such a view of differentiation assumes that a teacher will take a proactive stance—planning a variety of modes of learning, understanding, and expressing learning; assessing student readiness; matching learning options to student interest and need; using flexible groupings to ensure both challenge and equity; creating a flexible learning environment; assisting students in personal goal setting; serving as coach or mentor to students in reaching their goals: and assessing student progress based on individual goals and growth.

At Midland, what staff called differentiation was much more reactive than proactive. That is, there was pervasively a single lesson for all students—the same content, process, and product. However, if *students* indicated a need for adjustment in the lesson, the teacher would make minor modifications. For example, when a strong writer took her descriptive paragraph to the teacher to indicate that she had completed the assignment, the teacher whispered to her, "You seem to be okay with this, why don't you go back and add some dialogue." When a student in math indicated with considerable frustration that he "couldn't get" the problem, the math teacher said it would be, "okay for [him] to take it home and bring it back tomorrow." When a social studies student asked if she could word process her report, the teacher gave approval. In addition, teachers explained that they differentiated instruction by grading some students "a bit harder than others, so the kid who's having trouble is rewarded for trying and the kid who knows a lot doesn't get off too easy." Although this sort of individualization or tailoring is a kind of microdifferentiation and certainly shows more flexibility and awareness of students than a nondifferentiated classroom (see Figure 1), it nonetheless allows teachers to persist with a one-size-fits-all classroom and likely does not meet the academic needs of students for whom the pace of instruction is far too slow or too fast, for whom the amount of content is overwhelming or underchallenging, for whom different modes of processing ideas is essential, or for whom group goals are discouraging in their complexity or simplicity. It is certainly problematic when students rather than teachers bear the responsibility of prompting a lesson modification since some students elect to mask their learning differences or lack the skills or temperament to be a catalyst for change in the classroom.

A second finding which emerged from charting various enacted views of differentiation was that creating a differentiated classroom is not a yes/no proposition but rather a continuum along which teachers move as they develop skills of responsive teaching. That is, only a few teachers appeared largely inflexible in addressing student differences. Far more teachers were moving in the direction of developing strategies to acknowledge students' academic diversity. Even in that group, some teachers made fewer curricular and instructional modifications and others made more. In Midland, it was helpful for teachers to see the continuum (Figure 1), find their own location on it, and use it as one way to determine personal next steps in modifying instruction based on student needs. One teacher noted. "I feel better because I can see that I have already been growing and developing in the ways I teach, and I also feel better because I can get a sense of where I might go next." The continuum indicates that movement toward a more robust or macrodifferentiation is additive. That is, individualization or microdifferentiation will continue while new strategies

Figure 1   A Continuum of Differentiated Instruction Found Among Midland
Teachers

NO DIFFERENTIATION	*MICRODIFFERENTIATION*	*MACRODIFFERENTIATION*
Class works as a whole on most materials, exercise, projects	Adjusting questions in discussion	Articulated philosophy of student differences
Group pacing Group grading standards	Encouraging individuals to take an assignment further	Planned assessment/compacting Variable pacing is a given
Implied or stated philosophy that all of the students need same teaching/learning	Implied variations in grading expectations	Moving furniture
	Students pick own work groups	Planned variation in content/input
	If students finish work early, they can read, do puzzles, etc.	Planned variation in process/sense making Planned variation in product/output
Etc.	Occasional exceptions to standard pacing; may not need to show work, do all math problems	Consistent use of flexible groups
	Occasional adjustment in grading to reflect student effort and/or ability	Individual goal setting, assessment (grading)
	Etc.	Grading to reflect individual growth/progress
		Adopting a mentor role
		Etc.
	More Reactive	**More Proactive**
	More Dependent on Student Response	**More Dependent on Teacher Coaching**
	←	→
	More Fixed	**More Fluid**
	More Closed	**More Open**

are added to address students' interests and needs. "What we've been doing is a start, isn't it," one teacher said, "it's just not the end."

A working definition of differentiating instruction in Midland has now been developed and broadly discussed and disseminated. Differentiation has come to mean "consistently using a variety of instructional approaches to modify content, process, and/or products in response to learning readiness and interest of academically diverse students." The presence of a common definition earlier in the process might well have moved the discussion forward more quickly.

BARRIERS BUILT, BARRIERS REMOVED

"If they expect us to cover a certain number of chapters in a year, well then, differentiated instruction is a problem."

Asking teachers to move from a single-size classroom to one more accommodating to the learning needs and styles of academically diverse learners in heterogeneous classrooms was frightening to many Midland teachers because it indicated a need for major change in teaching practices. Change is disorienting and upsetting. Said one teacher: "We're supposed to be doing this because we're worried about the kids' self-esteem. Well, what about my self-esteem?" One response to potential change is to negate its usefulness. Teachers at Midland created a noteworthy list of "yes buts." "I don't see how they can expect us to have several things going on in rooms that are too crowded already." "If they want us to do this, they'll have to do a lot better with giving us materials." "I don't see how they can expect us to differentiate instruction when there are all those kids with all those needs in one class." "Middle school kids need more structure, not less." "We're doing too many things already."

While the list of detractors reflected an initial hope that the plan for differentiated classrooms at Midland would crumble under its own weight, the list also reflected salient concerns and genuine impediments. Understanding the conditions perceived by Midland staff as barriers to differentiated classrooms was essential in understanding the support needed by teachers in order to develop classrooms responsive to individual learning needs. Barriers perceived by Midland staff can be classified as (a) administrative issues, (b) issues of changing expectations, and (c) issues of professional support. In each instance, barriers also implied solutions, or at least countervailing approaches which might facilitate the goal of developing appropriately differentiated heterogeneous classrooms. A digest of key barriers and facilitating actions follows.

Administrative Barriers

Administrative barriers here mean those decisions made or actions taken by central office or building administrators which teachers perceived to be out of their control.

• **Top-down versus bottom-up decisions**—One administrator noted that the differentiation initiative in Midland was a top-down mandate, "reflecting a community reality, not a textbook change model." Another said, "Telling teachers what they have to do is a tough way to go, but then I have to ask myself whether we would have seen movement toward differentiated classrooms if we had waited until our staffs were ready to move on it." A teacher echoed the voice of many colleagues in stating, "When these things get mandated, it's a problem." Bandura (1986) posits that a sense of self-efficacy leads to motivation and positive behavior. When self-efficacy is lacking, the result is predictable. "If I'm not in the driver's seat, I'll only cooperate so far," said one Midland teacher. Another suggested, "They should do staff development for several years before something this big so there isn't culture shock." Given the reality of the top down mandate, Midland administrators provided many opportunities for teachers to explore the initiative, question it, and share feelings. That proved somewhat helpful, but, as one teacher explained: "I feel better after I vent, but it shouldn't have had to happen that way. It's backwards." The Midland experience indicates that initiatives which require major teacher change are likely to evoke less dissension if they arise from teacher reflection over time rather than from administrators or boards. As Fullan (1993) observed, it is difficult to mandate what matters. It may be that action from above is a useful catalyst, but judicious leaders need also to consider that unless the mandate can be transformed into motivation, positive and long-term change is unlikely.

• **Fear of faddism**—A consistent theme among Midland teachers and administrators was a sense that schools had become a "Fad of the Month" club. Thus teachers reluctant to accept changes required in a differentiated classroom found justification for their hesitancy. "It's just this year's thing," explained one teacher, "and by next year, it'll be something else." Another suggested, "I think we're only doing this because somebody thinks we have to show people we're up on the latest thing and changing all the time." An administrator reflected, "The hardest thing for us here is maintaining a focus on something important for long enough to make change possible." As an antidote to the prevailing skepticism, educational leaders have developed and shared long-term timelines for growth toward differentiated heterogeneous classrooms. Teacher doubt remains. "Every year we see last year's fix fade away." The Midland experience indicates a need for pervasive focus on differentiation over a period of several years if it is to become a reality and, in fact, if teachers are even to believe that it will.

• **Need for flexible blocks of time**—At roughly the same time the differentiation initiative was inaugurated, so was a seven-period day at Midland Middle School. In theory, the opportunity for flexible time blocks in the middle school existed. In reality, schedule rigidity was the order of the day. "My differentiation in science gets smashed with short periods and a lack of flexible scheduling. We say we have block scheduling, but there's a sense that if you run overtime, the next teacher is going to be plenty mad. If it happened to me too often, I'd be mad too. I can't get the students started on one thing before it's time to clean up. How could I get several activities started in such a short time?" Classroom observations made evident the sense of fragmentation resulting from short class periods, even in a single-approach classroom. A classroom in which tasks and time must be adapted for student needs benefits greatly from block time and flexible time use.

Issues Related to Changing Expectations

In order to develop a classroom which acknowledges and appropriately addresses broad academic diversity among students, older and more traditional pictures of schooling must give way to images built on a contemporary understanding of how students learn. Developing classrooms which were student-centered and in which students worked in a variety of ways to make sense of and apply key concepts called for major changes. Older approaches were comfortable; the newer ones, threatening. "I've been teaching for a long time in a good district where my kids get good scores. There's nothing wrong with that." "We're not malicious, but we sort of only know how to do school the way we used to when moving everybody past the same basic skills seemed to work." Figure 2 delineates skills undergirding instructionally differentiated classrooms which were troublesome for Midland teachers.

Leaders who work to facilitate differentiated instruction can take a lesson from Midland that developing academically responsive classrooms calls for a wide array of teaching skills not common in the practice of many teachers. It is important to diagnose and respond directly to needs of individual teachers as they develop core skills of instructional differentiation.

• **Multiple avenues to learning versus a single way**—Assessing student readiness and matching learning opportunity to student need, teaching with varied resources rather than a single text, encouraging expression of learning in varied ways rather than through a single test or project are key to classrooms which accommodate academic diversity. They were also unfamiliar to many teachers at Midland. An administrator reflected: "We've been shooting with water guns—a small stream of water down the middle of the class. We've got to figure out how to be oscillating sprinklers—and where to put the soak hoses from time to time." A teacher explained: "I think we really aren't sure how to see if a student has mastery enough to move to something new. Until we know how to assess, we can't really see that one student is ready to move on and another has missed the point. We don't know how to start it all. We don't know how to keep it going."

• **Management versus control**—For many Midland teachers, the great gremlin of a differentiated classroom was fear of losing control. Most of the teachers were skilled at controlling a single-focus classroom. They were less confident of their skill at coordinating multiple activities and at helping students develop self-management. "It's nuts to think these kids are old enough to discipline themselves to stay on task. Every time I give them group work to do, they start talking about all kinds of unrelated stuff. And that's when they are all doing the same thing," said one teacher. A teammate added: "It [having a classroom in which multiple activities take place] reminds me of my first year of teaching. I don't think I can handle that sense of impotence again." For many Midland teachers, managing multiple groups which were doing the *same* activity was often a skill which had to be mastered before a teacher could take the next step and adjust the activities for varied student needs.

• **Student-centeredness vs. teacher-centeredness**—Early observations at Midland revealed a preponderance of classrooms in which teachers were more active than students and in which relatively passive completion of whole group tasks prevailed. One teacher explained: "I think my lectures are about right. I'm working a bell shaped curve with the students. I challenge everybody." Another

Figure 2   Skills of Differentiation With Which Midland Teachers Experienced Difficulty

Skill of Differentiation	Explanation	Support Needed
1. Developing a Rationale for Differentiation	Teachers felt they already differentiated instruction, they were trapped by standardized test assessments, and it would take too much time to make robust adjustments.	Opportunity to talk about student diversity, discuss with students and parents "goodness of fit" of classroom for academically diverse students, chances to diagnose student readiness and learning to determine "what's working."
2. Preparing Students and Parents for a Differentiated Classroom	Teachers feared students and parents would think they were being unfair if tasks varied for different students. Also feared parent and student response to grades based on individual growth.	Guidance in preparing students and parents for differentiated classroom; skills in alternative assessment; permission to work with varied grading formats which may combine information from individual, class, school, national measures.
3. Managing a Differentiated Classroom	Teachers felt unprepared to work with multiple activities in the classroom.	Information, models, and coaching on establishing expectations for student behavior in a flexible classroom, using flexible groups, assigning students to flexible groups, giving directions for multiple assignments, monitoring group functioning, monitoring individual progress, record keeping.
4. Defining Key Concepts and Generalizations to Be Taught	Teachers were accustomed to teaching the text or curriculum guide in a linear way. Everything in the book/guide seemed important. Coverage for all students was highly valued. Teachers were not familiar with identifying pivotal concepts and generalizations which are focal for differentiated instruction.	Rationale for teaching by concept, opportunity to work with subject area experts to identify key concepts and generalizations in units of study, skill development, coaching in teaching by key generalizations.
5. Differentiating What Is to Be Taught	Teachers used a single-resource approach to provide information.	Availability of multiple resources for teaching key ideas (texts, trade books, computer programs, real-world investigations, etc.) and support understanding how to use them. Skill in conducting class discussions and sharing sessions when students have used varied resources.
6. Differentiating How Students Think About What Is Taught	In most instances, teachers used a single activity for practice regardless of level of student understanding of topic. Activities tended to be drill and practice or summary level—or "fun" without focus on essential understandings.	Information on and coaching in teaching for thinking, using varied instructional strategies to prompt thinking, developing a range of activities to assist students in sense making with essential ideas, extending activities for advanced learners.
7. Differentiating How Students Show What They Know	Most teachers used a single product/project assignment for all students. Product assignments seldom required students to revisit and expand on essential understanding about a topic.	Information and coaching on developing multiple product assignments on a single theme, varying product parameters and criteria for student interest/readiness, giving students a voice in product development, developing products which focus on real-world issues.

(Continued)

221

Figure 2 (Continued)

Skill of Differentiation	Explanation	Support Needed
8. Understanding/ Developing Models for Planning Differentiated Lessons	Most teachers lacked a framework for thinking about differentiated instruction as it might be translated into their classrooms.	Opportunity to work with a variety of teacher-developed heuristics of planning differentiated lessons and view sample differentiated lessons constructed from varied models which support appropriate differentiation.
9. Establishing Interdisciplinary Differentiated Lessons/Units	Interdisciplinary instruction was a Midland goal. It promotes connectedness of knowledge for students and lends itself well to differentiation. Midland teachers were unsure how to select appropriate concepts, coordinate planning among teachers, and develop interdisciplinary lessons. Standardized tests were a discourager.	Information and guidance in selecting appropriate concepts to support interdisciplinary instruction; assistance in team planning, execution and assessment of interdisciplinary units; curriculum guides with differentiated units; curriculum guides with interdisciplinary focus/options.
10. Expanding Instructional Strategies for Differentiating Content-Process-Product	Teachers generally lacked knowledge of or comfort with a range of instructional strategies which facilitate management of differentiated classrooms.	Information and coaching with varied instructional strategies which support differentiation (e.g., compacting, independent study, contracts, creative problem solving, graphic organizers, etc.).

said: "Right now I set the pace. That works. This new idea is that students might work at their own pace. It's not possible in the classroom." A key element of teacher-centeredness was moving systematically through texts to get ready for standardized tests. Midland teachers believed it was their job to ensure that students made it through prescribed curricula in time to fare well on end-of-year state and local assessments. "What if the scores fall?" worried a teacher. "Then it will be my fault because I didn't cover everything with everybody. It'll be my hide they're after." This fear was exacerbated when concept-based teaching was commended as key in differentiation. Extending activities for advanced students and ensuring meaningful and focused learning for students who have great difficulty in grasping material depend on teaching by concept rather than covering a mass of material which may be long since mastered by an advanced student and overwhelming to a struggling student. For Midland teachers, it was unfamiliar and frustrating to identify key concepts in texts and other classroom materials. "What differentiation says to us is that we have to know what the essential concepts are in our units and how to build learning on those concepts in a lot of ways. I don't think I can do that. At least not yet." Teaching by concepts was also threatening in light of the looming standardized tests. "It [teaching by concepts] scares me because of the end-of-year tests. We probably wouldn't cover everything, and what will happen to the [standardized test] scores?"

Midland teachers who were asked to develop student-centered, concept based classrooms but who remained aware that their own success and that of their students would be assessed according to fact-based standardized tests felt they were being asked to do the impossible. They were probably correct. Educational leaders would do well to deal with that conflicting message before teachers must do so.

Issues Related to Professional Support

Some antidotes to fears surrounding the changing expectations for Midland teachers lay in support which they felt would help them risk new behaviors in the classroom.

- **Need for an umbrella**—In any scenario Midland teachers could imagine, the effort required to develop a differentiated classroom seemed massive. They referred often to feeling fragmented. "We're going in too many directions. We have to have a focus." "I'm working so hard," said a teacher. "I don't know how I can add anything else." "This is one more thing for me to do, and I am already overwhelmed." A framework or umbrella to help teachers see the connectedness of varied district or school initiatives would be helpful to Midland staff in exactly the same way that a good interdisciplinary unit draws together concepts and insights for students. For example, the umbrella of "developing student-centered classrooms" could draw on such initiatives as writing workshops, teacher advisory, differentiation, cooperative learning, interdisciplinary curricula, multiculturalism, and many other practices which were being commended to the Midland staff but which they saw as separate mandates. Lacking such a framework for comprehensive change, Midland teachers felt pulled apart, splintered. "I'm stretched to the bone already." "It's like we've got all the mosaic pieces, but we can't see the picture they're supposed to make." A framework which serves as a gyroscope in an unsteady atmosphere of change can galvanize vision, energy, and effort.

• **Need for models**—In the beginning, Midland teachers wanted a recipe for differentiation. "Just tell us what to do and we'll do it. Isn't it on paper somewhere?" In time, many teachers began to understand that there were many ways to modify instruction based on student need and interest, the nature of the subject, range of available instructional strategies, and so forth. Several teams also began to devote regular team meetings to discussing differentiation. A member of one team said: "I think we spent the first part of the year as a team pulling one another down about differentiation. Then it occurred to us that among us we must surely have some skills at work already. We discovered we do, of course, and we've become a resource for one another." At that point, teachers willing to move ahead with differentiation spoke clearly of a need for concrete assistance in enacting differentiation. "We need somebody to sit down with us regularly and show us ways to do this with our own subjects." "We need somebody who can work with us in our classrooms on differentiation. It's like in college where they tell you all this stuff about teaching while you sit and listen, and it makes no sense at all until you start using it." Videotapes of classes in which differentiation was evident, examples of differentiated lesson and unit plans, opportunities to talk with teachers who utilized elements of differentiation, and accessible on site leadership were important at Midland. "It was amazing. She [an instructional leader] sat down with our team and in less than an hour we had really made progress on a differentiated product for our kids. We were really excited." "When I saw the tape, it came together for me. I guess I'm a visual learner, but for the first time I see how I could have different groups and individuals working in different ways on the same concept."

• **Teachers as learners and administrators differentiating learning**—Treating teachers as though they are all alike is an ineffective way of commending the importance of individual readiness and skill. In fact, middle school teachers at Midland were as diverse in readiness to make great leaps in learning as were the students they taught. Some had backgrounds as high school teachers where subject expertise was a source of comfort but flexibility in teaching style was rare. Others came from an elementary teaching background in which flexibility was more common but content confidence was sometimes lacking. Many had minimal training in teaching advanced learners or struggling learners—few had expertise with either. Some teachers, of course, remained intractably opposed to the changes suggested.

In such a setting, the opportunity is ripe for administrators to model principles of differentiated learning with their staff members. As in a differentiated classroom there could be goals common to the group and goals negotiated between the individual "learner" (in this case, the teacher) and the "teacher" (in this case, an instructional leader). There could be timelines for progress established in accordance with learner readiness which has been preassessed with classroom observation, learner reflection, and dialogue between teacher and learner. Varied learning resources could be provided in response to learner interest, style, and request. Throughout the year, the learner and teacher could come together in small and large groups to share work and insights, learning from one another and then focusing again on individual goals. It is likely that the concept of differentiation would become clearer and more compelling to a faculty which saw the diversity of its own members accepted and built upon. "We each have talents," said a Midland teacher. "We need to get credit for doing what we do well. We need that acknowledgment, and we could move on from there."

A SKETCH OF EARLY SUCCESS

"In this kind of class, weaker students excel—which is exciting—and strong students are challenged."

Just as there are advanced learners in many middle school classrooms, there were also advanced learners in regard to differentiation of instruction among the Midland staff. These "early subscribers." as one administrator called them, provided a profile of a teacher who learns to modify instruction in a heterogeneous setting and a profile of early attempts to develop personal heuristics for differentiation. Both are instructive for planning staff development leading toward classrooms which are appropriately differentiated for academic diversity.

Profile of Teachers Who Differentiated Instruction

During the first year of the Midland differentiation initiative, many teachers made only modest progress in developing classrooms which addressed academic diversity. Some made little, if any, observable progress. There was, however, a group of teachers who made major changes in their classroom management and instruction and who were advanced, at least in comparison with other colleagues, in their implementation of differentiated instruction in their classrooms.

Data for this portion of the study were derived from observations and interviews with a group of approximately 15 teachers designated by self and/or Midland administrators as ready for "advanced" work with differentiation during the second year of the project. Although a preponderance of the group came from Midland Middle School, some taught at other district middle schools. Their views thus represent those of "subscribers" rather than resisters. A look at teachers who did evidence progress in establishing differentiated classrooms is useful in assisting other teachers who demonstrate readiness to attempt differentiated instruction.

Both teachers and administrators in Midland speculated that age and length of professional experience might predict early success—the general theory being that younger teachers would be more likely to change. "Maybe some of us are too old," mused one veteran of many years. "When you've done something a certain way for 25 years, it's hard to change." "We've told them [more experienced teachers] for years that they are superstars," said an administrator, "and now we're taking that status away from them. Maybe it's not fair. Maybe we've taught them *not* to change." A young teacher drew a similar conclusion from a different vantage point. "It's hard for veteran teachers to change, but I'm new and everything is new to me, and I *have* to change in order to grow."

As the year progressed, however, it became apparent that the "new subscribers" were not defined by age. Some of the most experienced and most inexperienced Midland teachers were in the "advanced group." Early indications are that at least two traits were shared by those teachers who showed the greatest inclination and ability to move toward differentiated classrooms: (a) they were inquirers about students, and (b) they saw schooling as an organic enterprise in which disequilibrium or "disturbance" was a catalyst for growth. Regarding students, one teacher who made rapid and observable differences in her practice during the first year of differentiation in Midland explained: I've moved around a lot, taught in the inner city and in honors classes, I've learned to study kids and to meet them where they are." Another said, "My goal for my students is for them to see where they have strengths and weaknesses and then to help them set their own goals based on what they realize are their strengths and weaknesses." Regarding the role of risk in teaching, an "advanced" teacher reflected: "If I hit a brick wall with the kids today, well that's okay with me. I'll know to avoid it tomorrow—and I'll learn a lot about those bricks in the process. I'll learn about myself as a teacher, too. And if I'm lucky, the students will see that learning is often about *finding* answers, not *having* them." Another said: "Maybe more talking up front would have been good for us, but maybe not. Maybe folks have to get their feet wet in order to understand what it's [differentiation] all about. I subscribe to that ready-fire-aim principle, you know. I try it, and then I can figure out what's working and what's wrong." In fact, change among the faculty at large during the first year of differentiated instruction at Midland supports the idea that people are more likely to act their way into belief than to believe their way into acting. This suggests that experiencing success with a given classroom practice is more likely to bring about change in teacher behavior related to that practice than is trying to convince the teacher that the practice will be useful (Guskey, 1986).

Profiles of Early Teacher-Developed Heuristics

A major issue for Midland teachers in the early months of the differentiation initiative centered around how a differentiated classroom "would look," in other words, "I just don't see how you'd set it up so different students had different tasks at different times. Wouldn't it just be nuts?"

The "early subscribers" converted principles of differentiation to their own teaching styles, learner needs, and subject matter. As they discussed with one another how they implemented differentiation, their initial "models" or heuristics were implicit in their conversations. Figure 3 provides samples of ways in

Figure 3   Samples of Ways in Which Midland Teachers "Advanced in Differentiation" Routinized Management of a Differentiated Classroom

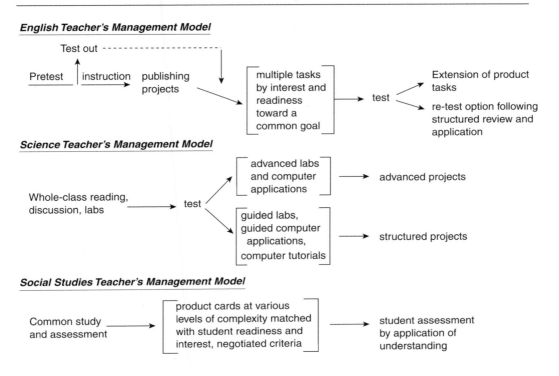

which three Midland teachers routinized the concept of differentiation. It is interesting and important to note that while the models have in common an intent to identify essential understandings, learner readiness, and strategies for matching content, process, and product to the learner, teachers applied these common principles to their classrooms in a variety of ways. This ability to understand and adapt elements of effective instruction is an important step away from formulaic teaching and toward a level of professionalism in which educators adapt their knowledge to the needs of their clients (Darling-Hammond & Goodwin, 1993).

SUMMARY

Qualitative research does not claim broad generalizability. Nonetheless, the Midland differentiation experience leads to some interesting and potentially useful insights which merit further study in other settings.

1. Academically diverse youngsters (e.g., advanced and struggling learners) report that they often do not find appropriate levels of challenge in one-size-fits-all classes.

2. Teachers in heterogeneous settings do not automatically know how to address academic diversity in those settings and often see no need to change teacher behaviors in order to do so.

3. Without clear definitions of what constitutes appropriately differentiated classes, teachers may believe that making occasional minor modifications in lessons is adequate to address academic diversity.

4. In order to assist teachers in establishing differentiated classrooms, educational leaders should be aware of specific impediments to differentiation as perceived by teachers, including administrative barriers and barriers presented by a paradigm shift which necessitates new ways of thinking about and practicing in classrooms.

5. Administrators should present specific classroom initiatives as interrelated means to accomplishing central instructional goals so that teachers do not feel pulled in many directions.

6. Teachers need models of how differentiation "looks" in classrooms, consistent on-site assistance in translating principles of differentiation into their own classrooms over an extended period of time.

7. Administrators should consider modeling differentiation for teachers as they move toward differentiated instruction, using the same rationale, format, and procedures that would benefit academically diverse learners in a classroom.

8. Teachers advanced in readiness to differentiate instruction in heterogeneous classrooms can provide momentum and models for a school or district moving toward differentiated instruction.

There is a need to move beyond an exploratory study of teachers as they begin to differentiate instruction for academic diversity and to investigate in depth the change sequences through which both subscribers and resisters proceed, management routines developed by teachers as they learn to differentiate instruction, teacher developed heuristics and models for differentiating instruction, and characteristics of administrators who are effective change agents toward differentiation. In addition, it is essential to examine relative long-term learner outcomes for academically diverse learners, including the gifted, in differentiated and nondifferentiated regular classrooms, as well as in specialized class settings.

REFERENCES

Archambault. F., Westberg, K., Brown, S. Hallmark, B., Zhang, W., & Emmons, C. (1993). Classroom practices used with gifted third and fourth grade students. *Journal for the Education of the Gifted, 16*, 103–119.

Bandura, A. (1986). *Social foundations of thought mid action: A social cognitive, theory.* Englewood Cliffs, NJ: Prentice-Hall.

Bateman, B. (1993). Learning disabilities: The changing landscape. *Journal of Learning Disabilities, 25*(1), 29–36.

Bogdan, R., & Biklen, S. (1982). *Qualitative research for education: An introduction to theory and methods.* Boston: Allyn & Bacon.

Carnegie Task Force on the Education of Young Adolescents. (1989). *Turning points: Preparing American youth for the 21st century.* Washington, DC: Carnegie Council on Adolescent Development.

Darling-Hammond, L., & Goodwin, A. (1993). Progress toward professionalism in teaching. In G. Calweti (Ed.). *Challenges and achievements of American education* (pp. 19–52). Alexandria, VA: Association for Supervision and Curriculum Development.

Fullan, M. (1993). *Change forces: Probing the depths of educational reform.* London: Falmer.

Glesne, C., & Peshkin, A. (1992). *Becoming qualitative researchers: An introduction.* White Plains, NY: Longman.

Goodlad, J. (1984). *A place called school: Prospects for the future.* New York: McGraw-Hill.

Guskey, T. (1986). Staff development and the process of teacher change. *Educational Researcher, 15*(5), 5–12.

Hallahan, D., & Kauffman, J. (1994). From mainstreaming to collaborative consultation. In J. Kauffman & D. Hallahan (Eds.), *The illusion of full inclusion* (pp. 3–17). Austin, TX: Pro-Ed.

International Institute for Advocacy for School Children. (1993). Heterogeneous grouping as discriminatory practice. *Effective School Practices, 12*(1), 61–62.

Kozol, J. (1991). *Savage inequalities: Children in America's schools.* New York: Crown.

Lincoln, Y., & Guba, E. (1985). *Naturalistic inquiry.* Beverly Hills, CA: Sage.

McIntosh, R., Vaughn, S., Schumm, J., Haager, D., & Lee, O. (1993). Observations of students with learning disabilities in general education classrooms. *Exceptional Children, 60*(3), 249–261.

Merriam, S. (1988). *Case study research in education: A qualitative approach.* San Francisco: Jossey-Bass.

National Middle School Association. (1992). *This we believe.* Columbus, OH: Author.

Oakes, J. (1985). *Keeping track: How schools structure inequality.* New Haven, CT: Yale University Press.

Page, R. (1991). *Lower track classrooms: A curricular and cultural perspective.* New York: Teachers College Press.

Shulman, L. (1987). Knowledge and teaching: Foundation of the new reform. *Harvard Educational Review, 57*(1), 1–22.

Sizer, T. (1984). *Horace's compromise: The dilemma of the American high school.* Boston: Houghton Mifflin.

Slavin, R. (1987). Ability grouping and student achievement in the elementary schools: A best evidence synthesis. *Review of Educational Research, 57*, 293–336.

Strauss, A. (1989). *Qualitative analysis for social scientists.* New York: Cambridge University Press.

Welsh. P. (1986). *Tales out of school.* New York: Viking.

Westberg, K., Archambault, F., Dobyns, S., & Salvin, T. (1993). The classroom practices observational study. *Journal for the Education of the Gifted. 16*, 120–146.

Wheelock, A. (1992). *Crossing the tracks: How "untracking" can save America's schools.* New York: The New Press.

Yin, R. (1989). *Case study research. Design and methods.* Newbury Park, CA: Sage.

Index

Note: References to tables or figures are indicated by *italic type* and the addition of *"t"* or *"f"* respectively.

**CORWIN
PRESS**

The Corwin Press logo—a raven striding across an open book—represents the union of courage and learning. Corwin Press is committed to improving education for all learners by publishing books and other professional development resources for those serving the field of K–12 education. By providing practical, hands-on materials, Corwin Press continues to carry out the promise of its motto: **"Helping Educators Do Their Work Better."**